By the Same Author

THIRTY PLAYS
HATH
NOVEMBER

Pain and Pleasure
in the Contemporary Theater

WALTER KERR

SIMON AND SCHUSTER · NEW YORK

Most of the articles and essays in this book appeared originally
in the New York Herald Tribune and The New York Times and
are reprinted here, with slight modifications in some cases, with
their permission. The essay on Shylock appeared in Horizon
Magazine, © 1960, American Heritage Publishing Co., Inc. and
is reprinted with their permission. The essay titled "The Comic
Country of the Blind" appeared originally as Mr. Kerr's After-
word on "The Cherry Orchard" in the book Five World Plays,
edited by V. Louise Higgins and Walter Kerr, © 1964, by Har-
court Brace Jovanovich, Inc., and is reprinted with their permission. The article titled "How to Be an Audience" was first published in the book New York, New York, by the Editors of the
New York Herald Tribune, published by The Dial Press, © 1964,
by the New York Herald Tribune, Inc. "The Vanishing Text"
appeared originally in Harper's Magazine, September 1966, under the title of "How Playwrights Lose." The article "Night
Sounds" was first published in Vogue Magazine, April 1963,
under the title of "Along Nightmare Alley." The translation of
Molière's School for Wives quoted on page 181 is by Morris
Bishop.

FIRST SIMON AND SCHUSTER PAPERBACK PRINTING 1970

SBN 671-20178-6 CLOTH
SBN 671-20736-9 PAPER
LIBRARY OF CONGRESS CATALOG CARD NUMBER: 69-14283
MANUFACTURED IN THE UNITED STATES OF AMERICA

for Peter and Mary

CONTENTS

THIRTY PLAYS
HATH
NOVEMBER

1
ME AND THEE

BACK HOME

IT TURNED OUT to be a tremendous relief to be getting the right kind of mail again.

You may or may not remember, but for some months a few years ago there was a newspaper strike, and while it was going on many things changed for the practicing reviewer: he became visible (on television), he became elusive (what time *was* that television show?), he became mourned as he has never been mourned and as he will not be upon his decease (oh, if only the reviews had been printed!). Speaking of myself, I became, according to one newsmagazine, "displaced," and, according to another, "a bundle of nerves." These were all innovations. But the biggest change, and the most shattering, was in the mail.

Things were all right again the minute the strike ended. In a trice I realized that I was truly home, back in touch with people once more. I came down to the office and succeeded in finding my desk after no more than a forty-minute search (while we were idle, our desks had not been; at one time or another during the three-month hiatus there had been a dance of desks—I like to think of it taking place near midnight, under a full moon—and oh! the joy and the zest and the tingle of the chase, with a heightened color to the cheeks and a happy, racing heart at the end of it!). At the end of it, I opened a drawer and there, along with a number of four-cent stamps that will never be used now, were some letters. Real letters.

"Dear Sir," the first one began, "I feel compelled to write you regarding what I feel is a gross injustice and complete lack of consideration on your part."

Recognition stirred. Hope grew in me like a tulip. I read on: "Your review of the recent opening of 'Sophie' is, in my opinion, truly a disgrace. . . . How in the world you could have written the review you did about 'Sophie' is beyond my comprehension. To my way of thinking 'Sophie' is, or rather 'was,' definitely an exceptionally fine performance, beautifully produced, far above average and certainly on a par with some of the so-called current hit shows."

There, I sat back and sighed, filled with a new sense of Belonging. Leaning forward again so quickly that the casters on my chair rolled away and had to be pedaled back to the desk, I snatched up the next two pieces of mail and opened them with fingers that trembled as they must have done on television. In a moment, I knew the best. "Dyspepsia, I'm sure, was the canker that gnawed in your candy-box last evening," came the words, crisp, well-typed, deeply outraged, and familiar as friendship. (These were in defense of *She Loves Me*, which I'd been alone among the reviewers in not loving, and they rolled on, heartfelt and heartwarming, for two and one-half pages, single-spaced.)

Peace at last, and deep contentment. The world was right side up again, and had I ever been away?

Now, it is possible that you think I'm kidding, and that reviewers really don't like to get letters suggesting that they had been asleep in the theater, or awake and fully incompetent. But that is because you may never have been on television. Let me tell you about television mail.

Here is one of the most interesting letters I received, early on. "Dear Sir," it opened, just like any other letter, "why do I never see your shirt-cuffs? Do you wear short-sleeved summer shirts in the winter time? You use your hands quite a lot when you're talking, and every time you do the sleeves of your jacket ride up, exposing your arm and producing a curiously naked effect. Is this intentional?"

(The question is important, and had better be answered. Every time I come near a typewriter, I roll up my sleeves so that the sleeves won't catch on the return-shift, the ribbon-reverse, or those little V-shaped things that are supposed to show you where the margins are if by chance the margins are where they're supposed to be. On television I always forgot to roll them down again until after that tiny red light went on—the tiny red light indicates that you are now in a million living rooms, though not necessarily that any one else is—and of course by that time it would have seemed undignified to be getting in and out of one's clothing.)

While I was worrying about the solution to this problem (false cuffs attached to the jacket, *letting* the sleeves get ripped to shreds by an only too eager typewriter?), I was given another. "Sir" (no "Dear" this time; the viewers of America were losing patience): "Since you cannot talk and smoke at the same time on television, why do you have to fill up the screen with smoke from a butt that you nervously keep waving up to your head and down again? I invested in a good set with a clear picture and don't need your inconsideration to mess it up."

(This correspondent is outspoken, but not quick. He is on the verge of uncovering my canny plan to lay down a smoke screen that would keep me from being recognized on the street afterward—a critic cannot be too careful—but he just misses it. It is not true, by the way, that you cannot smoke and talk at the same time. Many men, and some women, have done it. It is aesthetically undesirable, however, in a reviewer, since it makes him look like a fire-breathing monster. Personally, I stopped smoking.)

I think my favorite letter during the period, though, dealt with the matter of bifocals, which I wore on television not because I couldn't see the notes in front of me but because various members of my family have suggested that they give me a strength of character otherwise missing from my face. Bifocals, as you no doubt know, have a little line running horizontally across the center of the lenses, and by wiggling this line up or down you can either blur or bring into focus whatever you're looking at. I always used to do this while waiting for the red light to go on, partly to while away the time and partly to look surprised when the light did go on, which I always was. (It is part of television theory, I believe, to look surprised at the beginning of a sequence, sort of as though you didn't know you were coming and possibly should have called.) Anyway, my habit brought me this message:

"Dear Mr. Kerr: As a television viewer, and your optician, may I remind you that should your bifocals need realignment, or adjustment of any sort, you have only to bring them in to me, and they will be corrected without additional charge. Sincerely yours [name withheld, out of decency]."

By this time it may have become handsomely clear why the thundering anathema of the newspaper reader is infinitely to be preferred to the tenderest concern of the television viewer. The one thing that is obvious in all of this is that the television viewer hasn't heard a single word you said. He's just *looking* at you.

It's the newspaper reader who pays attention to what you say.

HOW DO YOU SAY?

It is not a reviewer's business to "sell" plays, but surely it is a playwright's business not to write plays in such a way that the barest, most gingerly mention of the plot material in a review will kill the play dead on the spot.

It is possible that you have never thought of this problem, though the trade thinks of it all the time. ("The trade" is a term used by insiders to show that they are inside it, and by outsiders to show that they are above it.)

For instance, there is something called a "money notice." This does not in the least mean that the reviewer's notice has been favorable. Quite the contrary. A favorable notice is a favorable notice, and let's hear no more of it except in the ads. A "money notice," on the other hand, is an unfavorable notice in which the reviewer has been so careless as to praise the actors extensively, or to admit that he laughed out loud three times due to surprise, or to give sufficient space to the fact that the play's content includes a sequence in which a mulatto homosexual is castrated by a nun. The reviewer, in short, has outfoxed himself, or been outfoxed by the playwright and producers: nothing he can say against the project will counteract the impression of sheer liveliness which his passing description is bound to give off.

Conversely, there are plays which the reviewer admires but which he cannot coax down from that sixteenth-story ledge upon which their authors have perched them. The plays are suicidally inclined, and trying to help them simply calls attention to their grim determination; it probably even hastens the jump. The reviewer can genuflect in admiration, he can fawn, he can flip. And every word he utters is a push into the great beyond.

The plays have signed their own death warrants by being too unmistakably *about* something. Now, I don't want to give you an example from plays of the recent past, because there are no doubt plays coming in any minute which closely resemble plays of the recent past, and I would seem to be signaling doom before the poor things had got past Boston. I have in my possession, however, a press release concerning a new novel published not too long ago, and I think it points up the particular difficulty of which I am speaking.

The press release begins by recapitulating the earlier stages of the novel, which fortunately include "an innocently incestuous love." "Innocently incestuous love" is all right, good even. It might be better if it were less innocent, but both the novelist and the release are on the right track for all that. Finally, however, we must come to the essence of the matter, to the nub of the plotting, the significance of what we are invited to spend time with. And here it is: "From then on, these three people become victims of what one might call the tragedy of erosion."

Were this a play, the scenery would be in the fire now. I make nothing of the word "victims." You can work "victims" into a review without frightening more than half the available population—"the extraordinarily beautiful Miss Elmwood, as the most passionate of the play's victims, lights a third-act bonfire that will be remembered for its heat long after the scorching of Chicago is forgotten." You see. You scarcely notice "victims" in all that heady pyromania.

But what in heaven's name are you going to do with "the tragedy of erosion" when finally you are required to mention it? You know perfectly well that only a very small number of people are ever going to pay twenty dollars for two seats to a tragedy of erosion. It's not that they don't know about erosion, or aren't willing to face it; they do know about it, they have faced it, and they don't like it. It doesn't sound like what they had in mind after dinner. They're not cowards. They know how the sea gradually eats into the soil and you get property losses. They know how arid winds gradually blow the topsoil away and you get Okies. They remember. They are also aware that human beings erode, and that the play is probably not about the Bering Straits or the dust bowl but about people. They have looked into their own mirrors and made the connection. The trouble is that the thought of an evening in which everything onstage slowly withers does not stimulate them. They're not hooked, so to speak.

But it is very, very difficult for a reviewer to bury "tragedy of erosion" in an otherwise hysterically happy notice. "The sheer exhilaration of this tragedy of erosion"—no, no, no, that won't do. Readers are not to be drawn into untimely speculation about the reviewer's sanity.

Try burying it in a parenthesis. "There are, in this tragedy of erosion, many heart-lifting things: moments of affection, moments of—" The reader has already caught you. You don't pull a parenthesis on him. Moments mean nothing. The reader knows perfectly well that the reviewer has a half column of space which he must fill up with "moments," no matter how ghastly the experience has been; he can't go on typing "ghastly" or "tragedy of erosion" paragraph after paragraph, can he? And the two mean the same thing, don't they?

The reviewer, sensing he is about to kill the thing he loves, broods. Does he *have* to say "erosion," even though that is plainly what the play is about? Can't he substitute a better word, perhaps "decay"? "The decay that spreads across the landscape like that beautiful weed, the morning-glory—" Out. How about "attrition"? A lot of people probably don't know what "attrition" means. "The process of attrition by means of which three charming people are reduced to—" Trouble ahead. "Reduced" is bad and leading to worse; the barometer is falling.

A bright idea strikes the reviewer. Perhaps he can falsify the content of the play by challenging its obvious interpretation. "Though the play seems to be a study in progressive deterioration, it is actually a bold affirmation of—" Hoist with his own petard. He has had to put the worst first in order to lead, kindly light that he is, to the little lie he meant to tell. He puts the gambit away regretfully: it would have been nice to propose an *original* interpretation of the play.

It is now eleven o'clock on opening night, with the presses ready to do what the movies call "roll," and there is nothing for it but to come at the whole problem candidly. This is the last, desperate, most devious course the reviewer has: to tell the simple truth. He writes:

"You will hear that the play is a tragedy of erosion. The play is in fact a tragedy of erosion. And erosion, to be sure, is not the most heartening spectacle a pleasure-seeker can seek on a sultry, late-season, summer's night. But seek it you must, for merit is in it."

He sends off the copy, enough integrity in his heart to carry him all the way home and through the first of two drinks. During the second drink he will have an awful premonition that the play will do four dollars and forty cents at the box office next week. He notices, too, upon rereading his review that in his last-ditch effort to win the reader with candor he has mentioned "erosion" rather more often than in any of his other contemplated sorties.

He cherished that play. And he couldn't so much as write about it without hurting it. Some plays are like that. They are written by lemmings.

The only solution to the whole problem that I can think of is this: playwrights who are deeply concerned with dissolution, falling hair, euthanasia and such other subjects as read like smallpox signs must so contrive their story lines that they sound, in the telling, as though they were saucy French sex-farces or perhaps highly suspenseful detective stories, with the smallpox content rubbed in along the way. Duerrenmatt does this, and I salute him for it. He helps a reviewer get a fellow into the theater.

Of course the best play of the coming season will be a tragedy of erosion and it will clean up.

MY MALIGNANT MIND

The trouble with reading too many murder mysteries is that you come to have a murder-mystery mind. Not that I have had time to read all that many murder mysteries lately. If you want to keep the least bit in touch with the trends and traumas of the contemporary theater you have got to devote your idle hours to reading people like Kierkegaard and Unamuno (not a corpse in a carload), and I must confess here and now that Helen MacInnes is a stranger to me, Len Deighton a name I see on the shelves as I pass, so forlornly, by.

But when the world was younger, and before I realized that hide-and-seek would have to be replaced with Heidegger if I wanted to understand what Jean-Paul Sartre was talking about, I did spend a great deal of time in the company of John Dickson Carr and his ilk, and the traces still show. I formed a way of thinking about mysteries that is peculiar only to the addict, with the result that I can't read a thriller or see one without behaving just as deviously as the author.

The murder-mystery mind has certain characteristics. It is not simply clue-conscious, ready to leap at a random word as though it were a street sign someone had turned the wrong way. That would be too easy. If a character says he has spent the entire evening in the billiard room alone, you know perfectly well he hasn't spent the entire evening in the billiard room alone. But you also know—if you are an aficionado with a head on his shoulders—that your quite correct deduction is utterly without significance. You will not be tricked by a plainly baited trap. What you instantly suspect is that the author, having led you to so cleverly spot a lie, is really trying to empty out that billiard room in your head *because* something did happen in it. In fact, the person you knew was lying was probably in it all the time, doing something you couldn't guess he was doing because you had mentally moved him out of it. Dirty pool of this sort is absolutely *de rigueur* in a decent mystery—the mystery is never in the plot but in the ploy for hiding the plot—and if you have any spunk at all in you, you play dirty pool back. You don't exactly become a doubter. You become a darer. You say to the author, "I *dare* you to lead me to think that I am cleverer than you. I'm clever enough to know better."

And so you join the game on equal terms, defiers both. The author says no weapon was found beside the body, and you don't start looking around the room wondering where the weapon is. You wonder where the body is, and if there was one. You've got to keep ahead, that's all. You have to be good at multiplication and long division to do it, and you have to realize that when a man carefully muffles his face he is probably trying to conceal his shoes (so that you will eventually figure out the switch and be misled by it), but in time you get the hang of things. You reverse to the *nth* power hoping your math will hold out, compounding the situations along with the author in hopes of confounding him, dog that he is. The murder-mystery mind becomes craft-conscious. It takes a sneak to catch a sneak, and you keep your slippers oiled.

The only trouble with this habit of thought is that the author may, God forgive him, be sometimes inept, or plainly irrational, in which case you will be leapfrogging ahead of him to no purpose at all. Let me give you an example. It has been widely noted by now that in Frederick Knott's thriller, *Wait Until Dark*, a certain oddity occurs. The heroine of *Wait Until Dark* is pretty, spunky, and blind. When three menacing figures slip into her Greenwich Village apartment, she can't see them. She can hear them, all right, because they talk interminably, and she can even detect a creaking of new shoes when her pursuers are silent; but she can't see them. In spite of this plainly established fact, one of the intruders keeps appearing in various disguises, apparently so that the blind girl won't recognize him on each succeeding entrance.

Now, I ask you, what are we to do with this? Mr. Knott is known to be a tricky deviser of deceptions: he did very well indeed with *Dial M for Murder*. We cannot really suppose that he is foolish enough to have overlooked the fact that the disguises are unnecessary, given the girl's inability to notice them. We are certainly not free to suppose that the actor playing the part just happens to have a fondness for putting on extra makeup, or that the director has gone out of his way to decorate the stage: the disguises are written into the busy dialogue.

I'll tell you what I did with it. Summoning up my vast scholarship in the genre, and assuming that Mr. Knott had *some* purpose in doing what was apparently uncalled for, I decided on the spot that we were being tricked on the double. There is only one conceivable reason why a character should change his wigs, his eyeglasses, and his walking sticks every time he appears before a blind girl. The reason: the girl isn't blind and the interloper knows it.

Aha, I thought, I've caught you, Knott. You're paving the way for an ultimate twist, and what seems a present goof will prove a form of upmanship. But no, I hadn't caught him, and no, he wasn't kidding. Two hours later lovely Lee Remick was still feeling her way around the furniture, sightless and brave, and I had long since abandoned my pretty sense of triumph. I was also feeling pretty deflated, I can tell you. What good had all my training been if mystery writers were going to start meaning what they said? And as for that fellow with all those costume changes, what *did* he have in mind? No one has ever said a writer must play fair in a mystery story. Crooked's crooked. But the characters—least of all the villains—shouldn't be chumps, should they? Personally, I want to have some respect for a villain if I am going to give him my experience and my time. We're not going to be able to preserve this valuable literary form if the scoundrels are going to insist on being silly.

Perhaps we can't save the form, even though *Wait Until Dark* did produce one big eruption of gooseflesh in its very last scene, with the women in the audience screeching and clutching their escorts' arms, causing their escorts' programs to fly into the aisles. We have come to know too much; we are so trigger-ready to spot false leads and turn them inside out that we want to turn *everything* inside out before the first curtain is halfway up. Certainly I did this as one curtain rose. It rose on a darkened stage, for the blind girl's husband was a professional photographer and he was developing film at the moment. Clever, I thought. Film. For producing evidence. Acid. For throwing when things got rough. A trick of darkening the lights to develop film when developing film wasn't at all the project in mind. (John Dickson Carr has a whole novel dependent upon projected film, in case you want to know where I get my bright ideas from.) Alas, I was overrehearsed again. The girl threw ammonia later, but forgot all about the acid. Nothing was ever photographed. And the husband himself absented himself from the apartment without darkening the door, or the room, again.

Even his disappearance foxed me. As the plot has it, the three intruders are searching for a child's doll, stuffed with heroin, which the husband has inadvertently, presumably innocently, brought home. They want the husband out of the house so that they can harry the girl in private, hoping she will lead them to the doll. So they lure him away to his studio on the pretext that a celebrity wants to have portrait studies made. There is no celebrity, of course, and the husband waits for more than two hours for the nonexistent creature to show up. Now—and I am sure you are with me—no man will wait two hours for anyone. Twenty minutes, patiently. Thirty minutes, restively. Perhaps thirty minutes furiously. But after thirty-one minutes of waiting most of the men I know will either start throwing things or go home. In the theater I assumed this. And when the husband didn't show up and was reported still patiently waiting past the two-hour limit, I jumped to an entirely natural, even necessary, conclusion: he was the ringleader of the whole business, he knew what was in the doll (after all, he *had* brought it home), and he was permitting his wife to undergo seven stages of fright for reasons which would come astonishingly clear in time for the final accounting, five scenes away.

Wrong, wrong, wrong. Rarely have I played the game so honorably and been so sternly rebuffed. For the simple fact of the matter is that Mr. Knott hadn't got any twists to his plot at all; he seemed not even to have heard of the double-dealing you and I grew up on and learned to master in our crafty, malicious, disbelieving way. Mr. Knott had an initial situation in which everyone was exactly what he or she seemed to be, and he was simply fiddling around for two acts *pretending* to be complicated while waiting until it was late enough to throw the Big Battle into the hopper. The battle proper was a wow, and there were probably many uncorrupted souls who were willing to settle for it.

I, poor overbusy soul, have been corrupted by the ingenuity of men who have fooled me and I am, no doubt and good riddance, a lost cause. John Dickson Carr has a nice habit of making you *like* the heroine so you will suspect she has surely done it, if you follow me, and that's the kind of cross-stitching I'm accustomed to. I don't think I can get used to blind girls who are really blind girls, innocent husbands who are really innocent husbands (waiting for two hours, for heaven's sake), dark rooms that are really darkrooms intended only for developing film. Not at my age. And I'm certainly not going to get used to character actors who disguise themselves just because

Sherlock Holmes did. Holmes wouldn't have stirred from that study if he hadn't thought someone was going to catch his act. I have been brought up on purposeful treachery, I have learned to be treacherous myself, and it's too late to make a trusting man of me now.

NATURAL THEATERGOING

I wish I could go to previews.

I can't, because that would be jumping the gun. The whole point of playing previews in recent years has been to expose a new play to randomly composed audiences before reviewers are permitted to get at it, and I'm wholly in favor of the practice. If I did try to slip into a preview before the official opening, I'd be canceling out its particular benefits: I'd be wearing out my responses to the play before the play had decided, by trial and error in front of some customers, just what those responses ought finally to be.

So, like other reviewers, I hide out, look the other way, pretend not to notice that the live theater is going on without me.

It is. As I understand matters, the livest theater currently available in New York is preview theater. Previews, I'm told, jump. They jump because the audience is directly, even passionately, engaged in what is going on, before the barrier of printed reviews has come between them and the occasion.

I'll have to give negative examples, and even these, of course, are hearsay. It seems that during the preview performances of one recent Broadway catastrophe—though it wasn't a critical catastrophe yet—audiences did more than mix catcalls with applause. On a certain evening a single member of the audience became so infuriated with what he had been watching, and felt so obligated to express himself, that he charged down the aisle toward the stage while the actors were taking their final bows and begged the rest of the audience not to applaud. "This is rubbish!" he is said to have shouted, and—if my information is correct—he succeeded in turning what might have been conventionally polite applause into a group demonstration of disapproval.

What's good about that? Everything (except, as it happened, the play). I have often marveled at the docility of contemporary audiences. Outspoken professionals like Mike Nichols or Gower Champion may nip the hand that feeds them, but audiences, whatever their actual feelings may be, keep their counsel in the playhouse. There is a good side to this reserve. If our audiences are undemonstrative, they are also remarkably patient, which means that they are willing to give every new play its decent chance. On opening nights they behave quietly and attentively for astonishing lengths of time. It is usually fairly clear, for instance, after the first twenty minutes or so of playing time what the general quality of the evening is to be. During the first twenty minutes a writer of comedy is apt to have tried out a couple of jokes, and the texture of what he thinks funny can be felt. The serious playwright is apt to have phrased a few thoughts, or written several extended speeches, in the style he considers suited to himself and the material; in twenty minutes the rhythm or the repetitiveness, the vigor or the vulgarity, of a style can be detected. But no matter what is being noticed, first-night audiences tend to hold fast much longer than that. They are determined to show respect, and to avoid forming hasty conclusions—which is good of them.

But ultimately the conduct of our post-preview audiences—whether on opening nights or thereafter—is evasive. Though an opening-night audience, to a man, may know at the final curtain that it has detested the play, it is secretive about the fact; the audience applauds, perhaps applauds a little bit more than is necessary in order to compensate for what it is going to think and say after it has got out of the theater; and it then gets out of the theater discreetly, looking neither to the right nor to the left, trying hard to betray nothing of its conviction of doom and feeling shamefaced into the bargain for being so furtive.

Glance at the faces of first-nighters who are slipping away from a bad experience and you may very well conclude that *they* have been the criminals of the occasion; they look it. First-night audiences live and leave apologetically.

After an opening, and after a barrage of notices has appeared in the press, a new set of circumstances comes into being. If the notices have been poor, and if the audience also dislikes the play, nothing noisy is going to happen: the reviewers *said* it was bad, didn't they, and what should be added to that? If the notices have been good and the audience also likes the play, there will of course be applause; but since there is now no sense of discovery, there is not much uncontrolled ecstasy in the aisles, either. Occasionally a situation arises in which an audience finds itself seriously disagreeing with the reviewers, this way or that. But the disagreement normally takes the form of a chaste, or even an intemperate, letter to the press. It does not provoke an explosion in the playhouse.

Somewhere between our habit of politeness and our habit of imagining that the newspaper reviews have intercepted and forestalled vigorous discussion on the spot, the air goes out of the audience. After a play has opened, the audience does not quite conceive of itself as the ultimate, and the immediate, arbiter; it feels that an intermediary has been there beforehand and has already said rather too much. If the audience does have another word to say, it will say it to the intermediary, not to the actors, not to the possibly present playwright.

Thus the only open, unself-conscious, fully personal relationship that now exists between performance and playgoers exists at previews. Here the issue is undecided, the experience fresh, the playwright in the wings, the expression of an opinion profitable. The audience knows that it, and it alone, is being played to; it senses its power, discovers its right to speak; and so it speaks.

Suddenly the true conditions of theater are in force once more: a playwright, through his actors, is contending head on with those who have come to believe or disbelieve. There isn't even a referee, just an honest-to-God wrestling match. If previews served no other function, if they weren't as useful as they are in trimming a play to its proper shape and weight, they would still be invaluable—indispensable, I'd say—for this reason alone. They bring the two essential parties face to face and let them talk.

It doesn't matter very much that most of the examples of free speech that we hear about are negative: cases of booing and wisecracking from the balcony and charging down the aisle toward the stage. Actually there are contrary instances: most of us have heard of exuberant demonstrations of approval at previews, approval that

wasn't always seconded in the press. If I am inclined to take somewhat more heart from rumors of forthright disapproval, it isn't because, being a reviewer, I have a natural taste for disapproval. It's
because the cheering can always be in part composed of our politeness, our traditional decency. But when members of the audience
take it upon themselves to break our regular patterns of behavior, to
go against the grain of what they have always done before, it must be
because they are feeling deeply involved in the situation at hand,
personally responsible for what comes of it, willing at last to play a
role in the theater they are entitled to play. Even when preview
audiences behave in a manner that some playwrights and actors find
rude, it means that they have been rudely awakened, or at least
awakened. (There are rude plays, too, plays which—in their anxiety
to press a point of view home—do not trouble to conceal their contempt for the lesser minds out front, but that is a subject better saved
for another time.)

It is especially important at this particular moment in our theatrical history that the audience be directly engaged and encouraged to
offer its responses directly. We are moving through a time of radical,
rather than routine, transition. Old narrative forms have been dis-
carded, by and large, as so much implausible manufacture. Attitudes
toward the characters onstage have shifted focus: good guys and bad
guys no longer exist as definable opposites. Logic, illusionism, and the
nature of language itself have all been called into question. A playwright setting out to do his work today can take nothing for granted.
Hand-me-downs are not available, or, where they are available, they
are too readily recognizable as junk.

The playwright, at present, has little more than his *own* authority
to walk with, to measure himself by. If his use of language works, if
his special assault upon the possibilities of the stage—however unfamiliar, however erratic, however unguaranteed—manages to remain
erect and energetic under a blaze of light and a blaze of eyes for
between two and three hours, then he is a functioning playwright.
Rules will get him nowhere; his voice must do the job alone.

But this is an unusually personal way of bringing "plays" into
being, an exercise in self-assertion that can profit very little from the
practices of the past. It is, in effect, an "I" on the stage, quite boldly

so; playwrights who used to be able to say "we," and share more or less standardized structures, were luckier.

This self-assertive "I," however, requires an equally assertive "I" in the auditorium. If a play, in our time of transition, can be judged only by the mysterious, intensely individual authority it displays, by the fact that it commands an audience instead of conforming to ancient expectations, then it is necessary for us to know whether or not the audience is in fact commanded.

And only the audience can tell us.

WHO WILL CHOOSE?

With the disappearance of the *World Journal Tribune*, the number of New York newspapers thought to have direct influence on theater-going habits was reduced to three. Three reviews of each new show. Three chances to win. The shudder along Shubert Alley is still felt.

For a very long time it has been widely believed that plays live on newspaper reviews. Without a big bowl of alphabet soup in the morning, the letters of the alphabet spelling out "smash" and "hurry" and in a pinch "irresistible," no show could hope to survive. A Yes from the daily reviewers meant years and years of profits, a No meant get the show out of the house by Saturday night, and anything between a fat Yes and a flat No meant those damned reviewers were pussyfooting again, which was as good as a No. Lines at the box office were thought to correlate precisely with hurriedly composed, hastily set, and instantly hawked lines of type.

This of course has never been true, though I am not going to tire you with one more long list of entertainments and/or serious ventures that have seen their third winters after indifferent daily notices or that have vanished in bafflement very soon after good ones. Even during the season in which the *World Journal Tribune* dropped out, with only four newspapers in hand and with *The New York Times* generally held to be putting up the most forbidding Stop and Go signs, the neat newspaper-audience correspondence didn't quite work

out. Harold Pinter's *The Homecoming* opened, as Sam Zolotow
pointed out in his news column, to two negative and two on-the-
fence notices. The rumor backstage, on the dawn that followed the
opening, was that the play had a life expectancy of not more than
three weeks. It ran for more than six months and won the New York
Critics Circle prize as the best play of the year. On the lighter side,
Woody Allen's *Don't Drink the Water* simply decided to look after
itself, well into its second year.

Plays can be damaged or encouraged by notices, but not controlled
by them. Plays don't live on print; they live on what people think of
them, say about them, or imagine them to be. The picture in the
prospective playgoer's head is finally decisive, and it is composed of
many things: stars, story, personal inclination, personal prejudice,
scandal, hearsay, adroit promotion, the passionate insistence of
friends, the need to know, the way the photographs look. Any
combination can act as a drag or a snowball; the notices get there
first, but they are forgotten in six weeks, provided the show lives to
see six weeks.

Still, with the number of daily notices shrunk to three and with
each of them thereby increasing its immediate impact, wasn't it less
and less likely that a mildly received show (or a wickedly trounced
show) could survive for six weeks, or for long enough to let the other
factors stir into motion? Yes, I think so. That, by the way, is why *The
New York Times* decided to split its vote, with separate daily and
Sunday reviewers to agree or disagree as they saw fit. That is also why,
at various times during the transitional season, the Sunday *Times*
solicited outside opinion known to differ from my own tea roses and
tantrums (mostly tantrums). The theater is really like a party, however seriously one may take it; it needs a number of voices going if it's
going to sound like a success. Three or four knells of the bell can
seem only funereal; a jangle suggests that a carnival is under way
somewhere. Furthermore, a range of opinion is needed precisely because it *is* opinion. One hopes that in every case the opinion will be
an informed one. But even an informed opinion is not the same
thing as a fact.

Would the new split vote help any, enough to take up the slack?
People were asking, and I couldn't blame them; the strain on the

theater was, and is, serious. (The *World Journal Tribune* had already taken steps toward diversity, adding Harold Clurman on Sundays; but that opportunity had now been lost.) Would the new breed of television reviewers, reaching millions with capsule rundowns confined to about a minute apiece, move into the breach and become the force that first sends theatergoers scurrying about for their checkbooks? If I say that I hoped not, it's only because the air time allotted is so skimpy that qualification (all right, pussyfooting) must be well-nigh ruled out; a Yes or No sounds more sudden and more final if a man can't even talk back to himself. (Strictly speaking, I could have no attitude toward television reviewers. I'd never heard one. I'd always been at the typewriter, shooing away copyboys, while they were delivering their sixty-second sermons. On the sidewalk they seemed like nice fellows, if that's any comfort to anybody.) Would theatergoing lose momentum altogether with so few, or such cursory, comments available to stimulate curiosity and spark talk? Whither?

I'll tell you where I think whither. I think that gradually, maybe sluggishly for a while, but finally and out of sheer desperation, the audience is going to take over. We're at a time of radical change in the order of things theatrical, a time when old habits and superstitions and handouts and lazinesses must perforce come to an end. The legend of "the power of the critics" cannot survive a dwindling down to the musings (however marvelous) of three or four men; there just aren't, and won't be, enough "critics." The theatergoer can no longer read a considerable cross-section and strike a balance; it will be hard for him to have a "favorite" critic when he hasn't really much choice.

He's going to be forced into deciding for himself what he feels he'd better go see, and arguing with the surviving reviewers who did or didn't like it later. In a way, he's always done this, though most often he's waited for a slowly gathering impression to take shape in his head. Now he'll have to do it in the first six weeks—*if* he wants any volume and variety in his theatergoing. My very best guess is that within five to ten years we'll have reversed both our preconceptions and our practices: "power" will have shifted away from a first-night concentration in print to a determination on the part of audiences to damn the torpedoes and stubborn speed ahead.

Surreptitiously, the shift is already under way—and has been since the beginning of the preview system. Surprise has been discovered as a way of life; in many cases interest is doubled by seeing the show first and seeing what is said about it afterward, playing what amounts to an outguessing game; the gamblers are on the increase. Off Broadway has been a factor in the new independence, too. Audiences have discovered that their own tastes are more extensive and unpredictable than they'd once thought; the sense of going out of one's way to try on a different cut of clothes, and to get a jump on the tides of change, has been growing. Some people like to go to coffeehouses where plays *aren't* reviewed; they find that they enjoy an unfiltered experience. Recently some playwrights have politely asked reviewers to leave them alone altogether; for the time being, they'd just like to get some work done. The seeds of a possible revolution are there, all right.

Am I trying to talk myself, or write myself, out of a job? Not a chance; no hopes should stir. What is almost always overlooked—and I forgive everybody for overlooking it—is that the reviewer yearns for this new state of affairs just as passionately as actors and playwrights and producers must do.

Reviewers—this will come as a shock to some people—aren't interested in power. Give any one of them the opportunity to kill or canonize a show simply by jotting down a bare Yes or No, without a single descriptive word added, and he'd walk away from the job—if not fly from it in panic.

Reviewers are interested in persuasion. They *do*, in their wistful or ardent or truculent ways, hope to convince someone—anyone—that the particular pleasure or pain they took in an entertainment was a justified pleasure or pain. They wish to do so because they are themselves both passionate partisans of the theater as such and, on top of that, compulsive talkers—babblers, really. The theater is the one thing in the world they simply cannot shut up about. They like it so much that they are willing to sit through it (not too many people today can make that claim). And having sat through it, they must speak or explode.

They want to be part of a conversation, not a catastrophe. They want to be free to say what they think no matter what anyone else says or thinks, and they are then willing to listen—I am giving you too many surprises here—to what everyone else says and thinks. They don't really want influence; they want exercise. The freedom to chatter on and on about the only matters that matter to them, the uninhibited opportunity to sing or to scold, is what is at stake here. It is a freedom, I should think, that could subtly be compromised. Tell a reviewer that his readers are really docile (he won't believe you, but what if it *should* be true?) and he'll right away begin to wonder if he's leading them to perdition. Tell a reviewer that his word means a great deal to the playwright's mother, to the producer's future relationship with the Internal Revenue Service, or to the very survival of playhouses (they'll all be garages someday), and he'll feel like a cad. Reviewers always do try to brush these piteous visions aside as irrelevant, because they *are* irrelevant to what went on on the stage of a certain evening. But the brushing aside might very well become harder if all conversation dwindled to a whisper; whispering suggests doom. Should a man tread softly in a corpse house? And what fun is that?

What the reviewer really needs to let his own heart free is some assurance that other folk are doing exactly what he is doing: going to the theater, exulting in the theater, berating the theater. With liveliness about him, he finds himself at complete liberty. If the whole town's talking, who needs watch his tongue?

Yes, the reviewer hopes to win the argument, if he can swing it. But first there must be an argument. On the day when the audience takes over—if it does—the air will be cleared, the subject up for grabs, everybody welcome and no holds barred. Perversely, the reviewer will not mourn any arbitrary influence he may lose; he will be the merrier for it, perhaps the more malicious for it, because he can huff and puff at his pleasure knowing the building won't fall down.

Hasten the day.

2

THE STRUGGLE
TO SEE

THE HEY, WAIT A MINUTE THEATER

It has generally been agreed that art has a right, and perhaps even an obligation, to exclude the gratuitous and the irrelevant. We have always understood that when a playwright writes a play he is leaving things out. He chooses an angle of attack upon his material, he arranges certain progressive steps that will advance and illuminate his concentrated vision, he lops off anything that would impede him or distract us. He simply does not bother to tell us, to use the traditional example, that his severely preoccupied characters also have to go to the bathroom; his omission does not bother us.

Or it did not, until recently. Recently the gratuitous, the apparently irrelevant, has come to call with a vengeance. In *Scuba Duba* a matronly woman parades about the premises with her exposed and overly ample breasts bobbling freely. There is no dramatic need for her to do so. In *Hair* four or five young men and several girls strip quickly beneath a rippling canvas to emerge nude and facing front. Nothing in the organization of the entertainment requires the display; it wasn't there when the entertainment was first mounted off Broadway. In *The Birthday Party* a man sat at center stage for quite a long time doing nothing but shred a newspaper—with a care that was

almost painful—along its column lines. The incident explained nothing about the man or the action in which he was engaged. In a casual
comedy called *Something Different* a husband and wife had twins
who were exactly alike except that one of them was colored. The joke
was compounded before the evening was over but not really accounted for. In each case, no need was followed by no comment.

Outrage has been the quick response in many quarters, though the
outrage takes a diversity of forms. Where nudity is involved, it is
frequently—and howlingly—held that sex is being cheaply exploited.
Where the irrelevance doesn't touch on such long-sensitive areas, as
it doesn't in the case of Harold Pinter's zombie shredding newspapers,
the author is accused of blandly manufacturing a put-on. (A celebrated letter to *The New York Times* demanded, in effect, that Mr.
Pinter explain his play or admit to being a fraud.) Where the play in
question is so light that no *serious* outrage seems called for, it is
called merely sloppy, as though the author hadn't worked hard
enough to tuck the proper pieces into place.

Criticism, in short, gallops off in all directions, certain that the
plays are doing the very same thing. But the plays, in point of fact,
are all headed in a single direction, moved by a single impulse. They
are one and all asking "What have we been leaving out?" and they
are asking it because it is suddenly important to know. We have
moved—for the time being but quite firmly, I think—into a kind of
theater in which the old selectivity, rather than the new randomness,
is regarded as a fraud. Selecting was cheating. Omitting was mis-
leading. We must have another look. And so the new Hey, Wait a
Minute Theater is with us—with us not because playwrights have
inexplicably become careless or secretive or pandering, but because
we want it.

We'd know that this was so if we paid any attention to our current
responses to traditional plays. One recent season virtually opened
with the traditional play in full blaze. A superb revival of Lillian
Hellman's *The Little Foxes* reminded us—very, very clearly—of what
it was like to have material fully organized for us. Miss Hellman had
known exactly what she was doing every step of the way as she
slipped into place just those character traits, just those lines, just
those decisive gestures that would build a trim dramatic house. *The*

Little Foxes is a confident play, and an airtight one. There are no loose ends left lying about, no moral ambiguities or unused plot threads, as the Hubbards progressively devour the earth and one another. The author knows the good guys from the bad guys, the right actions from the wrong ones, the telling movement that will help her make her point from the excrescence that will blur it. Everything is spare, appropriate, coherent. The play is beautifully sealed, made in the image and likeness of logic. What was the one criticism almost universally offered? That it was too well-made.

In our new state of mind we distrust what is orderly because we are now sharply aware that in everything ordered there is something extremely arbitrary. To have an order of any kind—political, religious, social, domestic—some of the things embraced must be arbitrarily embraced, whether they quite suit us or not; some of the things excluded must be arbitrarily excluded. We are terribly conscious—at this moment in time—of the fact that we do not really conform well to the roles and systems we have ourselves adopted. In shaping the roles and systems, too much of us was left out. We don't fit and we know it. The origins of this intense consciousness are many, crosshatched, cumulative; we can put them to one side here. What matters right now is our strong sense of having missed something vital along the way, along every way we have so carefully chosen to move: the political party to which we once pledged allegiance no longer contains us, the religion we believe in is seen to have neglected something actual that is in us, the posture we adopted when we became this sort of man or that sort of man does not house comfortably the man we are. Though the entire world is obviously and often violently engaged in the process of forcing all patterns open to see what has gone into their making—and what has failed to go into their making that ought to have been there—the mood is not truly despairing. It is determined. All of us must see more, hear more, risk more, embrace more, if we are to understand the bad fit and perhaps get a better one.

And so our heads swivel for a closer look. Above all, for a more inclusive look—without predisposition, without automatic exclusion of any kind, without *selection*. If we are going to select beforehand, we shall miss the same things we missed last time. Indeed, if any principle of selection is to function at all, it must be the principle of selecting now what was never selected before. *Nothing* can be called irrelevant if we are trying to find out what relevance is.

Thus the theater, like everything else in life, comes under two commands and a question. Say it. Show it. What *is* it?

That the theater has been desperately trying to Say It should be plain enough. Say what? Everything, before it has been edited. Take just one example: the onstage attitude toward the Negro. There are Negroes, by the way, in *The Little Foxes*. They serve the Hubbards, lighting their lights, answering their doorbells, tending their sick. Not much is made of them. Not much needs to be made of them because we know exactly where we stand in relation to them. They are among the oppressed. We sympathize with them and we like them. When the day of the Hubbards is done, if it ever is, we shall no doubt know them better and like them more. Our attitude is uncomplicated; it also leaves the Negro drawn in a single dimension. What else should be said?

The hero of Bruce Jay Friedman's *Scuba Duba* finds it imperative to say a great deal more. He is a liberal; he would have liked *The Little Foxes* and no doubt drawn his approving conclusions from it. He marched on Washington. Even then, though, he felt a little bit puzzled and a little bit guilty. It seems that he didn't quite listen to all of the speeches on that march. He spent too much time behind a tree with a colored girl. Of course, he has excuses. "Maybe it was her fault as much as mine," he says. "She was the colored one. She should have been listening."

Now he is thoroughly baffled. A Negro frogman seems to have run off with his wife and a sweet safe liberal one-dimensional attitude is no longer adequate to the situation. What does he *really* feel about Negroes? He doesn't know, which means that he must force to the surface everything he has ever felt at any time about Negroes, including all of the dirty lingering words he inherited during his boyhood. These last are still there, they *are* imbedded in his psyche, they *do* constitute a part of the total truth about himself, they rise like suds in an old-fashioned washing machine and spill over. Into the night, in a very funny comedy, go phrases like "dirty spade bastard," clacking against the moon. During his earlier liberal maturity, this man would of course never have used such words, would scarcely have acknowledged their existence in his vocabulary. He had an image of himself and also of the Negro, who would surely prove docile, grateful, and chummy once he'd been helped. Both images were fakes, something the Negro knew all along. The white man didn't know, he had *selected* himself too carefully for that, and now he must hurl his fakery at the skies—get it out into the open—if he is to discover who anyone is.

If the white man—in a play or, less readily, on the street—is finally risking Saying whatever is really lodged in his head, it was probably the black man who taught him to do so. Negro writers and speakers have been putting all the verbal cards on the table for quite some time now, without much caring which race their bluntness was aimed at. It was a Negro playwright who chose to call a play "The Electronic Nigger." Typically, the whites still lagged a bit. The title eventually had to be changed because, apparently, whites were so hesitant about pronouncing the words on the telephone or at the box office that sales were slowed down.

The process moves forward, though, and audiences who have settled in, at *The Boys in the Band,* to listen to homosexuals being entirely open with and about one another ("There's one thing to be said for masturbation, you don't have to look your best") are less than surprised to hear a white homosexual suggest to a Negro homosexual that he hush up and go eat his watermelon. A passion for watermelon was once a stock racist joke; it then became unmentionable out of what was thought to be sensitivity; it is now back on the playing field because its suppression was nothing more than *suppression.* Hiding the joke didn't exorcise the thought; indeed the hush in itself became a kind of inverted racism. Hopefully a truth between people will come of its laughing release.

Saying It, of course, is not confined to this single kind of example, isn't simply a matter of helping to surface information about Negro or homosexual minorities. It sweeps straight across the board, touching all of us in our standard pieties, our selective evasions. At the end of the rock musical, *Your Own Thing,* God the Father suggests that God the Son get a haircut. We are no longer to be silent about matters, humorous or otherwise, that we have furtively noticed and tastefully ignored. Silence can be, has been, dangerous; it is one of the things that made God the Father and God the Son seem irrelevant.

The business of Showing It takes exactly the same tack. Naturally it first tends to concentrate on whatever we have in the past most explicitly and insistently refrained from showing, which means sex. Those bobbling breasts are there because they haven't been there before. The nudes that have caused such a stir in *Hair* and *Tom Paine* are there for no other reason—if we are to accept them as something more than mere commercialism, which I do—than to let us look at something we might always have looked at and didn't. I find Groucho Marx's remark that he stayed home, stripped down in front of a mirror, and saved himself $7.50 very funny. But one of the things that make it funny is its astonishing literal truth. When the boys and girls strip in *Hair* nothing world-shaking happens; the most startling thing about the view is that it is, after all, so commonplace; we merely wonder what we'd been worrying about. Is that very little knowledge of ourselves to have gained? Very little; but it is something, given our tensions. (The nudes in *Tom Paine* were gauzily veiled, which took us back into the old titillating game of imagining that a real look would be shattering, a game that twists the truth out of all proportion.)

We have always had sex plays, particularly sex comedies. The curious thing about them was that there was no sex in them. They were talk plays. The actors may have chattered, chattered, chattered about sex the whole night long, with many a wistful glance toward the bedroom door, but the moment two of them went through that door the curtain came down. Traditionally, the sex play takes place in the living room. The closing door, with its falling curtain, also contained a promise of happily ever after. The battle was all in the words before bedtime. A play like *The Beard* goes through the door and comes back with another kind of report. Instead of happily ever after, a continuing, progressive, incantatory hostility is essential to sex play, up to and including the sex act itself (which is, to make the point, included). As it happens, I did not admire *The Beard*, mainly because of its monotonously repetitive use of ultimately flavorless words (Saying It can still mean Saying It Well). But I think I can see why it pursued its ritualistic standoff to a final, and most graphic, oral sex act. We had, all along, been talking and talking and talking about sex. But did we have in our mind's eye the thing we were talking about? Or were we painting, in the living room, an altogether different and quite unrealistic picture? Are we using anywhere near the right words for the action we're engaged in? Look at the action while it *is* an action, and then say.

Sex as a subject for this sort of exploration will probably tire rather soon. The range of investigation is limited, which means that the images must quickly become commonplace. Concentrating on skin in the theater isn't likely to get us much more than skin-deep. But Showing It has already invaded subtler and more provocative areas. I think we had no better play in 1968 than Peter Nichols' *Joe Egg*, and once again the first response of audiences thinking of going to see it was Not to Look. Joe Egg is a spastic child, a "vegetable." In life our instinct is to avert our eyes from this or any other sort of natural aberration—out of decency, we like to think. No one in the play would let us think so any longer, least of all a woman who came to the footlights to confess, in the most direct terms possible, that she physically loathed the sight of the child and would have "put it away" instantly if it had been hers. Harsh thoughts, ugly thoughts, pragmatic thoughts, unbearably loving thoughts crackled about the child while its "nappies" were being changed. We were inside a situation we have always—and not out of decency, either—stayed well outside of. We have refused knowledge out of fear: it is as simple as that. Knowledge does not wholly remove the fear, it cannot help being harsh; but because it is knowledge it can also be exhilarating and it can help to complete ourselves. Certainly we were doing nothing to complete ourselves when we were Not Looking. We were diminishing ourselves.

Harold Pinter normally refuses to tell us the plots of his plays, a fact which enrages some people and causes others to suppose him in some way incompetent. But Mr. Pinter isn't hiding his plot because he hasn't got one; he is hiding it so that we will look at something else. A plot can, in this new understanding, be enormously distracting; we tend to follow it so eagerly, pushing rapidly ahead, that we push all other things aside in our urgency; we don't pause to notice matters that don't help us hurry. What does Mr. Pinter want us to notice? Absolutely everything that has always been taken for granted. The way a man sits in a chair. The way he crosses his legs. The way he creases his trousers after he has crossed his legs. The way he lights his cigar. The way he waits. A vacuum is created where there used to be an external, ongoing, one might say *blinding* structure. Inside it now, sealed off and self-contained, sits existential life, life the way it happens, life itself to be looked at. Anyone who has seen a Pinter play well done knows how intensely our concentration focuses on just this sort of new/old detail: a woman handling a cup, a man putting a glass on a table.

What is accomplished by this sort of emphasis, especially considering that the detail has always been there to be observed (Laurence Olivier used to crease his trousers in *No Time for Comedy*, too) but was simply not observed because it seemed—in our narrative rush— unimportant? Oddly, what comes into being is increased mystery. Again, anyone who has seen a Pinter play well done has noticed that its most singular effect has been to make the stage, and the so minutely occupied people on it, seem to tingle—with apprehension, concern, awesome and perhaps faintly menacing life. As Ruth says in *The Homecoming* when the men have spent too much time discussing logical propositions, "Look at me. I . . . move my leg. That's all it is. But I wear . . . underwear . . . which moves with me . . . it captures your attention. Perhaps you misinterpret. The action is simple. It's a leg . . . moving. My lips move. Why don't you restrict your . . . observations to that? Perhaps the fact that they move is more significant . . . than the words which come through them. You must bear that . . . possibility . . . in mind." Perhaps we have, in our hurry toward the external, the abstract, the logical and the intellectually shapely, raced past the real mystery, the tremulous current that so often makes hash of our headwork. Logic, the effort at shapeliness, is not meant to be mysterious; it is meant to solve mystery and thereby kill it. Mystery comes back—we come back to the thrilling, agitating inexplicableness of ourselves—when we drop logic for close *attention*.

The letter to Mr. Pinter that ran in *The New York Times* was anti-mystery and demanded answers. A theatergoer who'd been to

The Birthday Party and who couldn't grasp why an unidentified lodger in a rooming house (Stanley) was being systematically destroyed by two unidentified invaders, insisted that Mr. Pinter tell her:

1. Who are the two men?
2. Where did Stanley come from?
3. Were they all supposed to be normal?

The theatergoer announced that she couldn't understand Mr. Pinter's play until he'd replied to her questions. Mr. Pinter replied that he couldn't understand her letter until *she'd* answered three questions of his:

1. Who are you?
2. Where do you come from?
3. Are you supposed to be normal?

In some quarters Mr. Pinter's reply was thought to be supercilious and evasive. Actually, he'd thrown his correspondent the one right curve. For, if she stops to think about it, she can't answer any of the questions. Ask someone where he came from and you will always get a quick answer: Scranton, Pennsylvania, or perhaps the West Coast. But he's only said where he was last, or where his parents happened to be when he was born. Where did *he* come from? From what unfathomable conjunction of genes, from how many untraceable generations back, has he now emerged to puzzle himself? ("I don't know where I got my red hair, or my singing ability, or my temper—it certainly doesn't run in my family!") No man can say where he's come from; it is the most challenging thing about him, and what makes him new.

Ask anyone "Who are you?" and again you'll get a quick answer: "I'm a teacher," "I'm a journalist," "I'm Ed's wife." But you will already have spotted the cop-out in that. The person answering hasn't specified an identity; he has mentioned a role he some time or other chose to play. The gap between identity and role must be obvious to us all. We *may* indeed function as teachers or journalists or housewives but we are by this time all too painfully aware that our functions are dress suits, that they do not in the least contain all that we are or that we might be, and that in actuality we do not even fill the limited role properly. Role is inadequate to identity, certainly to potentiality. In *The Homecoming* Ruth begins in the double role of wife and mother; by the end of the play she has agreed, without straining her identity, to become a whore. There was something else in her to be accounted for. Pinter uses the "whore" image repeatedly —it occurs in at least four of his later plays—not because he is obsessed with whores but because the whore is, by definition, undefined. She is no one and everybody—to anybody. Personality is seen to be without limits, without name.

Now, this is close to psychological baby-talk—we have heard enough about role playing in recent years to be ready to go on to something else—and we'll skip the all too stock question about what is and is not neurotic behavior. But if the plays succeed in making us more aware of how mysterious we are *to ourselves*, quite apart from the pretty little plots we have invented to provide a shape for our lives, if they remind us of the intense and baffling consciousness we have sometimes brought to the act of crossing our own legs ("I have done this before—why have I never noticed how peculiar it is?"), if they appeal to us *as questions* because we see that we are equally questions, then they will have focused the spotlight of Showing It on forgotten or neglected or unperceived thrusts and responses we do make but have rarely measured.

While this is going on, it is vital that no answers to the questions be attempted. Answers shape, somewhat arbitrarily, possibly prematurely. If we are going to take another look, a much more comprehensive look and one that does not begin in prejudgments and automatic exclusions, it will be necessary to spend an enormous amount of time just looking—to make sure that we get it all in. There is to be no leaping, not yet. That is why the most serious plays written in this vein—the plays that might be thought to get past the business of toying with questions into an attempted complexity and profundity capable of returning rough, overall answers—do not offer answers. Indeed answers are rigidly excluded. As we come, after having Said and Shown all that occurred to us or could be discovered, to the ultimate question—"What *is* it?"—we only dramatize the "What *is* it?" It is the asking that is acted out—and out and out and out until the lights fade.

In Tom Stoppard's *Rosencrantz and Guildenstern Are Dead*, the two principals very much want shape, coherence. They say so, often and sometimes loudly ("Come out—and come out talking!" one of them screams at the constantly disappearing residents of Elsinore). They want to get hold of the shape of Hamlet, the shape of the events in which Hamlet is involved, the shape of the play in which they themselves appear. They long for logic, and logic eludes them. There is a terrible need for them to know more. The fragmentary life of the castle that buzzes and bridles about them, throwing off sparks that won't come into a pattern, is a life to which they are denied access. But though life ignores them, they are still subject to death— to quick death as it happens, which they sense surely coming. They are going to die without having learned enough about the machinery that has trapped them to say who they are or why they have come or what is really happening to trap them. They can't get into life but they *are* in the play, and the play is going to kill them, no matter what. In the circumstances, their asking is understandably urgent. But to contrive an answer, given their present information, would be just that—to contrive, to fake, to put together a lie. The play will not put together a lie. Neither will they. The question mark must be permitted to quiver in midair to the bitter end, must be permitted to become the exclusive content of the encounter. For it is no better to die in a lie than in ignorance.

Teilhard de Chardin has remarked somewhere that we have just now come, along the evolutionary process, to an enormous expansion of consciousness. We have taken a great jump forward in what we *may* know. But of course at the moment of jumping, and of landing without road maps in territory vaster than we have negotiated before, we can only be bewildered. And we can only prod, test, kick with our feet and lift our noses to all winds, to see where we are and what untested solidities lie before us. We are very much in the position of infants who must try out all new objects with their teeth—or, short of teeth, their bare gums. We can't pretend to being natives. We are nothing more than clumsy explorers. But we had better be *attentive* explorers, ignoring nothing.

Thus our new plays are attentive to everything, ignore nothing, and defer conclusions. It doesn't matter that we have seen some of the things investigated before, that they once seemed too commonplace to deserve intensive study. They are being seen now in a new context, and that changes them, sometimes dangerously. We dare not assume that we know them, not in this heat, under this light. It may be a very long while before we dare assume anything. It is wise to postpone a shape that can be only an insecure shape.

Shape will come again, if only because man's mind has an instinct for putting building blocks on top of one another until they make a pyramid. I find, as I talk to university students here and there across the country, that the itch for shape, for form, for control of the new materials, stirs irresistibly even when an effort is being made to stay open, to embrace the possible without determining beforehand *what* is possible. Inside the present and necessary amorphousness, they ask in effect, isn't a seed already growing up, one that will organically reach out to use what is appropriate to it and discard what is inappropriate, selecting and rejecting until a new coherence is seen? They want the seed, while acknowledging that at the moment it remains invisible. I have no doubt they will find it, and make it adequate to those added materials that have so recently overwhelmed us. It will then do until the next increase in consciousness comes along.

Meantime, we must contend with this one, eyes and ears alert not for what is relevant or profitable—we don't know those things yet—but for what is there. No one need like all of the plays in which this kind of work is done; I suppose I must dislike half of them heartily. No one need call a bad play a good play simply because its tentacles are in the right place, though it does become a more difficult matter to say just why one thinks such a play good or bad. Old norms tend to shatter under such stretching, and one must go by instinct again; but that is a pleasantly personal, and directly engaged, way of responding to a play, and it conforms fairly closely to what we must now do in our out-of-the-theater lives.

Like such plays or rail against them, we are already involved in their effort; we are often surprised to find that we *can* take them, unprepared as we thought ourselves. The experience was with us before we set foot in the lobby. We may fight it; we can't pretend not to recognize it. I am told that in some university communities where *The Birthday Party* has been done, the older members of the audience were apt to decry the newspaper-shredding sequence as perfectly recognizable but utterly valueless; the younger members quickly adopted it as a game, as a self-explanatory and existential thing *done*. Questions of relevance, just now, need not be so agitating; it is possible to be cheerful while examining phenomena.

If I had to sum up the whole business in the fastest conceivable way, I'd simply say that we have moved from a logical theater into a phenomenological one. Look at the thing hard. What thing? Everything. And don't try to say what it is until you've had it long enough in hand to know its tricks. Shape will come again. Now, what about *shapes*?

THE MOMENT OF PINTER

I was quickly afraid that more people would be put off than turned on by Alan Schneider's production of Harold Pinter's *The Birthday Party*.

This was regrettable, because we had just then arrived at the Moment of Pinter. Every playwright whose work is genuinely original goes through a trial period of resistance and doubt, followed by a time of advancing rumor. On his first exposure to Broadway, with *The Caretaker*, Pinter had been banished after a short run. Subsequently his palm prints, like quiet messages left on moist plate-glass windows, had begun turning up off Broadway, one after another until the sign could become familiar. With each new short play done off Broadway the whisper and the commitment had grown: those who had seen only *The Collection* exchanged notes with those who had seen only *A Slight Ache*. But we were beginning to deal with multiples now, and after a while these multiples made a noise— enough noise to stir the sluggish, who hate to be left out even more than they hate to be pushed in. At last there came a time of turnover for Pinter, a Moment when it was necessary to know who and where he was, to know what sort of face might go with the rumored, disembodied hand. *The Homecoming* profited from the coming of the

Moment; a somewhat slack play, it arrived at exactly the right time to take up the slack.

With the larger audience hooked in now, or ready to make the connection, it became possible to rummage into Pinter's past and to mount on Broadway—ten years after its London trial-flight—the first full-length play he ever wrote. *The Birthday Party* is exceedingly simple in outline, simpler and more conventional—on the surface— than the sly, fetid, murmuring mysteries that so gradually built his reputation. An unshaven young man in a seaside boardinghouse scarcely ever goes out of doors. In at the doors come two strangers, ostensibly looking for lodgings, actually looking for the immediately fearful young man. They intend, in the most familiar melodrama terms we know, to "take him for a ride."

The parties to this contest do not know each other; the issue becomes violently physical, but it is not personal. The invaders—a genial, dapper Jew named Goldberg who conducts himself rather like a casket salesman, and a florid Irishman named McCann who can scarcely see the world beyond the bulk of his own chest—simply refer to an "organization" which the young man has betrayed and to which all (all of us) belong. Though the young man, Stanley, can no more remember what he may have done wrong than any standard Kafka hero can, he behaves guiltily, defending himself before he has really been accused. In the course of the play, Goldberg and McCann bait Stanley, rough him up, break his eyeglasses so that he must painfully bark his shins against the furniture, drive him so deep into nervous disarray that—with unstable flashlights cutting the gloom of a hollow party-game—he is discovered attempting to strangle and/or rape a neighborhood tart. After spending the early morning hours with him in his room, Goldberg and McCann bring Stanley down termite-crumpled stairs and take him away. It is his birthday, but he was born to be dead. There never was any other possible resolution to the struggle. What man escapes the "organization"?

In this single-minded destruction of a man who senses that he was created to be destroyed, there is a solid grounding for everything Pinter was to do later; there are sequences in which the special Pinter effect—a claw curls around the heart, though all the doctors' charts read "normal" and the nurses are laughing—comes off without fuss.

In fact, there are two ways in which the play ushers us into the isolation ward that is Pinter's world.

It accepts anxiety as man's principal experience of life, and then, instead of discussing anxiety, it becomes it. You will have noticed that the story offers us no facts, no history: no one knows what Stanley has done or whether or not he has done anything, not even Stanley; no one knows who Goldberg and McCann are or who sent them; no one knows where all three are going when they leave. Threat is without identity. So is guilt.

But it is precisely the nameless fear—the pain that can't be located, the strain that has come from no particular stress—that most haunts the contemporary mind. Anxiety, by definition, is apprehension without clear cause. By placing the uncaused terror on the stage, by making it actual without assigning it addresses or zip codes, Mr. Pinter has cut open for us, with a ragged blade, the particular can of eels we are all now trying to get down for our dinners. Exactly how masterly the playwright can be—at his sudden best—was clear from a fragmentary, unemphatic, recurring detail in the Broadway production of the play. Ruth White was the victim's landlady; she looked rather like an aging, frayed Little Bo-Peep for whom the sheep never had come home. She was terrified of one thing: that a van would draw up outside the house one day and that there would be a wheelbarrow in it. She didn't say why. We didn't need to be told. We only needed to watch her compress her lips, and seem to gather the folds of her flesh into a protective knot, whenever *anything* stopped on the street outside to know that the image—the image alone—had the power to drain her. When, at the sound of a car, she curled into a corner of the room as though the wallpaper might wrap its shielding arms around her, her fear was real because—with a few slight adjustments in the image—her fear was ours. The irrational demon exists.

The second Pinteresque effect that the play foreshadows, and occasionally makes concrete, is that of making us listen to what is going on *now*. Now only. There is nothing else to listen to, or to watch: no mortgage foreclosure at midnight, no promise that it will be a nice day tomorrow, no tomorrow. We are breathing, blinking, existing by the second hand on our watches: there are no hours or minutes on the dial, no promises, no pasts. The result is a tremendous concentration on the immediate, simply because it is immediate and because the immediate is all we really know. Thus we watched McCann, his oversize frame splayed loosely on a chair, slowly and painstakingly shred that newspaper into neat single-column strips, quite as though nothing more momentous could engage human fingers or faculties and as though a single slip or unwanted tear might bring an end to consciousness itself. We watched raptly, engaged in the action, unconcerned by its meaninglessness. It was important because it was taking place.

Stanley, distracted, surrounded, still alive (but for how long?), held himself barely in control at a table. He lighted a match, to watch it burn. The flame ate slowly along the stick. His eyes were filled with nothing else. He was not thinking; he was being, like the burning match. The match burned his fingers. But that happened in another second in time, and was not to have been anticipated. All intensity is rooted in the instant; the instant constitutes its own boundaries.

These things are discoveries—visual discoveries, theatrical discoveries, philosophical discoveries if you like—and Mr. Pinter is the first man to have brought them back alive. Even so, the production at hand was by and large a bore, and I could see little point in pretending that it was likely to make a great many converts.

What was off? Surprisingly, the acting and staging were subtly off. I was surprised for two reasons. The actors were all able, some of them thoroughly familiar with Pinter territory. And Alan Schneider is not only a skillful and perceptive director; he had already done (in *The Collection*) what may remain the definitive mounting of a Pinter play, controlling nuances as though he'd broken them in as colts.

Here, however, there was an essential thinness, an absence of density, solidity, reserved force. Goldberg and McCann did not seem inexorable powers, impossible to evade; a victim might well have watched his chance and given them the slip while they were doing a buck-and-wing exit against a flimsy vaudeville drop. Miss White's wheelbarrow, for all its invisibility, was more frightening. And the sequences involving Stanley, his landlords, and the girl from down the way were handled just a shade too casually, perhaps too realistically: we seemed to be watching a minor film of seedy British life which had unaccountably lost force in its sound track. The movement of the play, the visual patterning, was very nearly perfect; behind it there was not much secret sense of stored-up threat, of energy that might unpredictably be unleashed.

The play proper may be caught between two stages in Pinter's development. Being such an early play, it is dependent upon influences: the guilt-and-no-guilt line is Kafka, the hydraulic-drill clatter of non sequiturs with which Stanley's inquisitors derange him is Beckett. At the same time it shares with the playwright's later full-length plays a weakness at the base of the spine that beomes enervating. Mr. Pinter has not yet discovered how to sustain his unique command of the absolute "now" over two and one-half hours. Each long play builds to a single event; any one split-second along the way is apt to be mesmerizing; but in time, with the single event being held off, the separate split-seconds tend to become the same split-seconds and therefore monotonous. The playwright is being stingy, I think, not with information but with event. Since anything can happen, why doesn't more?

Pinter's best work thus far seems to me to have been done at lengths running up to an hour or an hour and fifteen minutes, not beyond that. Inside such a pressure chamber the intense absorption with what is happening in spite of the fact that we do not fully know what is happening, the alarming sense that the juggernaut is about to roll over us and that we do not know which of the characters harbors the power to set it in motion, can be kept alive, provocative, paralyzing, even grindingly funny. At such length one event is enough: it gets the curtain down. But after a certain span of time we tend to wish to do in the theater what we actually do in life: take steps. We swing into action as a means of dealing with our anxiety. The action we take may bring with it fresh states of anxiety; it often does— which simply means fresh fodder for the same playwright. But we do become impatient, and, in our impatience, mobile.

That is why I think the band of dedicated Pinterites—among whom I have long since counted myself—is more likely to be increased by exposure to *The Collection, A Slight Ache, The Dumb-*

Waiter, The Room and *The Lover* than by reluctant, and probably dissatisfied, first acquaintance with *The Homecoming* or *The Birthday Party*. We are constantly being promised revivals of these plays; let us have them, while Mr. Pinter keeps working.

THE FINGER OF GUILT

John Osborne's *Inadmissible Evidence* is an unattractive and highly original play.

The time is half-past Kafka. A thirty-nine-year-old solicitor never— not for a moment—ceases defending himself. Calling for glasses of water as though he were terrified of drying up, rubbing the flesh of his cheekbones until it folds back over his exhausted eyes, pacing the floor of his office with the irresolute alertness of a forest animal baffled beyond endurance by contradictory warning signals, he soils the air with the sound of his fear. But no one in the play ever accuses him of anything. He is defending himself against a silence.

More than anything else, silence leads a man to expect judgment. Silence *seems* the worst conceivable judgment. When the lawyer cannot badger a long-suffering, patiently enduring employee into attacking him openly, into admitting that he despises him, he drives the employee from him; an absent silence is better than a present one which must be looked at every day. When a business associate cannot be reached by telephone, the lawyer is certain that he *has* heard something on the other end of the wire. He is certain he has heard the associate's voice, saying to his secretary, "Tell him I'm out, will you?" Listening to the moment, watching the lawyer bite his lip in humiliated rage, we are not at all sure he has heard any such thing. He *wants* to hear something, wants to hear it so badly that he is capable of inventing it. Forced to invent, he can invent only what will diminish him.

When, in the early morning hours, he is wakened from a thrashing sleep under an overcoat on the office couch, he knows that he has been wakened by a shrill ringing. What? Which telephone? Which possible source of insult, which clean new trumpet of contempt? Half blinded in the dark, hung over, aching from one nightmare and plunging into another, he gropes breathlessly into cubicles, beyond frosted-glass panes, for the one phone that will deliver a voice. There is no one he wants to talk to: not his mistress, not his wife, not the clients he feels incompetent to deal with. Any call will be a demeaning call. Yet the stumbling race against the ringing, the reach for three, four, five instruments before the bell at last cuts off, has panic in it. For when the bell does cut off, curtly and finally, contempt will have become absolute. Better that someone had got him, charged him, defined any one of his guilts. Left to himself, in the still room, he is guilty of everything, without limit.

The silence at last becomes wholly literal. His daughter visits him in his office, at his request. He realizes that he has failed her, wants her to realize that he realizes it. He has always failed everyone. At work he has depended upon other people's efforts. He has been a bad father, a bad husband, a bad lover. He has never felt "with it," never been "representative of anything." It's not just that he can't *retain* things now, though he can't. He has a sluggish, small brain, and, to keep others from noticing too much, he "just runs it through quickly like a piece of film." Now, with his daughter, the film doubles, trebles its speed, blurs dizzily into the torrential tumble of a bombed building coming down.

Self-hatred spewing from him as though forty penitential lashes might somehow make him clean, he clutches at the girl for absolution, even tries to see in her generation an end to so much privately inflicted pain. Her generation moves along its own sidewalks, comes casually from its bedrooms, with ease and freedom and accomplished charm, it seems to him. Perhaps, having done everything "sensibly and stylishly," these youngsters will "subdue the earth for the first time." Mouth agape, perspiration streaming down his face, the lawyer waits for a word. His daughter leaves the scene without ever having spoken.

The play's originality consists, I think, in its having arrived at a stage form precisely calculated to echo and reecho a numbing paradox of our time. If contemporary man has been told one thing more often than another it is that he is not guilty. He may be sick, he may have been swindled by moralists, he may have inherited a thousand atavistic traits which are in themselves disturbingly antisocial; but he is not guilty. Guilt is a complex, something to be dissolved by right reason. The old order of anathemas, of judgments hurled at man by church, state, and unified community have lost their force, been exposed as social artifices meant to subjugate. Trial by anything outside the individual himself has been dismissed as unworkable. Nothing exists outside the individual himself; there are no fingers in the air pointing balefully, no voices crying shame. The air is empty of the power to convict. Therein lies the silence.

But under this dispensation an appalling thing has happened. Unconvicted by any roar from the heavens, or gossip from the neighbors next door, modern man has rushed his talent for self-inflicted torment into the breach. Guiltless, he is guiltier than ever before.

Appointing himself prosecutor, and prying without restraint into his feebleness, his failings, his most detestable motives, he can find no wish, thought, or deed in himself that is entirely blameless. Left to analyze himself rather than account for himself, he finds himself intolerable: unloving, disloyal, in his words and gestures fraudulent. He no longer has to face a defined accusation from a single, clear voice; he might always have dealt with that, might even have confidently lied in order to justify himself. Self-respect comes easiest when it is being maintained in public. Now, though, man need only answer to himself, for himself; as he does so, privately, he discovers that he is loathsome.

Worst of all, he is right. In Osborne's play there is no suggestion that the hero, or anti-hero, is mistaken about himself. The play is not built to show a distinguished man disintegrating. This lawyer, apparently, has for a time "got by" by leaning on better men than himself. He is not now competent to deal with clients; he is sexually miserable though sexually very active; he is coarse where he might be charming, and spiteful where he should be grateful. He calls himself "irredeemably mediocre" and the judgment, his own judgment, is accurate. Because the judgment is accurate, he cannot possibly forgive himself. And, because of the silence outside him, there is no one to whom he can appeal. His daughter walks away without comment; his mistress walks away in despair.

The play itself reserves comment, unless we are to take the mistress' parting shot, "You beggar and belittle yourself just to get out of the game," as something more than her own resentful view of things. But the mistress' words do not sound definitive; they sound small and irrelevant alongside the actual anguish we have been hearing, bearing, and in part sharing.

Overall, the play is not tendentious, not a diagnosis ending in a prescription. It is an abrasive rendering of a hopeless bind, an hour-by-hour and minute-by-minute accounting of what it is like to have nowhere to turn but inward, where hell is. The play describes the nightmare of a nonentity rigorously, promising the nonentity nothing in the way of relief.

For our part, we are allowed only the relief of Mr. Osborne's biting, non-mediocre, prose. The lawyer, reveling in corrosive candor, tells us that his daughter "is sure to marry an emerging African if she hasn't already given her virginity to Unicef." He feels confident, too, of the fate of a woman who rears her children as though she were serving Holy Communion: she'll "wind up with an empty chalice and hot flashes at fifty." The snarl is a quality snarl as often as not, and it helps to compensate for the fact that the author is, as a dramatist, belligerently single-minded in pursuit of his scented quarry. Having hit upon a fleeting truth—fleeting not in the sense of being half unreal but of being extraordinarily hard to lay hands on— he grits his teeth, clenches his fists, and makes tireless tracks through the desert. If we want to come along, that's up to us. He will not be dissuaded from his objective or from his stubborn, persistent indifference to creature comforts while following whatever it is that put the glint in his eye.

The play is no fun at all. It is long, repetitive, monotonous in feeling, though *not* boring. I have talked with people who found its claustrophobic atmosphere unendurable. But, as with several of his earlier plays, Mr. Osborne has tried to drive a nail through nothing-ness, and, hitting all our thumbs and getting the nail crooked to boot, he has succeeded in one disagreeable yet satisfying sense: he has opened a hole in the wall of our privacy, spilling out secret disturb-ances and apprehensions that, as modern men, we have truly fallen heir to but were keeping so secret that we didn't ourselves quite know we had them. It takes an original play to do just that, however ruthlessly or cavalierly it feels it must treat us in the process.

THE COMEDY THAT KILLS

After all these years of prattling on and on about Revenge Tragedy (with *Hamlet* as the supreme example of the good play that can be born of a merely bloodthirsty tradition) we have finally arrived at its dead opposite: Revenge Comedy.

Tom Stoppard's *Rosencrantz and Guildenstern Are Dead* is a Revenge Comedy in two senses of the term. On a superficial, and quite pleasant, level, the comedy takes its revenge on all of those people who have, for four hundred years, obstinately announced that they couldn't tell Rosencrantz and Guildenstern apart. Mr. Stoppard makes it clear that Rosencrantz and Guildenstern couldn't tell themselves apart.

On a much more serious, and finally most impressive, level, the comedy takes its revenge on that dirty trickster, Life, for being built the way it is. It is built like a honeycomb that is mostly plugged up, defying all the busy little bees who must work with it to get at it.

Rosencrantz and Guildenstern must live with the honeycomb that is Hamlet's house. They have been summoned by a messenger who came so early in the morning that they can scarcely remember what he looked like or what he said. Having arrived at a castle that seems so much melted-down wax, they are welcomed and then abandoned, left to toss coins in drafty corridors while the urgent business of the hour goes on in other rooms without them. They do not understand the task they are to perform, much less the crisis that has overtaken the occasional fugitives who slip by them to scream silently or perhaps to make an incomprehensible joke about knowing a hawk from a handsaw.

Guildenstern, a spare, gangling, fretful fellow who looks like both a hawk and a handsaw, is exasperated that he should so become "intrigued without ever being enlightened." Guildenstern expects something of the world he inhabits. He expects coherence, a pattern in which "each move is dictated by the previous one—that is the meaning of order." But here there are only fragments: Hamlet yanking at Ophelia's blond hair to whipsaw her head about, for no known savage reason; touring players rehearsing a dumb show in which the dead are blown away on the wind like nameless November leaves.

Rosencrantz is, for a time, more easygoing, if only because all the coins he tosses keep coming up heads: the probabilities, which no one can fathom, seem to be in his favor. Gradually, though, it becomes apparent that the universal drift is toward death—and toward a death that will come before anyone has quite grasped life. "Incidents! Incidents!" he cries out, shaking his fist at empty heavens as he begins to scent the woodsmoke of his own funeral pyre. "Dear God, is it too much to expect a little sustained action?"

The principal touring player gives neither of them comfort. He has long since ceased trying to make any sense of himself as a man; he is resigned to being nothing more than an actor, a creature of no settled identity. But he doesn't really suppose that acting is going to impose any shape on his wayward passage. He has long ago been "tricked out of the single assumption that makes our existence tolerable—that someone is watching." The play goes on, blindly, piecemeal. All of us are caught up in it. But it is being performed to deafness. Rosencrantz shakes his fist at no one.

The play is of course yet one more document in the unreeling existentialist catalogue. If I have anything against it, apart from its somewhat crushing overlength, it is that Mr. Stoppard himself is watching too closely, is too much with us. His two principal figures are not baffled and lost in their own ways. They are baffled and lost in his, speaking his words for him, placarding his thoughts. Thus there is a steady barrage of philosophical finger-pointing: "Which way did we come in—I've lost my sense of direction," "What have we got to go on?", "We're slipping off the map," "What does it all add up to?" The effect is to remove Rosencrantz and Guildenstern not only from the fevered life that is rumored about them but also from the arbitrary play that is surely going to execute them. They stand outside both, ignorant and omniscient at once, intellectualizing for their author. What this ultimately suggests is a Presence in the wings after all, a designer, a dictator, a listening God of some sort—and it tends to undercut the play's own premises.

But the evening's compensations grow upon one steadily as the stage lights turn from an autumnal gold to a tidal wave of blood-red. When Mr. Stoppard puts himself to digging beneath the outer layer of human experience, he is capable of bringing back chilling bulletins from the unknown front. Rosencrantz seems to catch his breath as from an invisible, sickening blow as he realizes that he cannot for the life of him recall when he first heard about death. Someone must have told him, undoubtedly when he was a child. News of such import must have lodged somewhere in his head. But it hasn't. Does anyone remember the moment of that first staggering announcement that he is destined to die? No, probably not. With his mouth scarcely able to form the necessary syllables, pallid from the implications he is trying to sort out in his brain, Rosencrantz makes the obvious deductions. No one remembers first hearing the news because everyone was born knowing it. A baby's first bleat rides on the breath of "an intuition of mortality."

The written moment, and Brian Murray's fiercely concentrated realization of it in performance, proved brilliant strokes of theater. So did the fidgety scurry of John Wood's slippered feet as Guildenstern tried, with caterpillar tactics, to evade the sound of what his companion was saying, huddling his toes together and clapping his hands over his ears as though his entire body could be blinded if he exerted himself enough. Again, the desperation with which Mr. Murray struggled to imagine England when he had not yet got there was original and telling exploration of the human consciousness, reminding us of those hundred half-forgotten—perhaps willfully forgotten— sensations we've had of the insubstantiality of all that is most familiar to us, of the images that wantonly dissolve the minute we decide to force them into sharp focus.

And humor is, in Mr. Stoppard's hands, the easy handmaiden of the frustrations we live with as we keep hot on the heels of a promised clarity. Either Rosencrantz or Guildenstern (it *is* hard to say which) wants to know why the players bother with a dumb show before the spoken play proper. The chief player explains that the unspoken is a good deal clearer. "You understand," he adds with a bitter flourish, "that we're tied down to a language which makes up in obscurity what it lacks in style."

Paul Hecht's chief player was breathtakingly good: a swaggering

Villon with a heart turned to ice, he put all of his belief into his own bravura, his upraised hand holding itself firm in the unanswering air, his stance angrily grounded upon an unresponsive earth. Theatrically speaking, everything about Derek Goldby's production was a joy to watch: the preoccupied people from *Hamlet* swirling by in their faintly frosted costumes, the dusty traveling harlequins creeping out of barrels on shipboard to surround Hamlet's two frightened friends in quiet but unhelpful sympathy. The evening's pantomime passages—a king retracting himself into sleep, a sweep of gray cloaks over the field of the dead—were beautifully mounted, and Richard Pilbrow's lighting seemed to swell inside the play and then diminish to the isolated pinpoints on which each of us must at last stand. The stage was managed as music might be; in time—and despite all reservations—we were overwhelmed by the visual sound.

APOLOGY FOR DYING

You'd have been neglecting a whisper in the wind if you hadn't looked in on *America Hurrah*.

There was something afoot here. And it was nothing so simple as the subtitle on the program—"3 Views of the U.S.A."—suggested. That suggested a montage of sorts, perhaps documentary in flavor, and the hint was rather depressingly reinforced by the fact that you noticed, as you wandered into the lobby of the off-Broadway Pocket Theater, a plastered-up assortment of photographs ranging from Louisa May Alcott to Wilbur and Orville Wright.

But you could forget the photographs. What was going on inside the blindingly white tile walls that enclosed the raked stage of the Pocket was a great deal more complex, more elusive, and more adventurous than that.

Take a slippery, and in the end rather chilling, moment in the first "view." We'd watched a handful of unemployed sit wistfully on square blocks while bland masked interviewers, sugared with smiles, hurled impertinent questions at them. We'd watched the stage dissolve into the city streets, the players dissolve into wailing sirens, whispered folk songs, the jumpy cacophony of marionettes rattling through a recording tape at the wrong speed. We'd noticed that the lurching through sound and space had an interior urgency about it that was odd indeed, especially since there wasn't the least trace of obvious narrative to lure us on. We lurched along willingly, bidden to do so by something original and personal in playwright Jean-Claude van Itallie's restrained voice.

Now a moment came when a full-throated siren alerted us to a corner accident. Someone had been killed by a car. The labored inhale-exhale of artificial respiration, made into a musical continuum by the same malleable actors who were saying all the lines, failed. A pretty girl—a girl with a strong sense of obligation—left the accident to go on to a party. She would have liked to tell everyone at the party about the accident, though no one would listen. Above all, she would have liked to apologize for being late. No accident is enough to make a person late for a party. Slowly, subtly, and with a sense of having been slapped in the face, we did grasp that it was the girl herself who had been killed and that she was apologizing for having been killed at such an inopportune moment. The dead must never be inconveniently dead. Not in America, not just now.

In his second and third bits of spying on the way it *feels* to be on this continent these days, the playwright offered us two strong, plain contrasts that were quietly and deftly kept from turning obvious. In a television studio three very normal workers glanced at the monitor now and then, where busy performers with striped faces—they looked like so many upended zebras—went through all of the violent, cloying, synthetic motions that pass for companionable entertainment on the national airwaves. But there was no relation between the workers and the work: a yawning gulf, big enough to drown us all, had opened between the real concerns of real people and the imaginary concerns of our imaginary archetypes.

One of the real workers nearly strangled to death on a bone in his chicken-salad sandwich. But the burly chanteuse who poured affection across the land as though she were an open fire hydrant of good will went right on beaming her thousand good-nights. Disaster is irrelevant in a time of eternally manufactured delight.

In a "respectable, decent, and homey" motel—we were in the last playlet now—a massive Mother Hubbard made of very rough clay revolved and revolved, like a warming beacon, welcoming the transient to a haven filled with the books of John Galsworthy and "toilets that flush of their own accord." Meantime two oversize grotesques, one male, one female, entered a paid-for room to strip to bodies that seemed made of flesh-tinted Band-Aids and then to destroy the room wantonly, book by book, toilet by toilet.

None of this was didactic. It was simply observant. None of it was labored. For the most part Mr. van Itallie trod gently across the sorrowing, inattentive earth. If some of the evening sounded as though the verse of e. e. cummings had been rearranged by Kenneth Fearing and then set to the intrusive rhythm of "Turkey in the Straw," that was all right. For one of the things the theater is trying to discover at the moment is a means of approaching poetic effect on the stage without relying upon arthritic forms. And these conscious "primitives" came to seem a valid, perhaps necessary, first try—almost as though we were Greeks again, searching out a right sound for the stage. Perhaps that was why there were so many garish Greek masks, and even elevated Greek boots, puffing up the plays at the Pocket.

The author was plainly someone to be watched, and wished well.

NIGHT SOUNDS

The atmosphere of the current theater is the atmosphere of a hospital corridor, with some of the doors opening and some closing, with some patches of bright light (harsh and metallic) and some of very dim, with birth taking place in some rooms and death in others, and with no one around to show us the particular room we are looking for. We walk this corridor carefully, looking right and left in wonder, prepared for regret and permitting ourselves just a little bit of hope.

Something is Happening. It can be heard happening on crowded sidewalks and it can be felt happening as we glance, in passing, up the side streets along Broadway where marquee lights are shining but shining down upon nobody. Over here is agitation and over there is stillness; both are bewildered.

By chance, the sidewalk that I used most often just a few years ago, a sidewalk that took me to my office past the Billy Rose Theatre, was a noisy one. I was generally hurrying back from early first-night curtains at the very moment when the customers for Edward Albee's *Who's Afraid of Virginia Woolf?* were having their second-act intermission cigarette, and it was impossible not to hear what the most excited voices were saying. "*You* were the one who wanted to come!" and "Since *when* did married people talk to each other like that?" were the commonest among the louder expostulations. It was as though people who hadn't quarreled publicly in years were compelled by the play to say that people don't, or shouldn't, raise their voices to one another. They nearly behaved like the play in order to deny the play; they were outraged by its behavior, and in theirs. One thing about them. They all went back in. Their nerves had been engaged and they had to finish scratching where it irritated. They wanted to reject, and they did not. What they were really doing was quarreling over a name for the baby.

The baby is still with us. It isn't very attractive just yet; its head is still a bit out of shape and it is hard to say what it will look like a little later on. All the same it has got to be listened to during the night, between curses and with some care. It is here now, and it does have lungs.

The baby is not, was not, simply Mr. Albee or his play. It is a tone of voice that is coming to be heard in the theater which makes the tones we were so used to seem pale and stale by comparison.

This has very little to do with specific shock effects. The fact that certain words we formerly excluded from dramatic conversation are spat out in rifle-fire rhythm in a number of new plays is of only temporary interest. Mr. Albee, for instance, peppers us with them as a kind of warning rattle, to make sure that our ears will be attentive when he decides really to burn them—with something else. The new tone of voice is actually weakest and most limited in its expletives, strongest and most flexible in its production of a sound pushed beyond the boundaries of the ordinary human throat.

If it is something like a scream, it is not like the hoarse, ragged, unsatisfactory scream we hear ourselves projecting when we actually do scream. It is closer to the sound we hear, but do not actually produce, when we dream that we are screaming; this seems to pour from us without any abrasive resistance in the vocal cords, to pierce the almost visible air with the swiftness of a flying knife, to travel farther because it has no muddying, or lifelike, reverberations. The sound doesn't wobble, or rattle; it shoots. In this connection, we have constantly to remind ourselves that Mr. Albee's play, like most other plays that have begun to exercise a nightmare freedom, is in no sense a realistic play. (Never mind the scenery: we are actually in an underground cave, or on top of Bald Mountain.) The form, at the moment, is always close to fantasy, close enough in Harold Pinter's plays to make us uncertain where the shoreline is. The plays are not saying what married people, or unmarried people, say; they are not even saying what people *would* say if they dared. They are saying all that *could* be said if the water pipes of personality had burst, all that it is possible to say—given an iconoclastic and sometimes despairing point of view—on any subject.

For content, we are undoubtedly indebted to the analyst's couch: everything must be dredged up, relevant or irrelevant, actual or potential. But for the ranging, clattering, hammering, unimpeded flow of inflection we must look beyond the couch, as though the couch had been inadequate. Speech, on the couch, is hesitant, dissatisfied with itself as an instrument, self-critical in its circumlocution, eternally unfinished. Here we go for a finish, go for soul-broke, opening all the taps and throwing away the buckets to see if inundation will do what judiciousness could not. Now more is said than is actually meant or understood. When the things we really think run out, we must improvise, keep the pressure high and the stream playing in the air until we see if it *has* any point of exhaustion. By the time we reach that point, if there is one, we will have said much that is untrue, as will any man who cannot—on principle—stop talking. Much will have been fabricated on the spur of the moment in sheer panic that the pressure will flag before the well has been drained.

But there is a hope inside the torrent: that some truth will rush out that we didn't know was in it, and that this truth—if it comes— will come with something of the unexpectedness of poetry.

Alongside this direct, prolonged, unedited cry, the old plays of neat habit, of lines tailored plainly to a foreseen purpose, of orderly bookkeeping done for a cost-accounting firm, must seem worn, too plainly ink-stained. These go about their business, sometimes well enough to call us back into the office briefly, as efficiently as they did before; but the windows are streaked, there is dust in the air, and one feels the need to ask them, please, to speak up.

3

TEXTS &
NON-TEXTS

THE CASE OF THE VANISHING TEXT

ONE OF THE more curious, and I think dangerous, developments in recent theater is the threat to abandon the dramatic text.

The movement afoot is heavy with ironies. Fifteen years ago the British theater, together with the more sharply critical members of the American intellectual Establishment, would have none of a director like Elia Kazan for the plain reason that he was known to tamper with texts. When Kazan staged a play by Tennessee Williams, say, he would ask Williams for revisions before and during rehearsals: not only emphases might be changed; the very ending of the play might be changed. Occasionally Williams himself would become sufficiently distressed with the alterations to publish the play, finally, in its original form or in an alternate form, rather as though he wished to say that he'd been willing to go along with the transformations wrought in the course of a collaborative production process but that now he wanted it *his* way. William Inge did much the same after Joshua Logan had got through putting his directorial imprint on *Picnic*, and the impression was spread that the American theater was a director's theater in which the playwright's text was regarded as little more than a shooting script and that, in fact, it was often shot down. Cries of outrage at this sort of rape were frequent.

Today the voices that were then raised loudest in dismay are the voices urging upon us the primacy of the director and the literary unimportance of the text. British critics, and even actors, were once outraged by the American director's high-handedness. Today they are the willing slaves of a Peter Brook or a Joan Littlewood. Mr. Brook recently brought us his *Marat/Sade* (full title upon request) and found as ready a public for its limited engagement here as he had for its repertory performances by the Royal Shakespeare Company in London. The effect of *Marat/Sade* was wholly a directorial effect, so much so that it was virtually impossible to get at Peter Weiss's text while watching a performance. Whenever Marat, or de Sade, prepared to make a statement of philosophical position, all creative hell broke loose around him. Actors, purporting to be lunatics, drooled spittle, masturbated, rattled chains in buckets, violated the promised sound of words by the sight and sound of spectacle.

The intense distraction was as deliberate as it was directorially brilliant. Mr. Brook explained that he had been happy to have, from Mr. Weiss, a text that was in effect incomplete. Mr. Weiss had provided him with what he regarded as a loose-leaf sheaf of notes; the looseness was welcomed as a virtue, since it left so much to be filled in by the imaginations of those performing the play. Mr. Weiss did not know, as he has explained in many an interview, whose side he was really on, Marat's or de Sade's; his preferences have varied, more or less with his changing political awareness, during the time that has passed since he "wrote" the play. Well and good. The director's obligation to communicate a point of view was diminished, his personal liberty increased. Further, Mr. Brook is enamored of a directorial principle which could be given free reign in such undefined territory. Mr. Brook believes in *not* suiting the action to the word. To reinforce the word with a gesture which parallels or directly amplifies it is to belabor it, to insist upon the obvious, to dull an audience's responses by making issues transparent enough to invite sleep. Better, in Mr. Brook's view, to play the gesture *against* the word, to have the actor say one thing and behave as though he were saying quite another. The word will thus be made more vivid, the audience's responses altered, through contrast and even conflict. Vertigo will challenge the audience to find out what *is* going on.

The only thing wrong with this last principle is that it isn't true and doesn't work. De Sade, let us say, is kneeling at the footlights preparing to make a speech of some importance. While he is doing it, he must be whipped by Charlotte Corday. Since the man speaking is the Marquis de Sade, the whipping is relevant enough. Conceivably a series of properly timed lashes could force from de Sade, and intelligibly punctuate, an aspect of his philosophy. This must not happen. Therefore Charlotte Corday whips de Sade not with a whip, which would parallel and illustrate the point being made, but with her soft, flowing hair. She twists her head this way and that, letting her locks strike the speaker's back in whiplike rhythm but of course without sound or forcible impact.

The image was visually striking, altogether original. Indeed, we watched it with such fascination that we did not hear what de Sade was saying. An arresting action always takes psychological precedence over speech; that is why non-speaking actors are ordinarily commanded to remain still and not busy themselves "catching flies" while one member of the company is speaking. The audience eye goes a-roving on the instant; anyone can steal a scene, or at least destroy it, by lighting a cigarette or twiddling his thumbs. And in this case what we *saw* was gentle. The image, taking quick precedence, did more than distract from de Sade. It denied de Sade, gave the lie to him. De Sade's meaning had not been reinforced; it had been reversed.

Yet the reversals brought about by one aspect of a theory are unimportant alongside the indifference accorded the written "play." The focus at all times was upon the mindless eyes, the spastic mouths, the cracked-egg skulls of the inmates of Charenton asylum, who had been assigned to perform the play-within-a-play that de Sade had composed. We said to ourselves, "How marvelous the actors are! How can they possibly sustain these rigid attitudes for so long? Doesn't it hurt?" The manner of performing was all we attended to or remembered; we sat through the evening, and then left the theater, feeling that the matter of the play needed scarcely to be investigated.

Indeed, the matter had not been investigated, either by author or by director. For instance, in the debate between Marat and de Sade over whether man should actively contend with the forces of nature or passively submit to them, there was a peculiarity: all of Marat's speeches had been written by de Sade. What did this mean? It surely should have meant something, given birth to some irony, opened up an intellectual interplay in which we realized, perhaps, that author de Sade had driven Marat more than half mad by giving him the worst of the argument or that he had, subtly and out of a yearning for something beyond himself, given him the best of it. Precisely *what* the device might have meant is not the issue. The issue is simply that the device was there—and was not used. No one onstage seemed aware of this interior dislocation in the text; the debate, so far as it was permitted any play at all, was played straight. In the audience we remained unaware of the promising oddity of the situation; or if we thought of it, we forgot it. It was quite as though no significance could be attached to the fact that in a debate one man had provided all that the other was to say. The text was so little regarded that it was not even required to pay attention to itself.

Mr. Brook is not alone in his devotion to "making" the play on the stage, out of the stage alone. Joan Littlewood has been there before him, happiest when she could assemble the fragments handed her by an unreliable Irishman or a nineteen-year-old novice. Brendan Behan was a talented man, though apparently not one with a passion for "writing out" plays. Miss Littlewood danced them out for him. Shelagh Delaney is, I firmly believe, talented, too, though I think we may fairly assume that *A Taste of Honey* had neither the completeness nor the coherence in manuscript that it had, physically, once Miss Littlewood had sewed it together with music and mime. Miss Littlewood may, just possibly, have been happiest of all when she had no playwright to feed upon. For *Oh What a Lovely War* she simply pasted up some ancient popular songs and threw before them, in ironic juxtaposition, improvised dialogue spelling out the horrors of the war the songs meant to romanticize. One can walk onto a rehearsal stage with no manuscript of any sort and build a complete entertainment from scratch, given the ability and the urge to behave in this way.

Mr. Brook and Miss Littlewood are both geniuses of a sort; that they have done their own work well is obvious. I wonder, though, if they are themselves aware of the capitulation that has taken place.

The British theater, at its most adventurous, has not simply surrendered to the Kazan image it deplored a short while ago. It has gone much further, out-Kazaning Kazan by light-years. It is conceivable that Kazan sometimes bullied his authors. But he always consulted them and he always saw to it that *they* did the writing. A text came into being, however collaboratively or under whatever pressure, and it was a text that stood firm and whole as a text. I do not think that *Marat/Sade* is going to look quite the same after Mr. Brook's personal imprint has vanished, that it is ever going to lead a satisfactory independent life of its own.

In this country much the same thing has happened where it was least expected. Formerly the manipulation of the text as though it were no more than an adjunct to performance was regarded, with considerable horror, as a "commercial" practice. It was a thing that terrible producers with cigars in their mouths, and overweening directors with egomania in their eyes, did to plays when plays were trying out on the road. What an author wrote was held to be the essence of the matter, and when a manuscript was subordinated to the improvisation of actors and directors, shocked protests against the "star system" or against "pandering to the audience" could be heard. The intellectual Establishment much preferred the purity of The Living Theater.

Yet it was precisely at The Living Theater that the primacy of the text went down the drain. This off-Broadway organization, driven from its local playhouse and at present surviving somehow in Europe, is fast becoming a culture myth, more acclaimed now that it is safely absent than it was attended when its doors were open. The *Tulane Drama Review* devoted an entire issue to citing its accomplishments and mourning its loss; and almost anyone who is dissatisfied with the present state of theatrical affairs—there are excellent grounds for dissatisfaction, provided the posture does not become a sort of fixed puritanical spite—will cite The Living Theater, lovingly, as an example of what might have been. There is a good bit of cant, and not too much common sense, in all of this. The Living Theater was weak in three transparent ways. It was creatively underequipped. Its moving spirits were Judith Malina and Julian Beck, both of whom acted and directed. But Mr. Beck was neither a good actor nor a good director, and Miss Malina was not a good actress though she was a fine director. That left its mainsprings with one out of four talents to live by. Their acting company was dedicated, but ingrown enough to be useful only in isolation. Its members never seemed flexible enough to work elsewhere; though most off-Broadway enterprises yield performers capable of asserting themselves in other company, this one did not do so. And, specifically aiming itself at an avant-garde audience of necessarily limited but hopefully loyal numbers, The Living Theater was unable to support itself on its own deliberately reduced terms. It did not find the audience it *sought*.

These unpleasant but theatrically important matters aside, The Living Theater made the contribution for which it is most remembered by finding in the rhythm of performance what was not present as text. The organization did of course produce some wholly written-out texts which it treated with deep respect, notably Brecht's *In the Jungle of Cities*. But Jack Gelber's *The Connection*, probably its best-attended and most widely publicized venture, depended not upon the words spoken, which were largely street talk set down literally, but upon areas of verbal silence: my own most vivid memory of the play is of a junkie stooped trancelike over a phonograph for minutes on end. A pulse could be detected during such sequences, but it was a performance pulse, not a written one. It is only in a later play, *Square in the Eye*, written away from The Living Theater, that Mr. Gelber began to develop a scene in its totality, with all values indicated in the words supplied to the actors. For a playwright who wishes to survive the departure of any one given director this is a vital step forward.

Miss Malina experimented a great deal with what she called the Theater of Chance. In the Theater of Chance the next word to be spoken, if any, is determined by a throw of the dice; the structural orchestration is not the playwright's, it is a thing of whim. The laws of mathematics, plus a talent for improvisation, take care of the matter. We are still hearing pious sighs—in some cases more than pious; the play is regarded as prophetic—over Kenneth H. Brown's *The Brig*, which was being performed when The Living Theater closed. *The Brig* is a didactic play, meant to arouse us to anger over the inhumane conditions in Marine Corps prisons. The program lists for us the intolerable rules and regulations governing the conduct of prison inmates; for instance, prisoners may not cross lines painted on the floor until commanded to do so:

> Sir, Prisoner Number Five requests permission to cross the white line, sir.
> I can't hear you.
> Sir, Prisoner Number Five requests permission to cross the white line, sir.
> I can't hear you.
> Sir, Prisoner Number Five requests permission to cross the white line, sir.

There is variation in the oral bullying meted out by warden and guards to the automated prisoners, though it is a variation strictly confined to the limited verbal resources of stupidly brutal men and to the routine, repetitive tasks of the day: latrine permission, cell inspection, floor scrubbing. There is, needless to say, no narrative progression or sequential development, save for a brief protest, moralistically flavored, toward the end of the play. The episodes of the text could be played in almost any order. More importantly, they can be indicated as satisfactorily by a stage direction as by endlessly, emptily echoed dialogue. Sample stage direction from *The Brig*:

> *All the prisoners run into the head in single file. Moments later, they begin at the inside exit from the head to exclaim, one by one,* "Sir, Prisoner Number One requests permission to cross the white line, sir," *and so on.* TEPPERMAN *stands at the door to the head and says,* "Cross," *as each one finishes this statement, using his own number. The prisoners then stop at the entrance to the compound and repeat the formality.* CORPORAL GRACE *is there uttering the same word,* "Cross," *and the prisoners enter the compound, return their soap and towels and pick up their manuals, stand at attention in front of their racks, and begin to read. . . . As* TEPPERMAN *issues the orders, the Brig becomes a veritable madhouse: prisoners requesting to cross the white lines, sweeping, swabbing, taking and returning materials from* THREE, *the storehouse man, and running in all directions.*

The essential effect of the spectacle depends upon the cumulative monotony of devices, which need only be *described* by the author, not realized as structured speech.

In these circumstances it is up to the director to discover a rhythm in the performing that will make the experience meaningful and tolerable. No, "meaningful" and "tolerable" are both wrong. The play's meaning is contained in the list of rules on the program; we can *learn* as much from reading the list as from seeing the play. And the experience is not meant to be tolerable; it is meant to be intolerable in order to inflame us. What the performance rhythm must do is persuade us that, beneath the extended boredom of our engagement with the work, a core of aesthetic pressure exists. This pressure should be sufficient to keep us in the playhouse until the director has done with us, and it should serve to suggest for the enterprise a subliminal shape.

But the rhythmic pressure is the director's gift to an author who has copied down reiterated commands without making a perceptive text of them. That is to say, perception depends upon what happens outside the actual words used, outside their specific arrangement, outside the manuscript as a piece of expressive, self-sufficient writing. Mr. Brown is wholly at the mercy of a production. He has not made the play as a composer makes a melody; he has instead extracted the keys from the piano, turned them over, and gone home.

A rationale can be offered for the kind of activity we are talking about. Various rationales, in fact. We live at a time when the words of the "formula" play are all too easily anticipated; because they have been used in the same sequence so often, they are now without intellectual force. If we are to hear them again, words must be used in an unprecedented way, either radically out of sequence as in the Theater of Chance or as independent counters, made abstract by reiteration, as in *The Brig*.

We live at a time when the formal surface is esteemed above what used to be called "content" (although *The Brig*, with its hammered-home preachment, did have content of an extremely old-fashioned sort). The relationship of shapes at the surface is held to be what "art" is about, more or less exclusively. Thus *Marat/Sade* needed no intelligible substructure; indeed, it was careful to dissolve the boundary between actor and madman on the stage, between audience onstage and in the auditorium, so that if we began to seek or scent a substructure we would be thrown back, denied access to precise meaning. We attended a ballet of white-jacketed nonentities and had to find satisfaction, or rather a new restlessness, in their varied, constantly mobile juxtaposition.

We live at a time—this is very nearly the reverse of the last point—when low definition, minimum explicitness, engages us more completely than an earlier literalness did. Marshall McLuhan has told us that when the information given us by a medium is severely limited, we enter the medium more wholeheartedly, plugging the gaps out of our own imaginations.

The catalogue of premises for what directors and some writers are up to could be extended indefinitely, and the fact that some of these tend to cancel one another out—we are to be more detached, we are to be more involved—is not terribly important. Certainly the theater needs to shake itself awake, by whatever means; certainly we need to reexamine not only the nature of words but the nature of our natures if we are to end the sleepwalking that has been our reflexive activity for so long.

I would like to think, however, that the fundamental work—whatever it may be and wherever it may lead us—was going to be done by the writer. The writer, to be sure, is not the whole of theater. Improvisational theater is possible and sometime ultimately profitable, as the Italian *commedia dell'arte* taught us centuries ago. No one can say with certainty whether a play is truly a play until he has seen it played; the text, isolated from actors and from their physical presence before audiences, is an uncertain guide. O'Neill can read like schoolboy babbling and play like the prosecution's summation. Spectacle has been on the list of drama's respectable appurtenances since Aristotle, and I would be one of the last to want to take it off. Manipulation of the tools of sheer "theater" is a valid way of revealing drama. When a theatricalist like Tyrone Guthrie shows me, in his staging of *Twelfth Night*, a deep sadness I hadn't known was in the play, I am startled and unexpectedly moved. But in this case Mr. Guthrie is employing markedly theatrical methods to underscore, and perhaps elaborate a bit, a quality *in* the text; by toying with the stage he has made me see that I was ignorant of something actual. When the same Mr. Guthrie makes use of his unceasing invention to play Petruchio as a shy fellow, a bumbler terrified of Kate and quite incapable of dominating her except in a spurious and accidental way, I am not so happy. The staging is not teasing a hidden truth out of the text; it is ignoring the text in favor of a "show."

Curiously, it is the avant-garde that is becoming more and more "show" business. Perhaps this is necessary for a time, until writers can grasp the revolution certain directors are urging upon them and learn to supply, with some fullness, a true matrix for what is now only a mock-up. But one must always beware a too great fascination with the tricky triumphs of stage direction, above all when the writer himself turns his mind to its opportunism. The writer who turns his mind to stage direction is probably running away from being a writer. Bertolt Brecht was at one time a writer. Our experience with *In the Jungle of Cities* makes that plain. Here, when one kind of situation is taken out of its normal environment and placed in an alien one, when one figure is picked up bodily and put down where he does not logically belong, the superimposition functions as metaphor does. Two logical wrongs coalesce to make a poetic right. And it is all on paper. Decent acting, without too much window-dressing supplied independently by a theatricalist-director, will reveal the play, make it "work" in its own elusive and unliteral way. But Brecht, over the years, became more and more obsessed with stage effect as such. His theories, of "epic theater" and of "alienation," are essentially theories of how to mount a play, how to make it behave in relation to an audience—often against what on paper seems to be the text. The text becomes at best a sort of negative, subject to proper or improper development in the laboratory backstage. In *The Caucasian Chalk Circle* a terrified woman, carrying an infant, is forced to cross a spindly, dangerously weakened suspension-bridge. If the sequence is taken at its face value, which is its text value, it will simply seem a clumsy, slightly parodistic echo of a silent-movie chase, as it did in performance at Lincoln Center. I am told, however, that when it was played at the Guthrie Theater in Minneapolis a season or two earlier, the suspension bridge was suspended on the shoulders of two Chinese-style supernumeraries, instantly divorcing it from its literal across-the-gorge source. I am also told that the effect was charming. But the charm is a gleam in director Brecht's eye; as a writer he has provided only a diagram, instructions for assembling the theatrical

toy on the night before Christmas, which is the last night of rehearsal. Brecht gradually came to *think* stage direction more or less in
opposition to what he wrote. The texts became less and less self-
contained, so much so that uninspired direction could actually invert
their meaning, as it has so often done in the case of *Mother Courage*.
Mother Courage is a romantic fool; she seems nobility incarnate in
mountings which are not careful to cancel, with stage cunning, the
events on the page.

Whenever I see a writer turning his focus away from the text
toward the *manner* in which it is to be done, I suspect a loss of nerve.
Creative writing is a harrowing business, a terrifying commitment to
an absolute. This is *it*, the writer must say to himself, and I must
stand or fall upon what I have put down. The degree of self-exposure
is crucifying. And doubt is a constant companion. "What if I am not
as good as I thought?" is a question that always nags, and can cripple.
Where, for whatever combination of reasons, there is a beginning
failure of faith, a flagging of self-assertion, the writer quite naturally
looks for a possible way out. If he is a dramatist, he can find it in the
theater. He can begin to shift some of the burden from pen to
production, from self to collaborative activity. He can begin to
imagine achieving on the stage what may not, after all, have to be
wholly realized in an enclosed text at such cost to his nerves and such
risk to his uncertain ego. I am inclined to think that some such
uncertainty—we may well be sympathetic to the creative man in
crisis—overtook Bertolt Brecht midway in his career and that both
theory and stage direction became his escape from an intolerable
situation.

True or not true in this particular case, any absorption on the part
of the *writer* with the mechanics of performance, any reliance upon
these mechanics to supply a substantial portion of his effect, is a sign
of creative faltering and a considerable loss to the theater itself. For
the theater should not have to feed on itself, to conjure up its dinner
out of thin air and devour it before it has vanished again. The fare
and the air both become thin indeed whenever this sleight-of-hand is
resorted to, as a glance at any nineteenth-century melodrama—with
its scenic effects supplanting all of the writing no one ever got around
to—will testify.

Have we so despaired of the writer that we must do his work for him? Perhaps. Or perhaps directors are simply trying to indicate to him the new kind of work he should do. Whatever may be happening as non-textual elements take over—and it may just be the current passion for a Happening that is happening—we had best not go about our practices blindly, supposing that we are enriching the theater's literature by eliminating it. Whether we deliberately violate the text or, in an uprush of independent invention, dismiss it, we will do well to keep a memory of its ultimate value in our heads. The text is the theater's body, the trunk to which its so animated arms and legs are attached. We don't want to wind up at a séance with detached arms and legs floating in the air about us, wigwagging felicitously but unable to find their way home.

When a production that is mainly dependent upon a performance rhythm vanishes, we are left with nothing. When a production built firmly on a text closes, we are left with a playwright.

THE DIRECTOR REVELS AND ROMPS AWAY

Some people were scandalized by *Futz* because its hero married a pig and the play proposed that it was the right match for him. I am going to have to pass this one. The pig—sow, I should say—did not appear in the play, and since I never got to see her I feel I am in no position to judge. I was scandalized by *Futz* nonetheless. I was scandalized that such slovenliness should have been permitted to masquerade as new art.

In the process of welcoming experiment and ruthlessly breaking old habits of thought, we should be just a bit careful not to lose our eyes and ears. Indeed it is urgent that our eyes and ears be in better working order than ever. The one thing we must do with a play that abandons an old-fashioned logical sequence for a poetry of discontinuity is *listen* to it. How are we to tell whether the colliding fragments that bombard us really connect—connect in our viscera or in our brains—unless we can hear them? The one thing we must do with a visual image that means to extend reality by contorting it—a man is hanged, say, and the entire stage erupts into a dance of jerked heads and clacked tongues—is *see* it, see it plainly and cleanly so that we can inhale its intention.

Director Tom O'Horgan would let us neither see nor hear the patterns he might have had in mind for Rochelle Owens' *Futz*. He was too busy boiling over, plunging onward, shouting abandon, loosing his actors toward a freedom that was only a freedom and almost never a firm design. Probably Miss Owens' play was an unimportant one in any case. When it could be detected through the blur of bodies and the whisper/whine of voices, it seemed remarkably sentimental. We were to feel instant compassion, once again, for the poor and terribly innocent "aberrant" chap who was hounded to death by the community for being different from the community— which the play was eager to point out he was not, the community being more piglike than his pig could possibly have been. But the issue was hypothetical, undramatized, ungraphic, without immediacy. The play took our sympathies for granted, it did not earn them; and unearned sympathies are sentimental sympathies. The play's language seemed unsure of its footing. A backwoods cretin turned to Futz, who was very, very proud that his bride had twelve teats or exactly ten more than any stupid woman has, and said of the community that "Anyways they would like the full freedom to do what you done." I don't think "the full freedom" is a cretin's phrase. I think it is Miss Owens' phrase, insensitively and tendentiously dropped in from the outside; it made me disbelieve in her cretins. The play's structure—if one may use such a conventional term in these outlands— was aimlessly disproportioned, spending far more time on a mother's boy who had slaughtered his sweetheart than was ever helpful to our presumed concern for Futz.

But the play, and any shadowy possibilities it may have possessed, had to be put to one side because Mr. O'Horgan had elbowed it to one side. "Elbowed" is more or less the proper term here. For Mr. O'Horgan's interest in life would seem to be elbows, ankles, twitched shoulders, headstands, the soles of the feet pasted together, slack jaws, lolling tongues, random couplings (a girl upended over a man's head so that he could get a grip on her bare feet and his head under her skirt at the same time), floorward nose-dives.

Now, an interest in elbows, ankles, etc., etc., is perfectly all right, particularly in a play which begins with a short film directly juxtaposing the physiological aspects of insect and animal life with human mammaries, flesh in the underbrush. Given the intentions of the play, these things become important to the play. I think they become important enough to the play to ask for definition, for precision, for economy and clarity of arc and emphasis. A dancer doing the material—or any one gesture inside the material—would discover a line for it. He would then draw the line for you.

Mr. O'Horgan was not able—apparently—to draw lines of any sort. He simply let his people go. When they took a twenty-seventh tumble to the floor, here or in his earlier production of *Tom Paine*, the tumble was only a tumble, a splatter. You did not feel that the fall had ever been rehearsed, and you did feel that the girl falling would one night hurt herself. (I was not in the least surprised to notice that one of the girls in *Futz* had a trussed-up left knee.) When an army of elbows shot into the air, it was an uncoordinated army, a flailing assortment of random and independent quiverings that canceled one another instead of reinforcing one another. The view was amorphous; the freedom was an amateur's freedom; the play called for a certain style—possibly the kind of style Joseph Chaikin applied to the first third of *America Hurrah*—and what it got was slapdash.

I have been searching for the word to describe Mr. O'Horgan's vocal techniques and I have found it. Yelling. Whether a player was confessing to a particularly bloodthirsty crime or a narrator was attempting to make himself heard through the grunts and mosquito-like drones of the night, he was not encouraged to inflect what he was saying. He was simply encouraged to adopt a pitch—high and shrill, low and throwaway, whatever trick would make him sound different for the moment—and stay with it until the next switch was due. Overlaps and speeches that run headlong into one another are common in this sort of play; they are meant to make an unpredictable music. In *Futz* they only trod upon one another, ultimately becoming a noise that defeated itself because the ear had tuned its sustained vibration out.

Mr. O'Horgan had been given considerable credit for *Hair*, and I think he deserved some, though it ought to have been remembered that he'd had an engaging and fairly well formed base to work from in Gerald Freedman's original staging of the musical downtown. He had also created, in *Tom Paine*, one striking visual image: a circle of hooded inquisitors sharpening knives on whetstones while their potential victim shivered. But the effects were occasional and rather surprising, considering the sheer clutter from which they emerged. As things stood, and overall, the director was by no means training performers to serve playwrights judiciously.

By contrast James Hammerstein's management of the rhythmic, mindless, cumulative snarl that became *The Indian Wants the Bronx* was a small miracle of tact. Israel Horovitz' play devoted itself almost exclusively to the idle, playful, improvised malice that began with two buddies mauling one another casually and ended with their concerted physical attack, savage and utterly purposeless, on a stranger who was merely waiting for a bus. Mr. Horovitz' quiet nightmare depended upon a rage that arose randomly, indifferently, out of the often grinning twists and turns that minds make when they are going nowhere in particular. There was no logical pattern to follow; we had to slip inside illogic to hear hate's heartbeat. Mr. Hammerstein got us there—honoring his author—by forming his actors' postures so economically, so liquidly, so *gracefully* really, that we enjoyed their manner of existing before we were forced to face up to the knife inside it. Each line of dialogue was a pebble skipped skillfully across the water's surface, its particular curve attended to; that a last well-aimed stone might have killed was perfectly reasonable. When the meaning is mysterious, the method had best have a rein on it so that we can advance warily, our antennae alert for all signals.

And when the meaning is much less mysterious and much more conventional, conscious control remains half of the game. During the week that *Futz* opened, Theodore Mann mounted a beautiful production of Eugene O'Neill's *A Moon for the Misbegotten* at Circle in the Square, reviving and in effect justifying one of O'Neill's final plays. The play *can* dissolve into a moonbath of self-pity; we'd seen it do that before. O'Neill's language is both too much and too little; performers can drown in its repetitions and starve to death of its ultimate poetic deficiencies. Energy, eagerness, misapplied enthusiasm will not get it through.

What got it through at Circle in the Square was the bold security with which Salome Jens stood astride the earth she so plainly owned, the reserve on everyone's part that husbanded implications and yielded them so gradually, so carefully, that we felt the larder was completely stocked, the supply of understanding inexhaustible. It was instructive to watch Miss Jens pretending to be a wanton as she taunted her irascible and conniving sot of a father. She did it very simply, by sitting on a stoop with her knees spread wide, her head pressed back against a shanty wall so that her hair billowed into a blowsy crown. She held the posture for a very long time; while she was holding it we could hear what she was saying; the posture said, in its composure, what the lines did. It was equally illuminating to watch Miss Jens and Mitchell Ryan, as the man she had cradled all night and forlornly surrendered at dawn, rise from their dreamworld in which sins had been forgiven and hope forever lost, to stretch their aching limbs and their altered psyches into the conventional shapes expected of them. They had been together, one, outside themselves. Now they were required to remake themselves into their artificial daylight images: she hearty and knowing, he glib and sporty. Their bones were stiff for the work. Their hearts were not in it. But in the uncreaking of their bodies—in the stiff, limited, cautious unlimbering—they painted a portrait absolute of unwilling birth. The picture was made of muscles, and had muscle; each tendon seemed separately explored for its meaning; nothing was used that was not useful. The text lived and was clarified by the painful act of putting a foot down.

Ankles are always with us. They should help a play walk.

INVITATION TO THE ORGY

My problem is that I'm not divine.

You're divine, as all the freest new plays are telling us, only when you do what you want to do. And somehow or other I never get to do what I want to do in those playhouses—and now garages—where the actors are having one hell of a time doing what *they* want to do.

In many of these playhouses—and now garages—the actors are very eager to have me join them. Take *Dionysus in '69*, which decided to let people into its downtown garage one at a time. (If you came with a date, one or the other of you had to go first, with that white door closing ominously on the back of whoever was bravest. Problem: did you, as a gentleman, defer to your date, abandoning her to the living jungle of flesh that was already writhing inside and leaving her with no one of her very own to cling to? Or did you, the intrepid explorer, precede her to tick off whatever booby traps there might be, allowing her to stand on the slowly darkening street alone, wondering if she'd ever see you again? But this was a conventional hangup, of which we must have no more.)

The actors in *Dionysus in '69*, which the ardently revolutionary Richard Schechner of *The Drama Review* had put together out of old bits and pieces of Euripides' *The Bacchae*, first of all wanted me to sit where they were writhing. They were all over the place, on the floor, on ladders, on raw wooden platforms. They didn't offer to move over, since they were very busy intoning hypnotic phrases like "Let the dance begin" and "Is Frank taking tickets?" so I looked around for an open spot that was not occupied by a woman's purse or a dancer's foot. I made a light leap (I am fairly agile in some ways) to a not entirely occupied platform, just above an attractive blond girl in a split jacket who was rolling her shoulders as though they were the well-oiled wheels of a locomotive engine, and I congratulated myself on at last being where the action was. Of course I couldn't be everywhere, not being divine, but on my pleasantly exposed perch I was in it, with it, of it. I dangled my legs devilishly.

I wasn't to get a free ride for long, though. Pretty soon the actors wanted me to dance. (Not just me, you understand; I didn't receive any sort of preferential treatment; *everybody* was invited to get in there.) The Dionysian revels had begun. The boys had stripped to less than loincloths. The boys had undulated on the floor while the girls marched astride them, bare feet planted between buttocks. The god Dionysus had appeared to his worshipers (all so like Euripides) to snap finger-cymbals and lift his skinny legs in rhythm beneath bushy hair, eyeglasses, and seedy mustache (not exactly like Euripides). The beat went faster, some of the girls went topless, the garage spun, customers were cooed at: "Will you dance with me?"

I do not dance divinely. When it comes to dancing, I'm an uptight person. (My wife has refused to dance with me for twenty-five years, having tried once.) In theory, to be sure, this made me just the man to be hauled onto that floor. Obviously, I need a breakthrough. But I am something of a realist and I was not wholly convinced that darting into the melee was going to make a dancer of me; I thought I was going to look pretty silly and maybe louse things up. This would have been especially unbecoming in a reviewer, who would thereafter have had to apportion himself a share of the blame. It just so happens that this isn't the particular breakthrough I want, and if this sort of group therapy is going to do any real good it's got to get at the actual trouble areas. Neither did I want to rush out and snatch one of the girls, if that's what you're thinking. I had got a pretty good look at some of the topless types by this time, and had reconsidered: there are girls and there are girls, and not all are equal. Or am I being too bold?

I didn't want to dance, I wanted to smoke. The evening was several hours long, there was no intermission (intermissions are bad for orgies, as I suppose even the Greeks knew), and I had a profound conviction that I would find my favorite brand of cigarette soothing. Aha. None of that. This was free theater, but not that free. It said plainly on the program, "No Smoking/No Cameras." I didn't care about the cameras, having forgotten to bring one, but it did seem strange to me that the theater of benevolent abandon should have been so surly with those No's. Did they want me really wound up? No doubt it was all because of the Fire Department, and you can't fight everything.

But there was another problem. Even more than I wanted to smoke, I wanted to think. I happen to admire Euripides' *The Bacchae* very much. I think it's one of the greatest plays ever written. I also understood perfectly clearly that *The Bacchae* was not to be presented as such but was to be tampered with at will in an effort to see how relevant it might be to the contemporary urge toward ecstasy and the contemporary urge toward violence. (In the original, the god Dionysus gives his followers great joy and great pain; that is simply what a god does.) I was curious, eager for illumination, not at all put off by the mauling of a text. *The Bacchae* will still be there when we're all through roughing it up.

Here I was really stuck. I wasn't distracted from thinking by the flesh, freckles, pimples, grunting, cavorting, or the clap-hands clamor for "Wine!"; I was kept from valuable meditation—I had hoped it would be valuable—by the performers', and Mr. Schechner's, careful determination that I get no hard information to work with. The suppression was deliberate. Speech was slurred, or underprojected, or blotted out by group cries; probably half the evening was unintelligible by design. When speech was intelligible, it was likely to be voided by a visual image. Pentheus, the puritanical young ruler who would have liked to put an end to revelry, announced himself disturbed by reports of excesses in the community. He made his announcement the moment after he himself had come slithering through a sea of sinuous flesh. Either his concern was meaningless or his memory extremely bad. The only possible conclusion one could see for the play, after Dionysus had streaked his own followers with rivers of blood, was an implication that the very openness and abandon we had been encouraged to share all evening long were an openness and an abandon that inevitably end in violence. Could this have been what the producers had in mind, or had we now pressed our own minds too far?

There was a point to the emphasis on the physical, the refusal to let our minds do all the work. Our theatergoing has been mainly headwork for quite a long while now, conventional headwork, dusty headwork; there has been very little kinetic response, engagement at the gut, in it. What greater engagement at the gut might be like was persuasively indicated by one prolonged passage in the experiment. Pentheus wished to silence the orgiastic impulse that had broken out all about him (and all about us, in far corners and over our shoulders). He tried to silence it physically, darting in and out among the mingled actors and spectators, clapping his hands over the mouths of Dionysiacs who were beginning to whisper ecstasy again. He could not go fast enough. For every whisper hushed there were three to break out elsewhere. The clatter crept up on him, surrounded him, washed over him, drove him to another kind (the same kind?) of frenzy. Though here there was no direct contact between performer and spectator—he was not putting his hand over *our* mouths—we were surrounded by mounting sound in just the way he was. The effect came off: we felt, as a physical presence, a rising pressure that could not be stopped, and we shared the pressure with the man who was trying to stop it.

There were other such interim successes, notably a wild flight in which Pentheus hurled himself, at breakneck speed, from platform to platform over our heads. His fear and his fury came quite close to us (I hoped they wouldn't come too close some night). Just enough of these provocations swept by to keep you attentive, and not restless. And just enough swept by to let you know that something kinetic is missing from our more routine experiences.

Still, the big question hovered. What is the best way to total empathy? Through actual hand-to-hand contact, shoulders brushed against the actor, direct muscular participation—with the mind lulled to sleep? Or is it best sought—as Euripides sought and did find it—in the awful penetration of words?

As things stood, the full contact did not work, had no cumulative possibilities short of rape, no staying power. We were intrigued but not truly involved. Those spectators who did join the dance danced feebly and were plainly glad to retire; one who submitted himself, at evening's end, to being pawed by a covey of Dionysiacs simply submitted himself, returning nothing.

It is only the actors who are liberated in this sort of meeting, and there is something arrogant, condescending, and self-indulgent about that. Clearly these actors enjoyed the unleashing of their own inhibitions. During an impromptu aside on opening night, an actress was asked by another performer how she felt about dancing on the night of Senator Kennedy's death. She thought intensely for a moment, then answered, "I have to. It's my statement."

But it was her statement, not ours. She and her colleagues were in control of the master plan. They were free to do what they wished to do. We were free to do only what *they* wished us to do or invited us to do. That is not engagement. It is surrender.

I'm still uptight.

THE METHOD OF "MACBIRD!"

Barbara Garson's *MacBird!* was both tasteless and irresponsible, but not in the way that is generally assumed.

Our first assumption was that the mere spectacle of Lyndon Johnson roaring naked-kneed about the stage in cowhide kilts borrowed secondhand from *Macbeth* while he plotted and carried through the murder of John F. Kennedy would be an affront to taste. It wasn't.

It might have been something else: defamation of character, perhaps. But it could not be an affront to taste because taste always has to do with something actual. If, for instance, we gabble on, noisily and thoughtlessly, about the chronic drunkenness and infidelity of a recently dead man in the presence of his widow, we are no doubt displaying quite poor taste. But our poor taste depends upon certain tangible realities: the time is inappropriate, the widow is vulnerable, the story is true. If the story weren't true, no one would arch eyebrows and call our remarks tasteless. They'd declare us insane and get us out of the room.

Taste is a response to the tangible, a way of dealing with the true. Good taste may handle the truth judiciously, tiptoeing when there is illness in the room; bad taste may use it clumsily, gratuitously, even cruelly. But questions of taste don't come up until there is a known truth to be skirted or stated, to be aired or suppressed, which is why the fellow who declares stoutly that the earth is flat or that the world ended at noon yesterday is never accused of lacking taste; he is accused of lacking other desirable qualities. Indeed, the connection between taste and truth is so close that the minute anyone began murmuring that it was in "poor taste" to show Johnson murdering Kennedy, the hint was already in the air that Johnson somehow really did do it and we'd best be as discreet about the matter as we could.

Now, no one who went to the off-Broadway Village Gate, to be seated either facing the stage or resolutely turned away from it at coffeehouse tables, went supposing that the content of the play was surreptitiously factual or that the parallels drawn between Shakespeare's ambitious usurper and a Johnson wielding a stuffed eagle for his scepter were meant to be genuine parallels. The author herself, in one interview or another, had suggested that only a remarkably naïve theatergoer would think for a moment that she intended, in transplanting Dunsinane to Texas, to imply any such thing. Heaven, and the Grassy Knoll Press, forbid. We were fantasticating tonight, the parallels weren't relevant, it was all so much moonshine, and we might just as well have been doing A *Midsummer Night's Dream*. Furthermore, caricature of the wildest sort is permissible in political cartooning; outrageous burlesque is legitimate behavior on page and stage. Nothing need be taken literally. And so, with truth put to one side, the question of taste could be brushed from the tabletops, too.

Yet a persistently sour flavor lingered on the lips at the Village Gate, growing rather stronger as the evening progressed. Where did it come from if not from any fear that what we were watching was treason? (And we didn't really sit there thinking treason because we saw that the handiwork was deliberately broad and because, after all, we are all big boys and girls now.) It came, in point of fact, not from the carefully outrageous content of the play but from Miss Garson's own shaky, squeaky selection of the darts she would use next. The tastelessness that marks the play lies in the stylistic choices the author has made, line by line, scene by scene.

Taste here consists not in being true to a fact but in being true to a tone, in maintaining a certain level of satirical thrust. Having set up her vast and clanking Shakespearean machinery for lampooning heartless Kennedys, cornpone Johnsons, a queasy Adlai Stevenson and a wishy-washy Earl Warren, the author was now required to deliver language that would cut, impale, distort and then disembowel on a scale exactly matching the brazen, but forthright, impudence of her material. She had to make the dare good, all the way. It would seem fortunate, at first sight, that she had all of Shakespeare to help her—and she did, by the time her work was done, manage to leaf through nearly all of Shakespeare, with *Macbeth* reduced to mere guideline.

Alas. Imagination crumpled alongside daring. Faced with her own challenge, Miss Garson rapidly collapsed into a frantic student chewing feverishly at two trots: one the Shakespeare Guide to Obvious Quotes, the other the contemporary television comedian's equivalent of Joe Miller's Jokebook. In this double-entry system, *anything* could be matched. "Screw your courage to the sticking-point" became, presumably, a pertinent and trenchant lift from *Macbeth* just so long as the actress playing Lady MacBird was careful to pronounce the first word "Scarew!", lingering fondly on both the

Southern-accent languor and the sexual double-entendre. The Southern accent joke was of course old-hat; no rich innovation here. And the sex overtone, if such it was, was without point in the situation. Neither had been linked, maliciously, to some sly meaning in the Shakespearean line. The gag was there because there had to be a gag; in desperation, any gag would do.

"This here is the winter of our discontent" was no better; we were simply playing that ancient darling of the high-school stages, *Aaron Slick from Punkin' Crick*, once again. For Johnson to sit morosely between scenes chanting "Don't Fence Me In" shifted the reference from Shakespeare to Cole Porter; it did not carry forward the promise that we were engaged in a new and more robust kind of political vaudeville.

Johnson, now become not only Macbeth but also Claudius watching Hamlet's play-within-a-play, sat listening to a chorus line sing "Massa's in de Cold, Cold Ground." That was not college humor; college humor is far fresher, much trickier. "Of all my foes I fear this twerp the least" substituted a single and out-of-date slang word as its sole contribution to making the Bard's line seem devilishly appropriate, which was scarcely work calling for skilled labor.

"To thine own self be true, and it will follow as the next depression" sounded, on first hearing, a trace better; the word "depression" surprised us, and seemed somehow to fit. As things turned out, however, it only fitted metrically. There was a depression neither in Shakespeare nor in Johnson's career to be needled, or related, by the remark.

In short, the jests were random, inconsequential, unmatched—and therein tastelessness lay. That is to say, no control had been exercised over what was and what was not to be thrown into the witches' pot; no standard of caustic, cauterizing humor had been established and insisted upon. Tone *is* a kind of truth; and that truth, in however bizarre an exercise, must be respected.

Tone finally went so far astray in *MacBird!* that satire was lost sight of altogether. In the sequences dramatizing Kennedy's assassination, the elevation of the doomed figure skyward as he became a sitting duck for bullets and the subsequent appearance of the play's other caricatures in mourning at his bier were moodily, melodramatically, and therefore disturbingly staged. The entertainment we had come for had been shattered by its own consequences; we looked at these moments through a gunsight quite different from the gunsight of parody, and we cringed.

The genuine satirist also has a peculiar kind of responsibility. It is not a responsibility to the apparently prevailing mores, to Boy Scout Oaths or the national code or the very latest Fireside Chat. The satirist stands apart from these things, having elected himself their gadfly. He wouldn't *be* a satirist if he took the pious at face value.

But he does have an obligation to keep his own hands clean while pointing out how dirty other hands are. He must not cheat, he must not beg, he must not stoop lower than the figures he is trying to bring low. In ridiculing the craft and the guile, the fatuity and the moral imbecility, of the fools who crowd about him, he must guard his own integrity. He must show craft or guile or any other quality for exactly what it is, but never for less than what it is. He isn't allowed to make the target easier for himself by falsifying its proportions. Lashing out at devils, he must give all devils their due.

Yet Miss Garson made jokes that were not only beneath the parodistic task she had set herself; she made jokes that were altogether beneath her victims. Adlai Stevenson, trying to make up his mind whether or not to gloss over Johnson's misbehavior and whether or not to go on serving such a man, soliloquized, "To see or not to see, that is the question."

To say that the punning was trite and right off the top of the head is beside the point. What was really wrong with the applied line was that Stevenson himself would certainly have done better. Stevenson was the sort of man who, when congratulated upon having received several editorial endorsements during a period of relative obscurity, could remark on the instant, "Yes, I seem to be emerging to a new failure." He was also a literate man, and had quite possibly read beyond Hamlet's textbook soliloquy. To reduce him in size in order to make him funny did not in fact make him funny; it simply made him unrecognizable and the satirist irresponsible.

John F. Kennedy was a man of some wit himself, carefully schooled in self-deprecation, dedicated to a balanced—indeed an overly balanced—rhetoric. To satirize him by having him say "Do not ask what you can profit off your country" was simply not to satirize *him* at all. Miss Garson had not cut her men down; she had mislaid them, and then merely cut loose.

Were there no successes in the performance of *MacBird!?* There were some. The early jockeying for power while Bobby Kennedy toyed with the notion of Johnson for Vice President and then found it hard to conceal his dismay over Johnson's ready acceptance was familiar but workable fun. William Devane, in a generally good company directed with remarkable élan by Roy Levine, was particularly effective as the tousled Bobby with a grin of ice. The stomping pomp of Stacy Keach's MacBird was robustly managed, too; Mr. Keach, wearing a laurel wreath as though he'd plucked it out of a haystack, proved himself a skilled caricaturist, and he was helped through the queasier portions of the entertainment by the fact that he didn't really look like Lyndon Johnson.

There may have been one more hidden virtue in the event. The very existence of *MacBird!*, and the interest it aroused, indicate how badly we need satirists who do not pussyfoot, how sorely starved we are for blunt irreverence. Unfortunately, Miss Garson did hide the virtue, not so much by pussyfooting as by corn-cribbing, not so much by failing to be blunt as by failing to be precise. Being a satirist is an honorable occupation. It should not be permitted to deteriorate into one of those children's games in which the child, blindfolded, is urged to pin the donkey's tail just any old where.

DREAMING WITH IONESCO

Eugène Ionesco is forever imagining a better play than he writes.

The imagination itself is original, bizarre, powerful. It would seem to begin, almost always, in something private and personal, in the kind of hallucination that often overtakes a man in his study and so fills the room that the walls threaten to burst. It is by nature expanding, then explosive. A portion of the universe, or the self, becomes monstrous, and suddenly the playwright sees the stage turning monstrous, adapting itself precisely to the ballooning proportions of his unbidden nightmare.

The program notes for the A.P.A.'s production of *Exit the King* told us that the play may well have begun, long ago, in an illness Ionesco endured. He had been having trouble with his liver. (Yes, the statement came out funny even in the sober program note. Why? And what does it have to do with the fact that Ionesco can never keep himself from giggling over the spectral enemies he most dreads?) In any case, he imagined himself getting out of bed, leaving the house, walking down a road, falling into a muddy ditch, and there watching his liver swell to a world-devouring size while his arms simply detached themselves from his body and sank into the mud. That is perhaps an ordinary kind of dream; what redeems it in a writer is his capacity for transforming it into an actual presence, bloated and pulsing, on the stage. It ceases being a dream from which any man can be awakened, and becomes waking.

There *is* such an imaginative transformation in *Exit the King*, to begin with. The play has to do with the coming of Death, exactly as *Everyman* does; it is, in fact, nothing more than *Everyman* rewritten by a twentieth-century sensibility. But that sensibility experiences dissolution very differently from the writer, or the hero, of a late medieval allegory. In fact, in the original *Everyman* the victim does not experience dissolution at all. Death comes for him—sliding a dark black hand over his heart while he chats at a banquet—and whisks him bodily and whole, to heaven or to hell, from a world that remains whole behind him. Nothing is dissolved or ended. The man is simply taken out of the world. In *Exit the King* exactly the opposite happens. The world is taken out of the man.

Example, and a good one. In the A.P.A.'s production, Richard Easton's body had begun to betray him. He had been king for a long time, absolute monarch of his "living room." We are all kings of our own consciousness. Mr. Easton's subjects were subjects simply because *he* saw them; they were dependent upon him for their very existence, were products of his awareness.

But when his damaged heart began to run amok, booming in his ears like ocean breakers that had gone crashingly out of rhythm, each giant thump inside him became a storm that blew his subjects violently away from him, tossing them toward invisibility as though they were so much soon-lost seaweed. It was not he who was disappearing; they were. To watch a black-robed Eva Le Gallienne, a frock-coated Richard Woods, an armored Clayton Corzatte go tumbling back and away, reeling, receding, ceasing to be, at every blow from a giant, unsynchronized pump was to catch in an instant the curious, inverted, deeply disturbing vision that the playwright had wrung from his private fears and made wholly public, entirely tangible. The sequence was not a trick; it was a stage truth.

There were others. Though the members of Mr. Easton's court were still able to obey their own orders, to move about when they wished to, they could not obey his. A loss of powers is a loss of power. His young second wife, romantically loyal and wishing to reassure him, begged him to give *her* a command; whatever anyone else did, she would obey. He gave the command and she stood paralyzed, straining against her own body, willing with intense eyes what could perfectly well happen for her but could never again happen for Mr. Easton. (Patricia Connolly performed this double impulse, urgent and impotent at once, most remarkably.) Beyond the transparent plastic walls of the palace the physical world was collapsing, too. Fissures had appeared in the ground; earth had vanished, irretrievably, through them; they were dismissed as earthquakes, but they were manquakes. Spring had departed abruptly, yesterday; it was now November. There were soothing considerations. "I always liked Mozart," mourned the King, clinging to what constituted life. "That's all right," Miss Le Gallienne seemed to say, parchment-pale and motherly, "you'll forget about it." The King did not die; Mozart did.

Now, this much was vivid and evocative—a series of unruly and troubling sensations impressed upon the theater, and upon us, by a mind with a unique, meaningfully out-of-focus eye. The performing was almost all very good: Miss Le Gallienne admirably suggested that there might be a degree of kindness in just letting the frost come; Pamela Payton-Wright bluntly ticked off the dreary routine of her day as housekeeper (so exciting to a king who would have no more chores to perform) with a fine peasant indifference; and if Mr. Easton could not possibly keep us attending to his every aborted gasp as the universe continued—and continued—to diminish, that was not necessarily his fault. We have come up against the inexplicable in Ionesco: that a man capable of taking us into a fevered, disjointed, persuasively and even overwhelmingly oppressive world cannot imagine doing anything more with us once he has got us there. Ionesco establishes and then repeats. He does not come to anything that hasn't been there from the beginning.

It's happened before—in all of his long plays, I think. *The Killer* creates, quite perfectly, a perfect world from which people forever vanish; it then lapses into a prolonged, unprogressive dialogue between one more victim and the vanishing agent (Death again). When the play is over we do not feel that we have discovered anything, except that Death does make people vanish from the most perfect of worlds—but we knew that, and the play has merely moved from mystery to banality. *Rhinoceros* does persuade us that people like to regress, that they like growing horns; but when, in the latter part of the play, we discover that one last lone man is not going to turn into a rhinoceros, the news is without significance. He, too, would like to. He simply cannot. His inability is unexplained, without body, cause, dimension. It is as though nothing existed beyond the façade, the first realized image that the playwright is able to mount inside the proscenium arch. He can see and he can paint. But we must not penetrate the canvas. The other side is empty. To go there is to discover less.

It can always be argued that this is part of Ionesco's point: that beyond the set of sensations which make up the distorted world we know there is no tangible nub, no further sort of knowledge to be gained, no profitable move that can be made in any direction. If so, two dramatic problems present themselves instantly. The play had better not run longer than the effective establishment of its initial alarming image. Two hours is likely to be too much; even the ninety minutes (without intermission) of *Exit the King* is something too much. We are first impressed; we are for a while fascinated; we are finally not paying as close attention as we should because, after all, Everyman is really saying again and again what he has so clearly said before (that he does not wish to die). The fires of the evening do not grow in intensity until they are unendurable for all of us who *are* to die; after a while they flicker and diminish—become quite tolerable, really—because there is no fresh kindling stored anywhere. We run out of awe.

Ionesco could possibly solve this first problem if he were more unmistakably, or perhaps more willingly, a poet. If what is happening is not going to change along the way, language might: it could probe deeper, and even if it were only going to bring back more of the same it might bring it back hardened into gold, or at least coal. Here, however, Ionesco insists upon his right to be banal. "The king must speak banalities," he tells us in his own program notes. "In this play he says what anybody would say on their deathbed." Life is banal, a man's last thoughts are certainly apt to be banal; let the language of the play be honestly banal, too.

But what this means is that we must listen to the stunned King repeat "I'm—dying!" incredulously four times over and then, after a little while, four times again. The effect is too literal—in this instance too unimaginative—to be moving; it almost becomes the kind of children's game in which the same sentence is repeated with differing emphases just to see how many different emphases are possible; it does not arrive at the intolerable cumulative despair of Lear's "Never, never, never, never, never." We do really wish he'd think of another way to phrase it. The phrase may be Everyman's, but it does not take us any distance into any man's heart. Does Ionesco insist upon so much banality because he is reluctant to do the real work of poetry?

Well, the man remains a puzzle, more of a puzzle than his plays. The plays begin well, then—somewhere along the way—seem to sigh a bit with weariness. Yet the man is not weary; he is inventive, and, in his criticism, persistently vigorous.

What *I* want doesn't matter much, but I'll tell you what it is. I want him not to call a play finished just because he's got the chilling landscape right. Painting one side of a naked street, with the overhead lamps casting garish shadows, is a fine thing to do. But drama— if we are to stay with it all the way—has got to walk across that street, translating landscape into motion, lengthening shadows into significant change.

ART AND FACT

Almost from the beginning, *The Deputy* outran itself.

Because Rolf Hochhuth had written a play in which a young Jesuit priest carried the cause of the Jews during World War II all the way to the feet of Pope Pius XII, only to be told that neither the Church nor Western civilization would be served by any formal condemnation of Hitler's death camps, the world was shocked into the realization that a question existed which had not been answered.

What were Pius' motives in remaining silent? Were they—could any conceivable combination of motives possibly be—adequate to account for what he did not do? The question is in the world's hands now, for scholars, for theologians, for Everyman to try to answer. Because no one can ever be certain that he has fully read one man's mind—Pius' mind—the question may never be answered. But short of an answer as we still are, it seems to me that genuine good has come of the mere forming of the question.

What I have read, in publications of every persuasion and of none, is so full of a necessary and honest anguish, of examination of consciences, and of shaming generosity (I am here thinking of what has been written by Jews), that the occasional violence the play has provoked seems the whimper of a spoiled child alongside the responsible speech, and the shouldering of a burden, by adults. Without the play we might not have looked into ourselves; and the looking—in my opinion, for what it is worth—is due, salutary, and profitable.

But *The Deputy* was presented to us as a work for the theater. It is astonishing that so flaccid, monotonous, and unsubtle a work for the theater should have moved the first mountain. We are faced here, I think, with an effect far greater than its cause.

Mr. Hochhuth's journey begins, briefly, at Auschwitz. Against a darkened cyclorama we see a straggle of prisoners slowly drifting toward death. Almost immediately we are listening to a papal nuncio in Berlin rather tamely and conventionally—with neither more intelligence nor more insight than that of some simple village priest—weigh the troublesome courses open to him. While he is wringing his hands for the benefit of the young Jesuit who has just arrived, an impassioned—and, it would seem, nearly deranged—storm trooper bursts in to offer evidence of the horrors of Auschwitz in an outbreak of highly impressionistic and somewhat self-defeating verse. We are sometimes on rational ground, and sometimes on mystical; the author exerts little or no formal control over the impulses that drive him from moment to moment.

As the Jesuit begins to clench his hands and to wonder what can be done, he visits his father who is a Vatican diplomat, he visits a friendly but fatuous cardinal, he visits his own superior who is hiding Jews and other refugees. In each sequence the motif is repeated, at approximately the same level of intensity: will Pius never speak? The pattern palls, where the crimes never can.

Ultimately we come to a confrontation with Pius himself. In the writing Pius is petty (he is terribly irritated with Roosevelt for having bombed San Lorenzo), Pius is supercilious (he can almost lightly equate the destruction of Jews with the destruction of books), Pius is concerned only that "our own throne is safe" and smugly certain that Hitler alone is preserving Europe from the East.

If the scene is anything it is a satirical scene, though it is not forcibly that. Mr. Hochhuth makes Pius a fool. That is a possible position for a historian to take and defend. It is a fatal position for a dramatist, because it enfeebles his play.

We have come this long way to little more than vapidity at teatime, where there is no real contest, no possible human alternative that might have been pursued. Six million have died for a mild insipidity. Given Mr. Hochhuth's convictions, for which he had gathered some serious documentation, there was a tragedy for him to write: the tragedy of an at least reasonably perceptive man who considered all of the choices open to him and then chose wrong. Instead of that tragedy, he pinned guilt on a straw man.

We were left with something less complex than a play. Mr. Hochhuth is not, I think, by affinity or equipment a dramatist. He chose the theater arbitrarily (when he was doing his research he had "no fixed plan to put the material into publishable form," he tells us) and the marks of arbitrariness are everywhere upon *The Deputy*.

Still and all, wasn't the event of such value that we had best silence as mere hair-splitting any criticism we may have of the drama as drama? Doesn't *The Deputy's* existence as a document, as a record of research done, as a repository of fact, as a reminder and a goad, supersede any and all theatrical considerations? In the circumstances does dramatic form count?

Mr. Hochhuth, incidentally, thinks it does. In the appendix to the published text of his play, he is careful to tell us that "what is offered here is not scholarly work and is not meant to be. But since neither the Vatican nor the Kremlin as yet permit free access to their archives, historians will have to wait before they can present a comprehensive account of these events. To intuitively combine the already available facts into a truthful whole becomes the noble and rarely realized function of art. Precisely because he is faced with such a plethora of raw material, as well as with such difficulties in collating it, the writer must hold fast to his freedom, which alone empowers him to give form to the matter."

The work, then, is not to be judged or especially justified as research. Because the man writing the play has adopted the freedoms of art—the freedom to alter, the freedom to invent, the freedom to combine fact with intuition—it must be judged as art. We have, really, no other course. Thus the author.

Most admirers of *The Deputy*, however, together with partisans of what is coming to be called the Theater of Fact, do take another course, and when they do we immediately begin to run into strange practical difficulties. If we suppress or dismiss the play's pretensions to art, reassuring one another that its standing as a documentary is the only thing that matters, we are at once confronted with a very odd beast: a theatrical documentary that cannot be documented in the theater.

Let me give an example of what I mean. In the climactic confrontation scene of the play, Pius rejects the plea that he explicitly condemn the mass murder of Jews, washing his hands of the burden with these words:

As the flowers
in the countryside wait beneath winter's mantle of snow
for the warm breezes of spring,
so the *Jews* must wait, praying and trusting
that the hour of heavenly comfort will come.

Pius has evaded his own duty by counseling Jews to pray and trust heaven. In the appendix to the play Mr. Hochhuth tells us that this is a "word-for-word quotation" from a speech by Pius. In the same sentence—and this is certainly to his credit—he goes on to point out that it is not. One word has been altered. Pius did not say "Jews." He was speaking of "Poles."

So long as we are giving careful attention to the printed play and its appendix, we are in a position to know precisely what degree of freedom has been taken with fact. Mr. Hochhuth has been open with us.

But what are we to do in the theater, where there is no appendix to counsel us? No one really conceives that, before or after seeing such a play, every member of the audience is going to familiarize himself with the aesthetic liberties taken, here or elsewhere (and how is an audience to know how much elsewhere is to be accounted for?).

There is a danger here, though it is a danger that comes into existence only when the documentary value of a play is exalted above its literary and theatrical nature. In part it is a danger of simple slovenliness of mind: told that the work is the product of research, an audience may conclude that it is seeing the research, whereas it is actually seeing something else—a play. And in part it is due to the questionable ability of the stage to function as a conveyer of fact. The moment an artist records a fact or an actor performs one, the fact is no longer what it was; something has been altered. It may be best, in the interests of the very truth that is being pursued, to insist that the audience place its primary focus not upon the issue as fact but upon the play as a kind of art.

I think it was the unself-conscious tendency to regard *The Deputy* as more document than free rearrangement that led so many to recoil, on opening night, from the portrait of Pius. In Hochhuth's view Pius was an evasive, vexed, uneasy and sarcastic man, marked by a coldness and hardness of face. (I have taken these adjectives from the stage directions in the text.) But Pius was a man of whom we have some impression, as we have some impression of Churchill or Stalin or Roosevelt; and our residual impression had somehow not been incorporated into Mr. Hochhuth's special vision.

Suddenly we saw the vision as really special, as an alteration, as a freedom taken. We had not been expecting that. We had been following the events of the evening principally as fact and were suddenly face to face, however artlessly, with art. We were confused, shaken in a way Mr. Hochhuth had not intended, set ambiguously afloat. What *had* we been watching—fact, intuition, invention, art?

The ambiguity exists in Mr. Hochhuth's own intentions for the play. On the one hand he tells us in the appendix to the text that "as a stage play the work requires no commentary." On the other he has explained in an interview that because the play can never be produced as it is written, his "book with its documentation is a necessary complement." The compass needle wavers.

I do not pretend to know the answers to all of the questions raised here. They do seem to me to merit some thought.

In the meantime—and without answers—we must remain grateful for a puzzle: that a work which is inadequate as art and uncertain as fact has nevertheless set off a chain reaction that may end by illuminating some very dark corners.

4
FILM, STAGE, NOVEL

FILM AND STAGE

A MAN CAN BE loyal to the theater and still tell himself the truth: nowadays he goes to the theater out of loyalty and to the movies out of interest. In the theater he knows exactly what to expect; he hopes he will get a good example of the expected, but he does not really look to be electrified. At the movies he has a fair, lively hope of having his eyes pop.

And this is so, now, for those of us who have been around for a while—not just for all of those buzzing arts majors in the incredibly equipped universities, clamoring for time with the camera equipment, time with the projection machines, time with the viewers and splicers. It is true for those of us for whom it shouldn't be true: those who have lived through the earliest, never-quite-to-be-recaptured excitements of films when Chaplin and Keaton and Ernst Lubitsch were yearly promises, lived through René Clair and the whole discovery of the European sound film, lived through Hitchcock when Hitchcock was something to be accompanied by popcorn rather than a devout running commentary by Truffaut. *Our* appetite should be sated; in point of fact we can remember where most of the new techniques came from; film should not seem so new, the theater not so threatened.

But there we are in one or another art house that is no longer called an art house, safely past the vending machines—or in more discreet environments the free coffee—straight up in our seats built for lounging, agog with discovery. The film seems to skid at us, take us off tracks we thought we knew, whistle past our ears dangerously, squirt color at us with a spray gun and erase it before it has stuck, stare at us in long silences that suggest too much light has been let in. We are jarred. We are alerted. And we jump. It is in the theater that we fish for mints to pass the time.

How come? Film is way out front these days, I think, for a very simple reason. It knows that it is film. The theater doesn't know that it is theater.

The strongest sensation I have whenever I go to a new movie is one of fingers. Fingers holding up a short, curled stretch of celluloid near a naked light-bulb. Fingers pressing film into the sprockets of a cutter and bearing down sharply with one thumb. Fingers running like a tarantula's legs across racks from which eight or ten or twenty strips of film can be snatched and simply hurled at one another, hoping the glue holds. Fingers, not story, making the rhythm. Fingers flinging blank or black snips of leader at us to remind us that it is all patched together, fingers so enamored of the *work* they do—and the material they play with—that they want us to share the crazy joy of the work and the tactile pleasure of the material. Fingers tampering with the film, running it at too fast or too slow speeds or suddenly turning it a solid blue, to call explicit attention to the fact that film is manipulable. Narrative is rarely in our eye. We are three-quarters through *A Man and a Woman* before we realize that until now the narrative has contained no threat and therefore wasn't really a narrative at all. Defined character is not much in our eye. *Persona* is about two women who are each other. The film opens and closes with utterly empty celluloid churning through the machine; between these two points images are impressed upon the celluloid but we are to remember that these are only impresses and that the celluloid is by nature empty, open; the film has something to do with the proposition that the women *are* film. Sustained atmosphere is not in our eye, as it always was with the old fade-out, fade-in picture; the faster atmosphere can be reversed or in some way violated the better. A finger is in our eye.

But montage has always been with us, hasn't it? Indeed montage—the rapid juxtaposition of separate pieces of film and separate camera angles to make a single intelligible mosaic—was the sacred cow of the earliest film exegetes. Nothing new here to account for such startling vitality. Long ago Eisenstein assembled shocking counterpoints for everyone to admire and virtually no one to imitate. If we find the unannounced juggling of five bands of time the only thing of real interest in *Two for the Road* (the film is five separate journeys through time treated as a single journey without respect for time), why should we find it interesting at all? D. W. Griffith kept four bands of time hopping in *Intolerance*, putting them neck to neck in the final reels, and earned no more than apathy and parody for his pains. The movies have been here before and not been so lucky.

There is a difference. Griffith failed with *Intolerance* because he failed to interest the audience in film as film. He wasn't even trying to do that. This was a new way of doing things, all right, rubbing ancient Babylon up against Model-T Fords. But the thing being done, the essential thing, was old: Griffith was primarily trying to interest the audience in history as history, in spectacle as spectacle, in morality as morality. There was no necessary relationship between the material at hand and the material *in* hand. The cutting in no way controlled, or even struck up a special relationship with, the content. The whole thing could have been done as an outdoor pageant somewhere, under religious auspices, and Griffith finally managed to recoup some of his losses by extracting one time-thread from his kaleidoscope and rereleasing it as a straightforward, strictly sequential, narrative (a trick that could not possibly be pulled off with *Two for the Road*; that film either stands on its fingering of time or falls altogether).

Even Eisenstein, who has surely played some part in reawakening film makers to the stuff they hold in their hands and whose individual images were often so brilliant that they are still locked in our skulls (the woman with the smashed eyeglasses, the dead horse slipping through the slowly opening bridge), was not fundamentally concerned with making the audience conscious of film. *He* was conscious of film; they were to become conscious of historical necessity, of horror, of a people. His audiences were in no way in the laboratory with the film editor; they were on the Odessa steps. The montages we admire most did not dictate the overall shape, or any part of the meaning, of the film; they were way-stops, stunning small explosions, in an essentially linear document. They were, in effect, absorbed into an experience not very much different from the experience of reading a novel or seeing a play. They were stylistic devices, not the control panel itself. Film had not yet insisted on growing the meaning out of the medium. It insisted less—if at all—as Hollywood took charge in the twenties and thirties. Instead of pointing a finger at the finger that was playing with slices of life as though they were so many slices of celluloid (because they *were* so many slices of celluloid), Hollywood steadily suppressed what was peculiar, arbitrary, and unique about film and did its level best to persuade the audience that it was coasting along as cozily as at novel pace, as directly as at stage pace. It often deliberately hid its own innate artifice. The transitional fade-out, fade-in that became standard in the period was, after all, a soothing effort to conceal the splice.

Now we want the splice, quick, jagged, breathless, bewildering, appropriate. (I have always been astonished that we did not want it sooner; I think I first saw a jump-cut in a Sacha Guitry film in the early thirties, and it was exciting then; but this sort of clobbering of time at the hands of a technician who literally held time curling up in his hands had to wait its turn, no doubt because Hollywood thought it had plenty of time.) We want film to do what *it* can do and no other medium can—rip time asunder, let space lurch, wipe the face of the world red or blue, tangle the threads like a computer already God, show its sprocket holes proudly. We want the *what* of its meaning to be made out of the *what* that film is. It is a negative, subject to impress. *Persona*. It is a spool, subject to speed changes. *Bonnie and Clyde*. *Tom Jones*. It is a lab wash, a filter. *Elvira Madigan*. *A Man and a Woman*. It is a cropping, a blowup. *Blow-Up*. (Interchange as many as you like.) Becoming conscious of itself, becoming *interested* in itself, film has become more completely itself. We're all happy.

There's more to it than that, naturally. I'm overstating the case for the man in the lab. Something in the world was waiting for just this uprush and outblast, if only Marshall McLuhan and his electronic circuitry. Notice, though, that there's virtually no difference in fundamental content between stage and film today. Whatever advantage the screen may have does not really lie in its subject matter. Both media have been up to their ears in the same thematic preoccuations: ruthless investigations of the anti-hero, dissections of fragmented personality, explorations of the existentialist void, simple but truth-telling genre studies, sex with the shirt off. *Alfie* was a play before *Alfie* was a film, and Harold Pinter works both sides of the street. If anything, the stage stays a bit ahead of the screen where *material* is concerned: Mr. Pinter's work for the stage is more radical than his work for film, and I haven't yet seen the cunnilingual sex of *The Beard* in my neighborhood movie house (or have I missed it?). Where content is concerned, about the only thing the stage lacks is automobiles: I sometimes come from films thinking they're no longer about people, they're about cars. But cars are right for film, of course. They do destroy time and dissolve landscapes. And as everyone knows, they invite tinkering. I suspect that the act of looking in the mirror to see where its teeth were, the fact of facing up to its face, was for film the single most important step toward all the unleashing, and all the plugging-in, that has come after.

The theater, lagging and lonely? Let's back into it through a piece of film. In 1924 Buster Keaton, who in his instinctive way was one of the first serious analysts of film, made a comedy called *Sherlock, Jr.* In it he played a film projectionist. Falling asleep at his machine, he dreamed himself leaving the projection booth, wandering down the center aisle of the theater, climbing onto the stage, and walking into the film. Once he was in the film, the film of course cut around him, wildly, unpredictably. But he didn't cut with it; he maintained continuity. This was dangerous. He might start to sit on what was plainly a garden bench and wind up sitting on a rock in mid-ocean. He might then dive into what was plainly water and wind up stuck in a snowbank. To this day the sequence is a small marvel of technical ingenuity. Keaton possessed such physical dexterity that he was able to place himself precisely in separately shot landscapes without dissolve, telltale lap-over, or any break in his own "outside" continuity. But the sequence is more than a stunt. It is film criticism. Keaton is pointing out to his audience how films are made, how they alter habits of perception, how they differ from experienced life, and so on. He is showing us that cutting is one thing and continuity another by letting us see both at once, in conflict.

There is a conflict here. Keaton doesn't belong in the sequence. He can't cut. He belongs back on the stage where he came from. And one of the things he is telling us, or at least one of the things that can be deduced from the risky conjunction, is what life back on that stage is all about. It is about continuity, about an eye-to-eye, toe-to-toe relationship between character and audience that is maintained without interruption of any sort until it becomes exhaustive and even unendurable, about intimacy so absolute that only a figurative death will relieve it (*all* plays must end in death, the Player King of *Rosencrantz and Guildenstern* insists), about a line that can't be broken until the hero or the audience is.

The stage is defined by, and lives on, the pressure that comes of this closeness, of the fact that no one can get out of there, cannot change his mind or even his angle of vision, not for a moment. (The primitive instinct that first made the playing area circular was a right one: the ring was meant to surround, to enclose, to prevent escape.) Film is like being bombarded. The stage is like being handcuffed. We are locked to the man up there, he is locked to us, and neither of us can make a move without moving the other. (I have developed a curious tic over years of playgoing. Whenever an actor on stage shrugs, I shrug. I can't help it, it just happens. But it never happens at the movies, only in the theater.)

Literally, we are bound hand and foot; our ankles chafe; our nerves may scream; any satisfaction we get is going to have to come from enduring our total exposure to one another until we have got past irritation into anguished, groaning, final and helpless commitment. The relationship *is* linear, which is why it may be out of vogue at the moment. Second by second, hour by hour, we are going to be with one another: time can't be shaken off, or space evaded. When, say, Hal Holbrook invites us in to spend an evening with Mark Twain, we are not to be allowed any more relief than he is. There are only so many places he can go: to a table to pick up a book, to a humidor to pick up a cigar, to a chair. We watch him track his way, the same way, across the carpet he doesn't dare leave (he can't vanish; that would end everything) until he seems to have dug a trench in the carpet. He *is* digging a trench, but he is digging it in us—in our skins, in our retinas, in our brain cells. He is never out of our sight, we are never out of his, and finally the two sights become so cemented that he can doze off for a catnap and we won't budge. We'll wait. Imprisoned by the continuity of the performance, we have no alternative. At higher levels we can't escape Phèdre or Oedipus or Lear, either; they are *at* us, they have invaded and are now occupying us, they won't shut up, won't take their clammy hands off our arms. The power of the theater is a particular kind of power: it is *staying* power, in every possible sense of the term.

This power isn't easily or randomly generated; it comes into being through specific means. These means aren't primarily visual (though all theater has visual elements, sometimes thoroughly monotonous ones). Marcel Marceau can transfix an audience by visual means alone, but he does so in short takes; when he attempts to press mime toward the duration and the complexity of an hour-long playlet, the pressure evaporates. Obviously—though not so obviously in contemporary theater practice—if we are going to endure the awful intensity of being bound hand and foot, minute by minute and mile by mile, to an alter ego we cannot escape even by closing our eyes, we must speak or go mad. Theater eases the pressure by expressing the pressure. Words are its out. It opens its mouth and howls its confinement. In so doing it also intensifies the closeness, completes it.

But not just any old words will do. Ordinary words, banal words, prosaic words, the humdrum words of our everyday experience, are not adequate to the task. No one wants to be chained to a bore who can't express himself, or who says the same thing all the time. The time is the same, the place is the same, the words don't dare be. They are the discovery that comes of the closeness, its climax, its purpose, its definition, its reward. Only language at its maximum intensity, displaying maximum revelation, generating maximum heat, can satisfy the awful demands of the situation, and that language of course is poetry.

Not poetry of movement, which belongs to ballet, or poetry of mood, which may belong to the short story, or poetry of pause.

Poetry of word, of meter; language thumping like heartbeat. Of course, Sophocles isn't at work now. Too bad. But the theater can still inch toward total outcry: the stir of imagery inside the prose of Tennessee Williams, the crackle of wit that polarizes our attention in *A Man for All Seasons* (more riveting on the stage because of our undeflected concentration on a mind), the undisguised rhetoric of Shaw and the onrushing epithetry of Albee and Osborne at their best all intimate the compulsion we have toward speech that sears, and, in the searing, seals. We hear where we are going, or at least want to go. Whenever we do get there, whenever the words flung in our faces persuade us that we have grasped the man facing us whole, we say that we have come through an experience of theater as theater to an experience of drama as drama. Theater placed us in position; drama spelled out the sensation. One has grown out of the other, each has needed the other. That is what the stage is about. It is about a binding of bodies that demands a loosing of tongues.

But that is not what the stage has thought it was about lately. While film has been leaping up and down proclaiming its very special nature, pockmarks and all, the stage has sheepishly been pretending to be half a dozen other things, including film. It has splintered its image, done its damnedest to splinter time and space, struggled, really, to diffuse the only pressure that will ever make it work. Look at a stage today, laboring to move as rapidly and as frequently as film: scenery flying away before our eyes, houses dropping in from the heavens, benches coming up through the floorboards, landscapes projected on white walls (are we ever *out* of the movie theater?), dissolve, dissolve, dissolve. Or, since stage machinery is rather sluggish, fade-out, fade-in. With a sound track.

Instead of competing by asserting what is distinctive about it, the stage has failed to compete by vainly imitating. The effort is vain, always was. No matter how fast the turntables turn or the treadmills roll (they had those in *Ben Hur*, for heaven's sake), they can never catch the coattails of film. If we're going to have a footrace, film will win. Playing it this way, the stage is bound to seem laggard, effortful, out-of-date, and not itself.

In the rush, in the gasp, it naturally has no time to create the particular pressure that demands language. A cliché, a routine epithet, a mere marker, will do in the scurry. Current stage language is not necessarily bad, mind you: it often has wit, in a quiet way it may have style, it can echo street sounds accurately. But—and this is the dead giveaway—it feels no need to be better than, or different from, the language used in film. (The closer the better; we'll get a movie sale.) I call this a dead giveaway because it says, perfectly plainly, that what is happening onstage does not call for any higher or more intense level of speech. There is nothing unique in its requirements, the pressure cooker isn't cooking. Language is only an accessory of film, not the dynamite that blows the bridge up; so long as the stage uses its essential tool as though it were a handy hairpin, a mere substitute for the master shot, it is going to be taken at its own valuation. Verbally it is no stronger than film; visually it is weaker. How should it hold its head up, or have a name worth asking for twice?

Indifference to language as the indispensable means of releasing and at the same time realizing the peculiar hothouse powers of the stage is not just a current accident, an absence of writers. It is an attitude. Not long ago Bruce Jay Friedman was quoted about his plans for the future. Mr. Friedman is a novelist who had just had his first success in the theater, a far-out, immensely funny comedy called *Scuba Duba*. It was undoubtedly proper of him, now that he was *in* the theater, to give its special nature some attention. But when he turned to the theater as theater, what did he make of it? Moving toward his next play, Mr. Friedman said, "This time I think I'll trust the medium more. With *Scuba Duba* I didn't trust the medium. I kept going straight to my trump, language."

No one thinks of language—a special kind of language under a special kind of pressure—as the theater's own trump any longer. Even a novelist riding on a stage success that was successful *because* of the run-on blare and tumble of its words was thinking of getting rid of some of the words. He was in the theater now.

It's almost a death wish, and widespread. Why the stage should have struggled for so long to be less than itself, why it should have breathlessly tried to overtake a camera it could never claim as its own, or why it should still feel compelled to lower its voice to accommodate the prosy ear of the script girl, would require separate and extended analysis, and perhaps a short course in the psychology of the defense mechanism. Fundamentally, I think, it has been intimidated for a hundred years by the onrushing sciences: by the social sciences that demanded documentary evidence, by the physical sciences that gave birth to so many means of literal reproduction. If literalness was to be the new vein, the one trustworthy vein, how could the stage not go along—even if going along meant tagging after?

Actually, it was quite a trick for film to make lively visual poetry out of literal pictures; film did it by defying its own literalness, by running the pictures out of rational or linear sequence. The stage couldn't manage that. Its own only means of escape lay in the flexibility of speech, in the power of non-literal, non-rational, non-linear combinations of words to penetrate and to ravage the subconscious. But in the new circumstances the stage didn't wish to seem out of step, out of touch. It decided to hold its tongue. Holding its tongue, it became superfluous. It is still standing there waiting for a re-awakening of the verb.

My own simple belief is that, somewhere short of eternity, the stage is going to deliver more that is powerful and more that is profound than the film can hope to do: the dispersed image, the essentially visual image, the busy image, has in the end less concentration. It is an exciting, often beautiful surface, and I love it. (I grew up on it.) I like being so constantly distracted. But when I feel like digging in and staying there, when I want an exhaustive rather than a lively panoramic experience, when I want to get under the blanket instead of being tossed in it, pulled centripetally instead of being exploded centrifugally, I go home to *Hamlet* or to *Heartbreak House*.

The stage *can* command all of us home again (at least for its fair share of the nights). Ironically, it can do it by learning from film the only thing it has not tried to learn from film. It can ask itself, "What am I, really?" and act on the answer.

BUT IN THE BEGINNING

I continue to see approving reference to a remark Elizabeth Hardwick made in *The New York Review of Books*, and I think we'd best take the garden shears to it before it leaps, like a pretty weed, across the landscape. Miss Hardwick, in her lively distemper, was out to drop a curse on the entire contemporary theater:

> The destruction of the American theater seems to have come from the fact that producers and directors and actors do not know that drama is a branch of literature. Those who have been told so do not truly believe it—not for our time, in any case. The last decade shows that the professionals, in whose pitiless subjection this great art lives, believe drama is an arresting idea or situation, projected by mechanical, theatrical devices, and embodied finally in the movements of stage stars. From the top to the bottom of the commercial theater this is the conviction —the only one they have. There is no sense that drama is first and last an act of literary composition.

There you have it, and much of what you have is—Aeschylus forgive us—true. But one statement is not true and it is the statement that is being most widely repeated: "drama is first and last an act of literary composition."

Drama is last an act of literary composition, but not first. Even when we say that it is last such an act, we are expressing a hope rather than stating a fact: the hope is that every two or three hundred years we will have an explosion of big and little Shakespeares; the fact is that we very often have to go for two or three hundred years living on a drama that is mere verbal indication ("By heaven!—it shall not be—a hundred pounds' reward for him!") and nothing close to literature. But we do somehow go on, and what we go on with is thought, at the time, to be drama.

We can yield a point at once: the sort of thing I have quoted above is not in the richest, ultimate, absolute sense drama; it is really a coarse kind of playacting, pantomime with verbalized exclamation marks. But a counter point must be insisted upon: buried inside every drama we are willing to call genuine, and not too far from the surface, is just this coarse kind of playacting, throbbing away like a motor. Either it is there, or the play, however finely conceived as literature, will not move on the boards.

I am sorry that we must entangle ourselves with such shopworn phrasing as "on the boards" and that we will no doubt wind up mentioning the *commedia dell'arte*, that convenient slapstick which is so regularly used to beat closet dramatists on the head with. But there is no getting around the theater's need for a motor that doesn't have to be, and most of the time isn't, literary. Drama *is* first a situation, a situation in motion: it must be if it is successfully to occupy the open space in which it takes place and if it is to sustain the attention of a diversified mob. When two furtive Dromios back toward one another from opposite sides of the stage, bump behinds, scream in terror and leap frantically for the wings, that is a situation in motion. It is also drama—primitive drama, but drama. (It involves action, discovery, change.) And it can be completed without speaking a word.

The *commedia dell'arte*—here we go—spoke many words, but all of them were improvised. For several hundreds of years actors bustled onto the stage with no more than a rough notion of the plot in their heads; they spent the rest of the evening improvising. It is not to be supposed that very much of their improvisation achieved the level of literature.

They were working close to, and making the very most of, the coarse underpinnings of drama that had already served, say, Plautus and Terence as a springboard to higher things. In due time they helped to provoke another literature, the high literature of Molière, the medium-high of Goldoni. Meantime, they understood the nature of the motor and so kept it running, dueling one another back to back, inventing spur-of-the-moment insults, tiptoeing downstage to trip someone up and to end the tripping in a somersault or a jeer.

What moved the occasion was the shook bones of the scenario: "Arlecchino the charlatan arranges the bench on which he is to mount and sell his goods. . . . Capitano salutes Flaminia and, recognizing Arlecchino as the man who has taken his sweetheart, pulls him off the bench; Orazio and Capitano fight; Arlecchino flees; Capitano flees; and in the midst of this uproar the bench falls over." Over and above and in and around these dancing bones the players might say what they wished, what was helpful, what was funny, but what they said was quite clearly not of the *first* importance. Today, remember, a great many performers are once more experimenting with improvisation and pantomime, perhaps in an effort to get the motor started again.

When the naked machinery is nakedly on view, when it becomes in effect all there is to the play, the quality of the play as sophisticated drama is not likely to be much. Most reasonably good playwrights refuse the machinery such bald exposure. They do not so much attempt to conceal or suppress it as to dress it freshly, to offer it in a perspective that is new, startling, and honestly come by, as Shakespeare offered every shabby but surefire device of the revenge melodrama in the staggering perspective of *Hamlet*. But most good playwrights—I would say all good playwrights—know that it is there and that it is not in its nature literary. Playwrights *pray* that it is there as they go about the final business of refining the lines and character complexities which may be called literary, knowing that if it isn't there not all of their refinements will ever make the play "work"—as not all of the refinements of Shelley, Browning, Byron, Coleridge, and Tennyson ever made their plays work.

And you will often find good playwrights deliberately using the skeleton in just a bit of its nakedness, as though to assert its presence and to claim its value. A man in mourning enters the stage and before he has said a word the audience is aroar with laughter; ah, yes, the true motor is running. A man hides beneath a table while his wife is being seduced and is of course unable to contribute to the "literary" content of the situation without giving himself away; his presence is as important to the success of the scene as anything that is being said above him. A woman enters a room at night and leaves it again without having uttered a sound: Chekhov, redirecting the sequence, took exquisite pains to get it just right. Under language, which is last and richest, lies a padding of feet, a grimace, a visible exercise of tough, coarse plot machinery. The circumstances in which drama takes place are themselves coarse; it is the marvel of the world that they should have produced a high literature as often as they have.

It may be objected that the bones—the tumbling bench, the footfall and the bumping back to back—are themselves a part of the initial "literary" concept, that the crude visual and spatial mechanics which guarantee sustained movement—something to *follow*, something to see—are literary to begin with. But unless we are willing to call, say, ballet a literary form, too, I am afraid the objection must be overruled. Not all deliberate composition is literary composition. And theater begins by putting a foot down. One, then another. The steps, so essential to survival in such a space, are not yet literary.

I know I'm not saying anything new. But I labor the point because there is such grave danger in persuading possible writers for the theater that what they are to write is first and last literary. That is a good way to lead them into failure, and we can't afford that. First it is their task to learn the nature of the space and time in which they must work, with a thousand breaths overhanging them. Afterward, let us all most prayerfully hope that motion, action, grimace, gesture can be caught up and crystallized in the loveliest or most searing of words, words that are better than the "abominable rhetoric" and "fraudulent sentiment" which Miss Hardwick tells us are now most commonly put before the public. On this last point, of course, Miss Hardwick is right enough.

STAGE SPEECH

My own first sigh of gratitude to William Alfred for his play *Hogan's Goat* came from having heard carefully wrought speech, speech that meant if possible to be literature, which was also and without effort stage speech. Our habits of thought these days tend to regard the two tones as enemies: we think of stage speech as a coarse makeshift satisfied merely to be "workable"; we think of carved language as belonging to a higher realm altogether—and we imagine that the only resolution to the battle is for one to kill off the other. Thus people who want the theater to be literature are willing to let it stop being theater; while practical craftsmen sneer and let better words pass them by. A ten-foot pole would not do to measure the cagey distance these opposed loyalties keep. And a good bit of bitterness comes of the estrangement: literary men who have felt themselves above learning the requirements of the working stage are bitter when that stage does not in fact support them; and practical craftsmen, persuaded that they must not try anything beyond the ordinarily serviceable, resent being called hacks.

Mr. Alfred's most immediately apparent virtue was that he gave no sign whatever that such a problem existed. He opened in a Brooklyn parlor, 1890. A taut, severely beautiful wife was furtively smoking a cigarette. Hurdy-gurdy sounds came through the windows, echoing a street that was as plausible as the gas lamps on the wall. A husband, a rough young Irish immigrant determined to strike for political power, bounded up the stairs to embrace his wife and then to turn on her vigorously for that "whore's habit," smoking.

In all of this there was no formal attempt to isolate either the behavior or the environment from the expected rhythms of life, no conscious artifice used to break through the naturalistic wall so that alien rhythms, the rhythms of verse, might enter. When Mr. Alfred wished to increase the intensity of his speech to the point where it would accommodate imagery, he did it by passion and by nothing else. The young Irishman was being badgered by his wife to marry her formally in the Catholic Church, but he had secrets that needed to be kept if he was to survive politically. To keep them now, from his wife, he took refuge in fury—and in the fury he simply climbed, stair by stair, the ascending platforms words could make.

This was almost always Mr. Alfred's method: to get the deeper penetration heightened language affords by stirring personal fires to such a pitch that they had to find right words to feed on or explode. A challenged priest would blare like a tarnished trumpet if his whole long history of conscience-chopping was called into question. A kind woman would find a way to venom if her generous instincts were sufficiently ravaged. A tinhorn politician, so worn from past wars that his face threatened to fold down about his cigar, would rise to fog-horn proportions given the proper needle. Touch a psyche, press it, badger it, doubt its worth for a moment, and scalding steam would escape from it, steam that condensed into apt phrases instantly.

It was only when the temperature was lower, the mood more reflective, that Mr. Alfred succumbed to the softness that comes of living in an offstage library. "Would you lecture me on courage?" is a standard rhetorical device, and "What am I that you take me for a fool?" is threadbare, though still garish, hand-me-down. There were also too many lilac veins in Agnes Hogan's throat.

But for nearly all of the long evening the author was showing no such self-conscious discomfort in edging toward a prepared speech. A speech, for him, was not so much what characters say as what characters do when they must. Here they are, standing upright, with feelings and lungs. Why should they not use both to cleave the air with evidence that they fully exist? What would reticence, emotional or verbal, gain them? What kind of tension is ever eased by hiding it? As the characters spoke up and spoke out, the tension flowed onto the stage and became the one thing we were watching. We saw what was said, and that is the mark of stage speech.

But I really began these remarks with the thought of calling attention to another of Mr. Alfred's virtues, also a rare one. His play had amplitude. *Hogan's Goat* was long but not self-indulgently long; we might well have wished for a greater concentration on the principal figure in the second act, but we were not apt to ask for cutting. Fundamentally, the play moved forward by a process of filling out rather than narrowing. We met the young husband and wife who were to be central and we grasped that the love between them was abrasively incomplete. We went then to a barroom, with swing doors and yellowed piano, where gossips of both sexes gathered to whisper of an impending death; in the scene and through the gossip we came to know, life-scale, the Agnes Hogan our young husband had abandoned and betrayed. But the scene was not expository or left-handed; it seemed to open the play to let another dimension of life into it. Thereafter the young politician, with his haunting Agnes finally dead, went to a priest to confess his sins and, hopefully, Agnes'. Trying to borrow redemption for a woman he had himself condemned, the husband swelled with complexity: he would be generous with the dead but only when they were dead.

The crossed wires of his own personality quickly crossed those of the priest listening to him, and the two were soon out of the confessional and into a donnybrook made of the compromised purposes of their lives. The scene was a powerful short stage piece, but that was not its special interest; what was specially interesting was that the priest—who never appeared again—had suddenly become a part of the life of the play, had added permanently to the increasing inhalations and exhalations that would constitute its enveloping, always more dense, atmosphere.

The scene that followed did not at first seem to follow at all: we met the crusty old political boss whose casual corruption was about to do him in and we listened to him pour informed contempt upon the just and the unjust alike. Here, in the fourth scene and deep into the first half, we were turning our complete attention to an altogether new character. That is a very odd, and usually a very awkward, way of building a play. But we were fascinated. For the old no-good, admirable in his vulgar energy, was not simply usurping stage; he was pushing it out one more measure, extending the reach we had to have—the acquaintance and the involvement—if we were to understand a younger man's self-destruction in its ultimate proportions. People do not come to their sorry ends on neatly appointed, narrow paths, and we know that. Most playwrights who want to show us how devious the course is generally focus on the falling hero and stay with him as he rattles, in increasing nightmare, through stranger and stranger labyrinths. Mr. Alfred worked otherwise: his play seemed to open steadily from the center until it was big enough to encompass and account for all the outskirts. We reached the back alleys, and the readiness for a fall, by starting in a parlor and then expanding through the neighborhood, by attending to two people and then discovering that twenty must answer for them. The final private tragedy was not a private tragedy; it was the circumference of all we had seen.

The method did not sustain itself absolutely. In the second half of the evening, while the ghost of Agnes was furtively reentering the young politician's ruthless course, the substantially drawn figures on the sidelines became too dominant. They did not lose interest, because they were so substantial; but they robbed the young politician of interest temporarily, so that he was dwindling a bit in size when he should have been growing dramatically fattest. The final scene jerked the slightly disintegrating mosaic into commanding shapeliness again, but some looseness had intervened, as had some too transparent melodrama. The melodrama of burrowing for ancient documents in a dead woman's strongbox could have been whisked away, or more sensibly managed, without loss.

But whatever undue space was taken up in the play's second half with the hangers-on of any man's destiny, we still must be grateful to the author for showing us that hangers-on are part of a man's destiny, part of the self that he tames or destroys. It might be said that almost all plays now being written are two-character plays, even when they contain ten characters. *Hogan's Goat* was a ten-character play, with the ten finally fusing to create the central two.

WINKING WITH WORDS

Everyone in *The Lion in Winter* spoke like an angel—like a fallen angel, I should say—and one of the special pleasures of James Goldman's play was that everyone knew it. Almost nothing was nicer than Eleanor of Aquitaine's deep gratification at having been thoroughly scalded by a caldron of seething syllables flung at her by the latest of her husband's mistresses. "I'm rather proud," she mused, once the mistress had vanished, riding the broomstick of her own invective. "I taught her all the rhetoric she knows."

The characters dearly loved the rhetoric with which they ravaged one another; they cherished the fact that it *was* rhetoric, and they seemed always to be squeezing their playwright's hand in gratitude for having given them such tongues. The play was about conspiracy, and it was a conspiracy. Mr. Goldman and his subjects had contrived among them a little game, a game in which the subjects would pretend to be Henry II of England and his court but in which they would always let us know exactly how much they were pretending by winking at us with words. The wink would bring the words wryly, and sometimes ruthlessly, up-to-date, so that anyone onstage could toss a bit of twentieth-century patois or a calculated anachronism into the hopper pretty much at will, but without in the least disturbing the impression that these were actual, untamable Plantagenets at work. What happened was that we joined the game, eager to let language scamper back and forth across the centuries, and if one hotheaded son of the realm called another a "stinker," we smiled twice; we smiled because the term is so coarsely contemporary and we smiled because Plantagenets, in 1183, must surely have thought of it.

Henry, snapping his royal head toward the light in pride of profile, brusquely remarked, "My finest angle—it's on all the coins," before bringing his official weight to bear on the problem of who needed a verbal thrashing next.

The playwright suspended us in a world made of epithets entirely, letting strict history go hang—along with certain other things—while the phrases with which we still loathe one another served to bind twelfth and twentieth centuries together. Candor at its most cantankerous is the common bond; the rate of exchange in insults cannot really have changed much since Henry whipped his three boys into such mettlesome shape that they were ready to murder him if their mother did not do the job first. But to suggest that *The Lion in Winter* achieved its bright and bristling effect by an adroit manipulation of colloquialisms alone would be to underestimate its energies. The colloquialisms simply opened the door to the wide room of speech, making it easier for us to go through into that playful, unlifelike place where long rolling periods and whole sunbursts of literate vituperation became possible.

During one spectacular battle between Henry and his long-locked-up wife, Eleanor of Aquitaine, all the changes of wind that ever swept through the castle keep seemed to descend upon these two people at once, picking them up like leaves and swirling them around and about each other in an insane dance of spleen.

Rosemary Harris, who first played Eleanor and who seemed to have turned slightly blue during her years of imprisonment, was now flushed as a freshly poked ember. Though she was perfectly capable of announcing that she was glad Henry had never loved her because it made it that much easier for her to manage him coolly, she was both in a fury of resentment and in love. Together they snarled until the thunderclaps grew so noisy that they were forced to fly to one another's arms to protect themselves against the dark sky they had made. While they clung they would console one another with hatred, and when they broke they would lacerate one another with old affection. The turbulence was emotional and always more than that: every verbal dagger-stroke was elegantly, eloquently formed, so that these two people would have nothing to repent when the main bout was over; they would have no need to go about for days afterwards thinking what they *should* have said, for the simple reason that they had said it, perfectly.

And then, in a little miracle of broken, descending rhythm, Miss Harris at last let the air out of her—and emptied the stage of its whirlwind—by sighing, most philosophically and with a sweet smile of self-mockery, "What family doesn't have its ups and downs?" If there have rarely been such violent ups and if there have rarely been such dizzying downs, there has even more rarely been so slyly preposterous a period put to them. Mr. Preston was splendid in his bullying and admirably foolish when he tried to turn crafty-bland, though his author had not given him quite as many colors to try on as Miss Harris got: I shall certainly cherish for some time the memory of this Henry raising a goblet to his aging but still much too vigorous wife and offering a toast "to your interminable health." As for Miss Harris, I can only tell you that she was giving one of the ten or twelve best performances anyone is likely to run across in a lifetime. I am altogether serious.

The play was a roundabout game rather than an advancing structure, and that caused it some trouble on Broadway. Mr. Goldman was proposing, more or less, that power tends to erupt and that absolute power tends to erupt absolutely. He was interested in the eruptions for their own sake, in the splattering bubbles of sulphur that plopped open when the pond was hot enough; and he was fascinated by the chicanery, the deviousness, the spying behind tapestries ("That's what tapestries are for"), the lunatic bargains and the lies that made the heat. He was not interested in arriving at a moral, or even at any coherent end to what he had so maliciously begun. I suspect that he had let his play take the course he thought power struggles generally do take: the course of self-defeating sound and fury, signifying greed. But to build a play as circuitously as kings contrive their kingdoms is to risk the same degree of self-defeat: there are apt to be so many machinations that the mind begs for a brief release; the end of the struggle is apt to be flat; the motives that drive men to such deviousness will most probably remain obscure (it was a bother to us while we watched the play that Henry should for so long wish to settle the crown upon the biggest booby among his sons). Mr. Goldman's decision to mirror the idiot and endless intricacies of plot and counterplot, rather than give us someone to cheer for or some plain goal to anticipate, had in effect denied him a conventional plot, a sense of moving forward purposively; and that, I think, is why *The Lion in Winter* drew a mixed first-night press. Nor could anyone promise an audience that the wintry lion would find his spring; in the play he could only shrug and agree to one last compromise.

But, so far as I am concerned, the richness of the performing under Noel Willman's direction together with the raciness and the vigor of the unexpectedly well-turned speech were altogether enough. There is a further sense in which the mazelike trickiness of the structure might be said to have justified itself: it exposed its own meaning and it tumbled headlong into scene after reverberating scene. (We must sometime speak of tidier, more progressive plays which have no *scenes* that are worth acting.) This is a kind of theater—literate, virile, urgent enough to demand that the actors train themselves to do arias—which few young writers aspire to and for which we are all long starved. I looked up Mr. Goldman's credits to see where his energetic command of language could have come from, and was confounded to discover that after having written one so-so contemporary comedy of Army life and one mildly promising musical comedy he seemed to have plucked his latest style out of the blue, where bolts come from. He once studied to be a music critic. That must be it. In any case, he should most emphatically be urged to go on doing what he has so inexplicably learned to do.

ONE PLUS ONE EQUALS ONE

Brian Friel's very moving play, *Philadelphia, Here I Come,* seemed utterly incapable of making a mistake, which was all the more interesting because it risked so many. It took its biggest risk right off.

Young Gareth O'Donnell—not quite young any longer, but not truly feeling himself a man, either—is putting his few things together in the small town of Ballybeg, Ireland, before flying off to Philadelphia, where he will work in a hotel and occupy the spare bedroom in the apartment of his Irish-American fright of an aunt. He is leaving behind him a father who hasn't said an unexpected word in twenty years, a girl who has married someone else, and a pubful of cronies who were once fun to be with but are now fast fading into "ignorant bloody louts."

Gar, as he is called by everyone who knows him and knows him so little, can no longer really speak to the world of his childhood or of his buoyant near-coming-of-age: each passing year has robbed him a little of the use of his tongue, and when he puts out a hand to touch a presence or a memory it cannot reach the whole way. Everything is as it always was, only it has grown silent and closeted, frostbitten by all the days that have drifted by in the diminishing hush of habit. Not to have opened one's heart of a Sunday means to have lost a part of it by Monday, and there are now so many Mondays multiplied that the very calendar of feeling has turned brown on the wall. Weeks do not matter much in solitary confinement; and the weeks are swiftly folding into forever.

The leap to America promises Gar little. There is more talk in America, but Gar has heard some of it, and it is the talk that fends meaning off, talk so noisy with affection that it fears its own pauses; pauses tend to call a man's bluff. Determined to make himself cheerful between an actual old silence and a threatened new one, Gar goes into his bedroom—where the mold-green wallpaper and the lithograph of the Sacred Heart have matted themselves together like the bottom newspapers in an attic—singing out his destination to the tune of "California, Here I Come."

In the bedroom alone he is not so alone as he was. Every other line of the song is taken by a voice that seems to belong to the wallpaper and the battered suitcase and the mirror before which Gar ties his tie. It is a voice that shares the room, unobtrusively, with Gar, and in a moment or so it acquires a body.

The second Gar that slips from the closet with a chiding tongue and a wicked eye for emotional detail was called, on the program, the "private" Gar, and yes, author Friel was planning to double our vision, giving us two central figures in occult counterpoint—sometimes gesturing in unison, sometimes giving one another the lie—all evening long. While the "public" Gar was making a painfully ragged botch of his last meeting with a girl he once loved, while he was testing his father in hopes of rekindling an ancient kindness or doing his best to believe his buddies as they promised themselves a wild night with the town wenches, his ever so animated shadow was to be on hand to demand the truth of things, to prod and tease and mock and pry until we should have the whole of Gar's head in our heads, until the auditorium could be filled with its mocking, brutal, funny and heartbreaking rattle.

The device worked superbly, on the instant and to the end. Why did it? After all, Eugene O'Neill made a failure of his try at it, and in the nature of things it is perilously close to a trick. Well, there are several too obvious and too easy answers to the question. One is that director Hilton Edwards had, in performance, managed the visual and vocal dance of joined identities with such scampering adroitness and elusive grace that we never had a moment to wrench the two halves apart. It was astonishing how naturally we accepted two deliberately unlike faces as indispensable partners in a single psyche. We didn't look from one to the other, seeking contrasts. We saw both at the same time, making fools of one another, suffering one another not at all, but irrevocably one; to let either figure vanish, even for a very short time, was to cleave the stage. Of course only the "private" Gar could vanish; when he did, we felt as strangled as the "public" Gar did and wanted him back.

The second easy answer was that actor Donal Donnelly was so insidiously commanding as the secret self that we would scarcely have dared doubt him for fear of interrupting our own sad and malicious delight. Mr. Donnelly had gone beyond the twelve-tone scale into some unfathomable mathematics of style, so that he could at one moment sneer sorry home-truths while a rosary was being recited and at another linger over language with great longing: a phrase like "and left the girls dangling their feet in the water" seemed to catch the broken mirror of moonlight as music might.

But there has to be a still better answer to explain the play's power of openly affecting audiences—by openly I mean to unrestrained tears—while keeping its sassiness intact and its central trick busy. The answer, I think, is that the play *needed* its trick if it was ever going to tell its truth. The conceit of the double person was something absolutely demanded by the material, not something ingeniously added to it. The play was about man's failure to speak what he feels; but we could not have had the play at all—not naturalistically, and not in prose—if we had not had one dumb ox who failed to speak and one dancing devil who felt. The core of the play was rent by contradiction; it had to have twins to plead its case.

On top of that, the doubleness was true. Every last one of us— "Have pity on every god damn man jack of us!" was the cry phrased in the play—literally talks to himself, upbraids himself, insults himself, every hour of the day. Playwright Friel showed a sure instinct for the trivial self-accusations that cause us our deepest agonies. One thing for which Gar could not forgive himself was as silly as it was painful: in an excess of romantic confidence he had blabbed to his girl about the "egg money," the small change he picked up on the side from farm to farm that his father knew nothing about. The secret was not very humiliating; Gar was humiliated because it *was* a secret he meant to keep and he could not curse himself roundly enough for having exposed the crazy workings of his mind. We all have covenants with ourselves we betray; and when we turn sick with the signs of our weakness, it is the "private" in ourselves, stupid but unrelenting, that makes us ill.

We all have ears we didn't ask for, ears that hear the awfulness in the speech of those we love. Gar "public" wanted to like his aunt and uncle from America, if only for selfish reasons; Gar "private" could not help hear the aunt saying that, upon their arrival in another country, a friend "treated us like we was his own skin and bones." The garbled phrase was an ugliness, funny but repellent; it was picked up only by the recording ear, the invisible radar, that would never pretend to have noticed it. Gar liked his old schoolmaster, drunk that he was, and perhaps was grateful to be given a volume of the decaying fellow's poems, "privately printed," as a going-away remembrance. All the same, one part of him listened to the schoolmaster's coy, self-protective, falsely candid remark that of the poems "some are mawkish" and heard each disingenuous inflection for precisely what it was. Two men stand at attention for one man at all times—in life as on the stage, separately alert. The play found the one right and easy means of saying so.

Mr. Friel cross-lighted the stage, subtly sending one shaft down where it would intersect with its opposite, blending fact and feeling at a center point where both could burn together. The play's two-handed reach caught hold of almost everything in a constricted, but so very complicated, world: the way an appalling aunt proclaimed her resemblance to a beloved but unremembered mother, the way an unsalted codfish of a father recalled a suit the boy once wore, the way a curt crone of a housekeeper bribed a lad's friends to be friendly, the way a tongue that wanted to be kind raced ahead of itself in its hurry to hurt, the way a clod quickly colored with embarrassment when he was at last impelled to be generous. *Philadelphia, Here I Come* could conventionally be called bittersweet, but it was not so romantically rueful as that. It was plainspoken in order to prod out hidden poetry; it was funny to be fair-minded, cruel to be kind. It simultaneously imprisoned and liberated its hero, letting him suffer his failure to speak and letting him speak his savage heart out, as though to say, "It *is* necessarily so." Life is a halfway house in which a man meets and stumbles over himself. As with any stumble, there is hilarity in the clodhopper's clumsiness and in his fall a real hurt. Both were on the stage.

DIGGING IN

I have been having a bit of correspondence with an agreeable, if patently misguided, reader who wants to persuade me that the novel is a superior form to drama because of the enormous freedom with which the novelist is able to work and because of the vast territories he is able to occupy. I really hesitate to enter the argument; it is so rare to find an ardent soul taking up arms on behalf of the novel these days that the temptation is to leave the good fellow alone and hope that he will succeed in convincing *someone* that the novel is not in fact dead.

But there is a fundamental misconception abroad about the method with which the two forms do their work, and it is a misconception that has lately crept into the theater itself, rather blurring its nature. So I shall go on, contending that drama is at least the equal of the obviously freer form (secretly I think it is the greater of the two, though I pretend on panel discussions to be utterly unbiased), and insisting that freedom does not necessarily generate the maximum force.

A novel is like a grand tour. A play is like a mine shaft. I don't mean to hint by this comparison that the novel isn't capable of depth. Clearly, it gets its depth through complexity, through being here, there, and everywhere at will, through being able to report the objective incident and the subjective experience of it simultaneously. Its dimension is made of an overlay. Scurry around a thousand corners, burrow into a thousand minds, one at a time or in whatever fits and starts please the novelist, and as the successive pages pile up on top of one another the thickness of the world is virtually held in our hands. Words, scenes, men and women and states of mind accumulate; the last presses down on the first; weight comes of all the superimpositions that have taken place between first and last.

The power of, say, Günter Grass's *The Tin Drum*, which is like the power of approaching headlights reflected against a smeared windshield, is not a concentrated but a dizzily distributed power. If every paragraph takes care of itself, which is to say that every paragraph is independently readable, the effect of the book is an aftereffect: you didn't know what it was going to be until you'd arrived at an inn for the night and discovered what language the natives spoke. Along the way you were pretty much blinded by the glare, deprived of a sense of direction but happy to stay the crooked course. The real lust of a true novel is wanderlust. Think of *Tom Jones* or *Lolita* or *War and Peace* or *Catch-22* and maybe you'll see what I mean.

The theater's fundamental method isn't a bit like this. Oh, Shakespeare does wander a bit, and it may take a computer to keep track of the side issues in *Lear*; but no matter how far afield the subplots may stray we always have the feeling that they are pressing inward, not opening outward, and that the magnetic center about which they are gathering is a single rigid man, whether he is Hamlet or Lear. And *Othello* is much more typical of what the theater is about: two men could stand still and play it all. Racine did sometimes have two people stand still and play it all—as the Greeks did, with Creon and Antigone rooted to tiny plots of ground from which neither could budge—and when we make jokes nowadays about plays which limit themselves to five characters or to two, we are wrong in supposing that some canny playwright is keeping his costs down; he is instinctively stripping himself of distraction to see if he can get at the root of the theatrical matter. Aeschylus got along with no more than two actors until Sophocles, behaving rashly, raised the number to three.

The theater's penetration is downward, rather as though if you stood on one spot long enough, stamping your feet in agony or in simple determination, you would eventually work your way through to China, or, short of China, to the core of your own being. Don't disperse yourself in diversified activity, the playhouse seems to suggest to its inmates, or you will turn out like Peer Gynt, who had no more core than an onion. Hold fast, think hard, feel fiercely, and the ground will give beneath your feet.

I sometimes think that is why the Greek theater had a chorus—to fence the contenders in. Ring them around so they can't go away and you'll see them exhaust themselves, explore and reveal themselves, in plain view. No assembled reports from far-flung outposts are required to assess the situation; all the news is here and now, self-contained, self-examined, self-devoured. Every art form needs an artifice to say from the outset what kind of thing it is; the original chorus said that it was a bonfire in a protected, carefully circumscribed place. Prometheus was chained to a rock so he *couldn't* move; it didn't keep him from making a play.

Needless to say, I have nothing against action. But the action of drama is a vertical thrust, not a horizontal reach, and the two things become crossed at their mutual peril. There is a good bit of crossing going on at the moment. Entranced as we are by "epic theater" or by that rather vague substitute for it which is called "total theater" (this usually means neglecting drama to play with the light board or to run up the costume bill), we are often to be found fragmenting our plays, scattering concentration this way and that in order to embrace the maximum number of persons, places, and points of view, in imitation either of the novel or of film. Interestingly enough, such plays survive—if they survive at all—on the strength of scenes in which the clutter is got rid of and two or three survivors are left stranded at stage center. *Now*, the play seems to say, we can get down to business. More often, as in John Whiting's *The Devils*, the dispersal of forces is so great and the sense of dissipation so strong that we feel our eyes have begun to fail us and that we are victims of overexposure to double exposure; in the absence of any clear priority, we blink and withdraw. Ronald Ribman's *The Journey of the Fifth Horse*, derived from Turgenev, added to its source; but what it added was flashbackery calculated to give us vertigo with its straying. The play was lost, strayed, *and* stolen by the time it was done.

Novelists who turn to the theater generally bring their habits of mind with them, habits good enough when they are on home ground (which, as it happens, is anywhere the novelist wants to be at the moment) but not very helpful when it comes to putting a fist straight through one inch of earth. Even so distinguished a literary man as Robert Lowell—and God knows the theater needs poets if it can only persuade them that the theater is a mistress with a little wriggle all her own—fails, in his *Benito Cereno*, to scent the single-mindedness with which the stage traps its quarry. Mr. Lowell builds his play like a teeter-totter, touching now this bit of ground and now that. But we are looking at a needle with too wide a swing; what we want is a needle that will pick a patch of flesh and *jab*. A play with more than one center will seem to vacillate; plays drive stakes through themselves, as through Dracula's heart, and trust that profundity will come of the wholly committed, intensely fixed plunge.

5

THE PLAYERS

INSTANT STARS

I HAVE AN incoherent letter here, one much too incoherent ever to have reached the Letters to the Editor column of my newspaper, and it will take a certain amount of detailed textual analysis to get us through it. But I don't think we should avert our eyes from these things.

The letter reads:

DEAR MR. KERR,
You are without doubt approaching the age.

What a pity for the American theater that no actress past a certain age can call forth the ecstasies you enjoy in Miss Barbara Harris. (I have taken into consideration your descriptive references to most of the American actresses you wrote of in your many reviews over the years.)

However, I do thank you for some of your references on behalf of Miss Harris.*

Of course, you cannot know that you have sown the seed of her future dilemmas, etc.

What man is going to live up to Miss Harris?

Poor Barbara! For those who gather around, and they will be

many, will do so, not so much for what she is, but for what has
been written!

Ever sincerely yours,

———————————

Founder and President of the Society
for the Protection of Cruelty to
Actresses of the United States of
America.

There, I think that's all of it. No, I forgot the asterisk. The asterisk
refers to a remark crowded onto the bottom of the page, as follows:

*Although you seem to be more susceptible to the firmly
fleshed than to the firm of mind.

Obviously, there are four or five mysteries and/or canards which
must be cleared away before we can get to the true nub of this
complaint. Let's dispose of the asterisk first. I am very susceptible to
firm-minded women or I would not have married the woman I did.
Of course, I see no reason why a firm-minded woman shouldn't also
put on a little weight. I said a little weight.

Otherwise:

(a) I am not approaching the age. I have always *been* the age, and
do not intend to make changes now.

(b) I certainly don't know what man is going to live up to Miss
Harris, after all those notices. I imagine quite a few would be willing
to try, though.

(c) The signature *does* read "for the Protection of Cruelty" as
opposed to the customary "Prevention of Cruelty." This is either a
mental lapse on the part of the president, whose name I am with-
holding so that men will feel freer to live up to her, or it is a small
joke. I have an awful lot of trouble with small jokes these days.

Enough analysis. There is a perfectly sound point buried deep
inside the minor, and in some cases rather deplorable, inaccuracies,
and I would like to say "Amen" to it as soon as we can find it. It is, I
think, this. There is too much sudden overpraise swooping down upon
the young. (I am not going to take anything back, Barbara; these are
going to be general statements, and you can just look the other way.)

The overpraise of the young that infects our theater, and ends up
doing perfectly real damage to the young, is not really due to the fact
that they are young, pretty, firmly fleshed, or in other dubious ways

desirable. Neither are young men praised, when they are praised, for being plainly virile. They are one and all hallelujahed so hysterically simply because they are *new*.

Not new in years, new to us. (The first time Eileen Herlie came here, say, she had already played Hamlet's mother; the fact didn't keep anyone from dancing in the streets, nor should it have. And the most passionate notice *I* ever wrote, according to my lawyer who was worried about what her husband would think, was written about Margaret Rutherford. So there.)

But there is a very real distinction to be drawn between ecstatic salutes to the mature and accomplished on the one hand and ecstatic salutes to chicks fresh from the shell, male or female, on the other. The mature have learned their business and probably won't lose an ounce of technique while reading hyperthyroid notices about themselves. The young *haven't* completed their theatrical educations and there is a very strong chance that, showered early with adulation and swiftly elevated to stardom, they'll never bother to complete it. They may never even be given another chance to do so. Stars quickly become too busy, too sought after, to learn.

As I say, the problem is real and we'll stop making light of it here and now. The American theater is greedy for fresh talent. In part this is so because it has always been so: who isn't happy to be in on the dawn of a Duse? But it is more emphatically so nowadays because the theatrical turnover is terribly rapid: films and television lure away, and eat up, so much of the talent the theater does discover that the theater is forced constantly to increase its discovery rate. Audrey Hepburn was welcomed with open arms in *Gigi* when she was scarcely old enough to be out alone without her governess. That was seventeen years ago. She's been back to Broadway exactly once since. The theater, meantime, has had to keep right on discovering new Audrey Hepburns night after night, just to keep its marquees occupied. It is an institution that has had to learn to make do with instantly replaceable parts.

But the fact that the problem stems from both a natural appetite on the part of playgoers and a genuine desperation on the part of producers doesn't make matters any prettier for the young actors involved. What happens is this. A youngster makes a first dazzling impression, the impression is duly recorded in the press and rewarded by the public, and the actor, his agent, and his accountant (he needs one now) are all happy. The player is suddenly a star and is expected to deliver—the next time around—with the force of a star. Because he is personable, he may get away with it the next time around: reviewers and playgoers are notoriously reluctant to let a new "star" down too soon.

But because he is offered only starring roles now, and as a rule starring roles that are closely related in style and feeling to the first impression he has made, he is literally forbidden—at a very early age—to learn anything. He is expected to maintain his box-office draw by replaying the original record at maximum volume; he winds up wearing it away as rapidly as possible. The fact that he *had* a quality makes it all the sadder; we watch that one quality being eroded steadily through overuse and undernourishment. An intelligent young actor like George Grizzard, well known but not a walloping star, may find it possible to wash his hands of Broadway offers for several years running and go wandering about the campuses of the country looking for things he hasn't done before. But the lad or lassie who has got the full treatment, which means that his or her face has ballooned into a full-page ad, is quickly locked in the prison of too swift, much too fulsome, praise.

The result is that we lose "stars" as fast as we make them, and we don't just lose them to films or to television; we lose them because, after a short time, they cease being stars. Looking at *The Diary of Anne Frank* thirteen years ago, I'd have sworn that Susan Strasberg would be one of Broadway's brightest ornaments today. Looking at *Bernardine* sixteen years ago, I certainly expected that I'd be seeing John Kerr regularly, and rewardingly, in the 1960's. Both were promptly starred. Neither has been in the vicinity lately. I don't know the precise why, of course, in either case, and I'm not prying. But I feel cheated of a pleasure that ought to have grown.

Were the first reports wrong, the first raptures undeserved? No, I don't think so. The equipment was there, the appeal was real. Everything is no doubt still there, as potential. But along the way there was no chance for a change of tune, for unembarrassed experimentation, for ordinary hard labor at ordinary cost. All costs were too high: the cost of appearing in a failure, the cost of trying something else, the cost of keeping press agents well fed and producers in pocket money. It would seem that we often make synthetic legends of our youngsters before they are ready and then lose all interest in them before they are ripe. Indeed, we help keep them from ripening, and that's a crime we must answer for. The fact that we do it out of surprise, delight, exhilaration and genuine admiration doesn't quite square matters.

We really must learn—you and I both—to make gentler noises over the pleasures we come upon of an evening, especially when the pleasures are still very young.

THE WRONG RULES

I am not against actors, I am not against Actors Equity, and I am not a picket-kicker. (In the event that you don't know what a picket-kicker is, I'll tell you. A distinguished American producer who is also a very conservative fellow once explained to me that he deliberately sought out places of business that were being picketed, drove up to them in his car, dismounted and entered the building, carefully—and apparently by accident—kicking a picket in the heel along the way. Sometimes he manages to kick as many as four or five pickets in a day. I have always thought the term should go into the language.)

But I must confess to overriding distress on one point that emerged during the flap over the signing of Anthony Quayle to star in *Galileo*, and Margaret Leighton to appear in *The Little Foxes*, at Lincoln Center. Mr. Quayle and Miss Leighton are, of course, British actors, and their casting was protested on the grounds that American actors might have done just as well in the parts.

Actually, these two particular issues turned out not to be issues. It was quickly discovered that Miss Leighton, who has worked here as much as she has abroad in recent years, now has the status of a "resident alien," and is therefore employable without any sort of special permission. And Mr. Quayle had been invited to appear with the repertory troupe at the Vivian Beaumont only after an American actor, Rod Steiger, had defaulted due to illness. Some unofficial picketing of the playhouse continued in Mr. Quayle's case; but Equity, having earlier approved the substitution, disclaimed any responsibility for the maneuver.

Let's put these two matters aside, then, and look at the fine print. What disturbed me mightily, in the accounts of the fracas that appeared in the newspapers, was the hitherto unpublicized information that "The repertory theater's agreement differs from that between the unions and the Broadway theater, where a producer may hire alien performers of his choice, subject to approval of immigration authorities." The Lincoln Center Repertory Theater's agreement with Actors Equity "prohibits the employment of aliens without approval of the union's 72-man governing council."

In short, there is one standard for Broadway and another for rep. Broadway has the easier time of it: if a commercial, and usually a contemporary, play can well use the services of a talented outsider, its chances of getting that outsider into the country—and into the company—are reasonably good. If, however, a repertory theater wants someone to come in and help do *The Alchemist*, *The Changeling*, or *The Country Wife*, its chances are much, much slimmer, if not altogether nil.

This, if I may say so, strikes me as insane. Repertory is precisely where we need the presence, the assistance, the prior training of people who have had some experience with period styles, with theatrical artifice, with verse—with, in short, the whole range of what we usually call repertory. Broadway, which for the most part does plays that are in the American or at least the modern naturalistic tradition, can far easier get along with talent that's been homegrown. The regulations are upside down.

There is, of course, a premise behind the prohibition. British—and no doubt Continental—performers are barred from joining our permanent acting companies because we need so desperately to develop native talent in classical roles. Our performers haven't had adequate opportunity to test themselves in Sheridan, Shakespeare, Congreve, Molière. Brilliant as they may be—and, indeed, are—in the collected works of Tennessee Williams, they mumble and stumble in periwigs and houppelandes, in manipulating snuffboxes and in tossing off iambic pentameter. (We shall not even discuss Alexandrines.) The only likelihood of their improving themselves in these unfamiliar departments lies in their getting out on the stage and tangling with the stuff. If we're going to import the people who *know* how to do it, our own people will never, never learn.

But the premise really works the other way around, or could just as readily. The notion that our own actors are going to learn how to do *The Changeling* just by doing *The Changeling* is a sweet one, a pretty one, an innocent one. In all truth, they probably would learn to do by doing—in time. Our actors are not unintelligent. But the time involved, I'd say, would be anywhere from ten to fifteen years. To speak for myself, I'm not raring to wait.

Even if we all take a vow that we are willing to endure the mishaps and downright catastrophes of the next ten to fifteen years, while our good folk are working out in sweat what could be picked up in observation in a much shorter period, we run two hidden risks. One is that we won't find the native directors who can crystallize a variety of playing styles, conveying to Method-bred performers the nuances of getting Ben Jonson out of hock. Directors of this sort are in dreadfully short supply—there are perhaps two or three directors in the country today who can manage, at most, two or three different styles, which explains why Tyrone Guthrie is in such demand that if his long frame could be sawed in half twenty cities across the land would be happy to have the halvings, no questions asked—and what we undoubtedly need to do is to import British and Continental directors at least as rapidly as we do players.

The other risk—a crushingly real one—is that the whole repertory movement will be dead before ten or fifteen years can be marked off on the theatrical abacus. Audiences give up, and who can blame them? Just how real this risk is can be measured by the fact that Lincoln Center, after no more than two years of doing *The Country Wife* and *The Alchemist* in the Vivian Beaumont, was ready to lease the Vivian Beaumont, part time, to outside, contemporary, ordinarily commercial productions. The chipping-away has begun, and, barring a miracle on 65th Street, it's going to get worse. Something has to pay off the mortgage. More than that. Something has to keep the well-intentioned customers from surreptitiously gathering up their coats and stoles and slipping into the night during the first and second intermissions. The traffic flow at the Beaumont during intermissions has sometimes been fierce. And all Departures, no Arrivals.

All right. The quickest way to teach American actors to inhale style and artifice and verse and variety, so that we *shall* have genuinely American acting troupes before we all go to our graves, is to place them in the contending company of performers who have long since tucked the right tricks up their sleeves. You'd be surprised how rapidly a man can improve his speech (Elizabethan or Restoration), teach his body to respond stylistically (so that he can cut around the artificial corners of *The School for Wives*), and learn to *hear* the heartbeat that does thump steadily beneath costumes that aren't quite dungarees when he is forced, nightly, to deal face to face with colleagues who are going to make him look a fool if he doesn't fight back. Styles are caught on the wind, in the ear and in the air, not by thinking about them bookishly in the brood of the study. Put an Eileen Herlie or an Irene Worth or a Christopher Plummer on the stage and everybody perks up. "Oh, is *that* how it's done?" the tyro says to himself, lifting his inflections to see if he can't match theirs and catch Sheridan's. Gilt by association, let's call it.

Eileen Herlie is about somewhere, by the way. Why isn't she overemployed? Irene Worth, American-born, British-trained, is probably persuadable. She does a dandy Clytemnestra. Mr. Plummer is half missing his career shuttling between occasional successes in London and occasional condescensions to films. Why hasn't someone offered him an Orestes, or a Richard III, here? (Well, we can all go to Canada and see him do an Antony now and again; Canada, linked by history to a range of theatrical traditions, plainly has a better knack for these things than Connecticut does, and Connecticut isn't getting any better going it alone.)

If there is *one* place where an open-door policy should prevail it is in repertory. Think of it selfishly. The sooner we get effective productions on the stage, the happier audiences will be to support this time of transition. And the more challenged our very own, very dear performers will be. Challenge is what is wanted, not mucking about in the dark.

Well, I have probably now lost the last three actors who were speaking to me. Perhaps I shall be picketed. If so, I will kick no one. But do let's please use the little common sense that is left to us.

SLIPPING THROUGH OUR FINGERS

Mike Nichols' brilliant production of *The Little Foxes* at Lincoln Center left me filled with admiration and a kind of panic.

Its one unmistakable message was that we could have an American National Theater any time we wanted to. The materials were all there, ample and imperious and holding firm ground, on the stage of the Vivian Beaumont. My panic stemmed from the fear that we wouldn't and won't get it, that we wouldn't hear what was being said, that having come right to the edge of a discovery of our present powers we would permit the vision to dissolve and the powers to scatter again as we always have through all of our long history.

First a word about what was there. The play is an American one, not a great play perhaps, perhaps not a play that will be performed three hundred years from now, but a play virtually perfect of its kind, lean and candid, muscular and mettlesome in the bold black-and-white strokes it makes against a money-gilded world. Melodrama? It is that. But watch Lillian Hellman, telling her tale of sharp-clawed Hubbards who mean to inherit the earth, take hold of the altogether familiar business of valuable bonds that are suddenly missing from the family cashbox. Miss Hellman is no theatrical innocent, no mere purveyor of tin thrills. Quietly, and with a knowing and level eye, she absorbs all that is standard about the business into the cunning of her characters, letting them treat the situation as simply something to be expected in a wryly wicked age. An eyebrow lifts slightly, a nose wrinkles in suspicion, a prying voice keeps its tone down: ferreting out the culprit calls for a cheerfully amoral, ruefully sophisticated calm. It isn't only the author who knows what she is doing; the characters know, too. Craft, and more than craft, is here at work. For the very plainness of the situation, the single-mindedness with which it is pursued, reflects a way of thinking, a habit of handling bonds and personalities as though they were equally negotiable, that did once exist in the American crazy quilt and that may continue to characterize an age for some time to come. America *was* melodrama in 1900. It may still be.

In Mr. Nichols' production, the level of the performing literally made you hold your breath. You held it for fear that the next time the drawing-room doors swept open you might miss a flash of George C. Scott or Margaret Leighton or Anne Bancroft or E. G. Marshall. The stage was flooded with quality—I have not mentioned everyone—and with quality in contention, bound together, matching quarter-notes. Most of those present were what are called stars. Isolate their scenes and you might have been able to detect "star turns." Margaret Leighton stumbling into the room in a wrapper like a gaunt pink ghost, reaching out to comfort a man though her own back seemed cruelly broken; George C. Scott discovering he'd been had and toppling backward onto a sofa in a whoop of admiring laughter, then rising to tap Anne Bancroft's marble cheek lightly as though to say he'd be back for a tasty revenge; E. G. Marshall, who may never have given a better performance, turning red in the face with fury and—at the very pitch of his fury—crumpling at the heart; Maria Tucci, newly bereaved, beginning to smile uncontrollably as the vultures about her offered their unfelt condolences. All of these, and more, could readily have been put down as Moments.

But Mike Nichols had not asked for moments; he had asked for an insidious drift and a curling interplay not unlike the faint, swirling fogbank that seemed to come from the armored cigars the male Hubbards were eternally lighting up. The staging was severe, disciplined, brooding with intimation. Housekeeper Beah Richards became a silent chorus framing the coolly rapacious action, turning up the gas lamps that would shine ever so briefly on a rising clan, turning them down again as every kind of dark descended. A straight high staircase bolted upward as toward an ultimate tomb. The scurry of passing footsteps up and down it marked the rhythm of success, failure, greed, groan. At the point of disaster a flurry of pale, rattled figures vanished into sheer black beneath the stairs; Hubbards could be wiped from the face of the earth without so much as going out of doors. Mr. Nichols had previously been known as a director of comedy; here he wrapped his arms around another sound altogether, gathered its overtones, compressed them to a still, clear signal, sustained in space. Play and players were the same creature.

My panic. All of this was there in our hands. But it had come into being out of bounds and against the rules. The rules hold that if we are ever to have a national company it must be a permanent company, with the same actors bound together, bound to the same house, similarly trained, forever. We have a notion that the performers who will ultimately represent us at our best must be snatched as children, more or less as ballet dancers are, and carefully nursed over a very prolonged period in a wide variety of styles until sometime—ten years from now, twenty years from now—we will at last be ready to announce that we are ready, grown-up, qualified to compete in the international arena. I don't dismiss this dream, this long-range vision. I'm for it.

But in the meantime, out of old fears and new shibboleths, we are denying ourselves the intense pleasure, the pride and the gratification we might have. The country is full of good actors; otherwise there wouldn't have been so many of them on the Vivian Beaumont stage. Five or six other companies just as good as the *Little Foxes* company could be called together instantly if anyone cared, or had the power, to call them together. We *could* have five or six productions a year just as rich, just as resonant, just as indigenous, just as serenely confident, as the show we've been talking about. We could if we were willing to improvise, to chuck our preconceptions over our shoulders.

Just how inhibiting our preconceptions are can be seen from the fact that this particular treasure-trove at the Beaumont was highly suspect. We had no sooner come from our special sensation of having seen the American theater at its best than we were chopping it up for firewood. Yes, of course the acting was splendid, but who had put the package together? A commercial manager and Mike Nichols. It was a one-shot and of no further possible significance. Yes, it did seem a kind of call to arms because it had been done in a municipal playhouse, but it didn't really belong to the playhouse; it was being moved to Broadway shortly, its posture of strength was an illusion. Yes, it was fascinating to watch, but the play wasn't Shakespeare or even Strindberg, and until our actors can do Shakespeare and Strindberg we can't really claim any importance for them. And so on well down 65th Street.

It is conceivable that the questions we ask ourselves, and the answers we give as we put our brief excitement behind us, are the wrong questions and answers for this particular moment in time.

Appropriate in the light of eternity? Certainly. But are we masochists now, or partisans of the hair shirt, that we should deny ourselves delights that are demonstrably available provided we are willing to take them on their own terms?

We might be better off learning to grab. If Saint Subber and Mike Nichols can put such a company together, let them do it. Let Alan Schneider or Gene Saks or Joseph Hardy—whoever has the strongest twisting-arm—do the next. If George C. Scott or Walter Matthau or Arthur Hill or George Grizzard is willing to come for a short time only, let him come; he can be replaced as fast as the British National Theater replaces the wandering minstrels who first appear in its productions. If the Beaumont half turns into a booking house, and if the booking possesses the sting and the amplitude, the reach and the rightness, of this *Little Foxes*, let it. Ideals are excellent. Being an idealist, I'm sure they'll win in the end. But it is really very foolish to let them, in their still inchoate state, stand in the way of another excellence that can be held in the fist.

In a way, I hated seeing *The Little Foxes* because it showed me—all too plainly—what I could be reveling in regularly and what no one, neither a commercial nor a municipal management, is offering me at all regularly now. Given a choice, I'd be rash. I'd be willing to start the American National Theater with this one production and then holler for help. I'll bet that another, by hook or by crook, would come.

I haven't always thought this way. But something actual stared me in the face.

INDELIBLES

Benny, Martin, Preston

It isn't easy to say what turns a performer into an absolute stage image, so absolute that you can be coming down the aisle in the dark, looking for your seat, and still know instantly—out of the corner of your eye—that the stage is already alive with a presence which will refuse to change its outlines for you as long as your memory holds. But musical comedies, in particular, have a way of presenting us with such presences, and an effort should be made to account for them.

If I speak of coming down the aisle in the dark it's not because I am in the habit of arriving late on opening nights. The sensation has stuck with me because, one summer not long ago, I happened to drop in at the Tappan Zee Playhouse, which is somewhere on the other side of that lazy cobra of a bridge, to see Jack Benny giving a solo performance, and I *was* a few minutes late and I *was* stumbling about in an unfamiliar aisle when I realized that somewhere in front of me, silhouetted in a white spotlight, an ineradicable posture I couldn't quite see yet was functioning all by itself with the simple authority of the Parthenon.

Not that Jack Benny resembles the Parthenon. The Parthenon is more rectangular. But in the give of one idle knee, in the huddle of elbows that permits two hands to wring themselves out regularly, and in the reflectively cocked head that endures the slings and arrows of this world with such quietly exasperated tolerance, there was a single bold line that might have done for a poster by Toulouse-Lautrec. That was an icon up there onstage, a relief map of one of comedy's countries, as unavoidable as the eyes of Al Jolson, as graspable as the spectacles of Bobby Clark. You didn't look for details, or need to. The man came all of a piece, with his bones tucked out of sight and only an attitude left to stand up for him. *He* wasn't standing there; his stance was.

Mary Martin, who was one-half of the entire company of *I Do! I Do!*, was as defined as though she had been sculpted in ice cream, a very special ice cream guaranteed not to melt. There is nothing pinker in the spectrum, nothing cooler or more composed in the refrigerator, than she; apples may yet come to be known as Mary Martin-cheeked.

Her smile, curiously, is not in her smile: it is in the breadth of her face, which beams all by itself before she has quite told us whether she is happy or not. When she *does* smile, the smile swallows itself, contentedly, leaving only a pair of bright eyes and a poised intimation of deep merriment behind. The face is the kind of face children learn to make out of interlocked circles when they are first being taught to draw. It still has the children's astonished pleasure at their discovery in it, open and rounded and happily exclaiming "Oh!"

It was Miss Martin's business in the entertainment derived from Jan de Hartog's *The Fourposter* to be a wife, the sort of illustrated picture-book wife who hooks a clothesline clear across stage to hang out the kiddies' underthings, who scoops up rocking horses and blue bicycles with the finesse of an empress who has come to houseclean, who shows her temper with a sprinkle of fingers and a brisk "Out, out, out!" and who manages her slightly pompous and sometimes straying husband by beginning her reproofs with a seductively silken "Now, I don't say this to hurt your feelings, darling."

What she brought to these steadily sentimental, overly familiar, and not very inventively rewritten snapshots of everybody's married life (as the comic strips fancy it) was the soothing gloss of a spirit that had long since reduced itself to a few basic, indispensable, confidently fetching ingredients. The first sound we heard from the orchestra as the evening got under way was nothing more than two alternating piano notes, a plink, then a plunk, as regular and delicate as clockwork. Miss Martin worked in much the same way, whether she was singing or skipping or speaking her knowing mind. She struck a tone, then a sly countertone, and then suspended the two together as though filling the stage with pleasure were a mere matter of juggling whatever simple objects might come to hand in the kitchen.

Robert Preston is a different sort of stage drawing, an itch and an energy and a kind of Teddy Roosevelt bristle. Even his voice reverberates as though he'd been shooting arrows with his vocal cords and couldn't silence the twanging, while his foot seems to keep on tapping long after he's decided to stand still. It was really quite right, in *I Do! I Do!*, that a muted brass-band orchestration should have accompanied his urgent efforts to get himself into nightgown and tasseled nightcap: something had to compete with, or accompany, the rat-a-tat-tat of his pulse. Right, too, that when he was scolding his spouse for the bills she had run up, composer Harvey Schmidt should have given him a racing House-That-Jack-Built recitative to contain the rhythm of his outrage.

Mr. Preston exuded impatience, impatience to get on with the hurried bringing up of children (we watched his unseen daughter grow as he whipped larger and larger frocks onto a clothes rack), impatience to take off into the faster freedoms of music. Though he hadn't been given the wittiest of lyrics to spend his diesel-powered drive on, he didn't really miss them; start a tune going, give him a top hat, a walking stick, and some open stage floor and he was off like a high-strung thoroughbred, leaving the track in a daze behind him.

If Miss Martin forms a gleaming "Oh!" Mr. Preston always becomes an insatiable "More!" The urgency of the moment is never quite enough for him; somewhere beyond it lies a starting gun he hasn't heard yet. Even when he has a very good joke, he goes at it as though sniffing out the next one. In the show, the couple rode on in the merry-go-round of a bed that Oliver Smith had designed for them and rose from it dizzily, early in the second act, with their New Year's Eve paper hats still aslant on their heads and with champagne glasses still clutched in their fists. The celebration had clearly been extensive, and they had only barely slept it off. Coming to, Mr. Preston murmured casually, "Oh, maybe we should have gone out after all."

The moment was delightful, the joke a genuine surprise. But when I say that the actor murmured the line, or that he got it off casually, I mean he did that and something more. His murmur is actually a throb, and his casualness is already searching the wings feverishly for the next six or seven scenes or perhaps another carload of songs. He is an actor who is in dynamic control of himself while already wishing it were next week. The stage burns his feet, I think, and the resulting vibrations all reach us.

Lillie

I am haunted by an image, which has come into my head from nowhere. I see a producer's office. The producer is doing a musical. He has sent the script of the musical to Beatrice Lillie, together with a nice little note saying that he hopes she will consider appearing in it. Now the producer, together with his composer, his librettist, his director and perhaps his pastor, is sitting awaiting Miss Lillie's arrival. Today she will give her answer.

Miss Lillie is announced. Miss Lillie enters, as one and all leap to their feet from the leather chairs which have contained them. With her husbanded smile—it is the smile of a rector's wife who knows altogether too much about the rector and secretly puts fresh spiders in his psalmbook every Sunday—and with a motherly nod that is just a bit cheeky for Mother, the lady composes herself, looks about absently, and then remembers that it is she who is supposed to speak. She speaks, and what she says is merely something I have imagined, to my personal and profound horror. "My dears, I just love the part!" she says. "Now, what do you want me to *do?*"

I wonder if you see the nature of the problem here. This is a question that calls for an answer from one or another of the gentlemen present if the interview is not to bog down into a shuffle of silences and if Miss Lillie is not to go away unrequited. But what in heaven's name would a man say to her? He couldn't begin by repeating the plot.

I don't for a moment suppose that anyone connected with *High Spirits*, which was a musical-comedy version of Noel Coward's *Blithe Spirit*, ever sat forward in his chair and, distinctly articulating his words, pointed out that Miss Lillie was to play Mme. Arcati, a medium, that she was to conduct a séance at which a man's recently departed wife would materialize, that the entire narrative development depended upon Mme. Arcati's ability to get that ghost back where she belonged again, and that at the end of the entertainment Mme. Arcati, like the other principals, would take a slug of a potion which would render her stone-dead, though cheerfully so. No one said, "Miss Lillie, these are the things you do." I feel sure of that.

For who has ever hired Miss Lillie to do what a playwright put down on paper, of all things? Who has ever supposed that the progressive events of an evening could be in any way related to, or supported by, or kept in coherence with, the tentative one-foot jig the star would probably be doing the moment everyone's back—but not the audience's—was turned? One does not ask Miss Lillie in to go where a show is going. One asks her in to keep it from getting there. That is her specialty: total distraction from what everyone should be paying the strictest attention to. She is the roadblock that refreshes, the pause in the day's occupation that is known as the adults' hour. Children can do things in orderly fashion, a step at a time, if they care to; grown-ups know that nothing works out that way. Miss Lillie is grown-up. And gone, real gone, if I may put it that way. If she does not always say "Shoo!" to the plot right out loud as she comes on, it's only because that is no longer necessary; plots have heard of her, and hide.

Very well. These facts are known. But if you couldn't answer Miss Lillie's question by talking sensibly about something you'd already surrendered, and glad of it, what then? Would you say, "Well, Miss Lillie, we'd like you to be singing a song and right in the middle of it, for no reason at all, you start to yodel a bit and right in the middle of the yodel, also for no reason at all, you yawn"? Would you *really* say that? What if she said, "Why?" You'd be in great trouble.

Or would you perhaps suggest that she tie a teddy bear to the rear end of her bicycle, wear a canary on her hat, and from time to time adjust a rearview mirror attached to the handlebars? Do you hear yourself hinting that in another scene you'd like her to appear with what seems to be one of those tin horns used to celebrate New Year's pierced straight through her head, and that the two halves of this horn might turn out to be adjustable so that she could treat them as antennae and apparently tune in Mars now and again? I imagine you'd get a pretty frosty look from Miss Lillie.

No, you couldn't tell her what the show was about, because that would be irrelevant, and you couldn't tell her what you'd like her to do instead of it, because that would be silly of you. In fact, I believe I have succeeded in inventing, hypothetically, an utterly unanswerable question, a riddle not even an Oedipus could unravel. There isn't a thing in the world you could mention to Miss Lillie, except possibly her salary—which could never, in the circumstances, be enough. All you could do is shake her hand and get out of the way. I don't even see why you'd send her a script.

We are confronted—let us slip into deep thought now—with mystery, for all I know with myth. (Myth is very fashionable in literary circles these days, and it has to do with what is communicated without being understood or with what is understood without being communicated. Miss Lillie is a perfect example either way.) Miss Lillie is simply What Happens, existentially speaking, when What

Happens is hilarious. She consistently wears enough beads to buy Manhattan back again, but I don't think she has real estate on her mind. Sometimes she stops everything to hum "O dem golden slippers," and she is clearly happy doing it; but she has no golden slippers, she has some very soggy loafers with small rabbits riding on them which she stops to examine closely though without reaching any conclusions. She wears a Nesselrode pudding on her head when she chooses, if it is a Nesselrode pudding; at other times she appears as Robin Hood going on Superman. She always seems to be seriously occupied, and I am glad to know that she has an interest in life. I don't ask to know what it is.

Working steadily downwind, Miss Lillie is absent without leave, present without cause. Off comes her granny's nightcap, out comes her Ouija board; across the stage on tiptoe she teeters, sweetly snarling at the floorboards. When the audience applauds her, she freezes haughtily. What has she been doing to attract such attention or to provoke so noisy a demonstration? What, indeed? She has been cultivating her own garden, where the Nesselrode grows, minding her own business, refining her own soul. She is a private person, not to be intruded upon by plots or producers or philosophers who like to feel that humor can in some way be explained. She does what she does, that is all. And it is all delicious.

Caldwell

Jean Brodie, the regal, frumpy, frightening and raffishly endearing heroine of Muriel Spark's novel and then Jay Presson Allen's play *The Prime of Miss Jean Brodie*, is a creature for whom the world must glow. Glow, or she washes her hands of it.

For Jean Brodie everything must be extraordinary—the times, the girls she teaches, the dark forces that are waiting to assassinate her the moment she teaches her girls too much, the very floorboards on which she so precariously and so arrogantly places her winged-Mercury toes.

It is the only way she can make herself extraordinary, or account for the extraordinary thing that happened to her when she was younger, before her prime. She'd been engaged to be married and her man was killed in the war. Now she turns to her charges and tells them "It was for you that Hugh died" as she urges them to a distinction that will trample on the Philistines and redeem a thoughtless, empty world. However inadequate the girls' equipment may be, they are to sing *Traviata*, fight for Franco, become magnificent courtesans the minute they turn eighteen.

No matter that enemies lurk or that, after one scandal or another, Miss Brodie may be dispossessed of her job in a Scottish boarding school. She has had it out with the headmistress many a time; she has met other, lesser teachers in the corridors and noticed "the predestination in their smiles." The truly distinguished are beyond fear. Miss Brodie has had an ancestor, a good craftsman and a bold man, who "died on a gibbet of his own devising." Gibbets are built high.

In New York this anything-but-gray eminence was played by Zoe Caldwell, and what she was up to was extraordinary, too. Miss Caldwell was not precisely acting a character; she was inventing, in clear amber light, a mobile nightmare—intense, wildly proportioned, antic and slippery, chilling. An enormous secret came onto the stage with her, a secret of such power that she could scarcely contain it: it made her head duck low in a graceful humility as she turned corners (brushing the corners out of her way); it gave her the ectoplasmic security of a snake placed in charge of the garden; it escorted her out of rooms with the breathless dignity of a blown daffodil; it led her to fingering the buttons of her salmon-colored blouse with such a trembling nervous overcharge that you felt she was trying to quiet the salmon that must have been leaping inside. She was a haughty quiver, a wicked guardian angel, a clown damaged by cruelty who was suing the universe, sure of winning. There was sweetness, and steel, in her way.

Giotto was her special taste; displaying a reproduction for her students, she seemed literally to wear it, snuggling into it sensually, warmly, with a lyric proprietary coo that might have belonged to a high-priced fashion model out to buy herself a dress, or a soul. Miss Caldwell rippled across the lawns of Edinburgh beneath an umbrella, exuding the liquid syllables of "The Lady of Shalott," as though the supple, shimmering ladies of La Grande Jatte had been given singing lessons by a myna bird; inside the classrooms she seemed a spill from the stained-glass windows. "There is no contradiction between being ridiculous and magnificent," a frustrated lover said of her. Miss Caldwell proved it.

Under glass on a turntable, this specimen was seen from all sides, most of them preposterous, several very touching. When, once an ultimate scandal had done its inevitable work, Miss Caldwell came in shock to visit a student who might have been able to explain the blow that had fallen, there was no real self-pity in the woman, only a pale and dogged effort to comprehend. After a reflective skip in the rhythm, she said, "Sandy, I believe I am past my prime." You dissolved. She didn't, quite.

The funny, swooping, playing-with-fire complexity of the performance wasn't all Miss Caldwell's, though she had stamped it with a bizarre imagination of her own. Jay Allen's text was that very lucky thing, an adaptation that amplified its source materials without diminishing their personal tone. Muriel Spark cannot conceivably be an easy novelist to dramatize. She works glancingly, with a razor blade. Reading her is like hearing every whisper of one side of a telephone conversation. One side only. We are intimate and detached at once. In order to open the work up for the stage, Miss Allen had of course had to let us in on what else was being said all the time, and this did rob her of one final effect: we could not have the sharp impact of discovering which of the girls had "betrayed" Miss Brodie when we had been with the betrayal, watching the girl, all along. But the adapter had done two difficult things very well. She had not broken Miss Spark's slant of line: it remained odd, overheard, hypnotic. And she made the evening move on a double curve, letting the curves intersect. We swept, with fondness and fear, along a Brodie curve: from being amused to being appalled to being sorry. Inside this, and against it, we inched steadily along the path a rebellious pupil was taking: from jealousy to spite to icy sternness. We had always two choices before us, affection and rejection. The play was built to permit us to cling to both.

Channing, Bailey

Hello, Dolly! was a musical-comedy dream, with Carol Channing as the girl of it. Almost literally it was a dream, a drunken carnival, a

happy nightmare, a wayward circus in which the mistress of ceremonies opened wide her big-as-millstones eyes, spread her white-
gloved arms in ecstatic abandon, trotted out onto a circular runway
that surrounded the orchestra and proceeded to dance rings around
the conductor. Personally, I thought the whole paw-pointing, hoof-
pounding, proud and prancing show was really being performed by
circus ponies as people.

But let's calm down and take rational account of what was going
on at the St. James. *Hello, Dolly!* had been suggested, as the program
phrased it, by Thornton Wilder's *The Matchmaker,* which was a
dizzying enough proposition to begin with. Designer Oliver Smith
had leafed his way back into the beer-and-pretzel, "Brilliantine and
dime cigar" world of horsecars in Yonkers and milliners with hats
like maypoles, festooning it with milk-chocolate fire escapes until it
seemed to drip rotogravure.

Composer Jerry Herman had torn up a hurdy-gurdy and scattered
its tinkling waltzes and mellow quartets and tipsy polkas all over
Union Square, and then director Gower Champion had come along
to stage—to squander, in fact—an apparently inexhaustible supply of
what may have been the most exhilaratingly straightforward, head-on,
old-fashioned, rabble-rousing numbers since Harrigan and Hart rolled
down the curtain.

Mr. Champion's dancers began by exploding through the floor,
wrapping themselves around rafters, and vaulting over the roof beams
as David Burns tried to sweep them away with a hay-and-feed-store
broom in an uproar called "It Takes a Woman." You wondered if
Mr. Champion hadn't worn out the men of the company. But a few
shrill whistles later, after he had shot a whole series of quick tintypes
out of his choreographic repeating rifle, he was ready again with a
wild waltz, listed simply and appropriately as "Dancing," which took
to the air on an invisible trapeze and then simmered down, magically,
to a quaintly mismatched twosome: tiny Sondra Lee drifting like a
disabled duck around twice-her-size Carol Channing.

Enough? Not at all. The second act opened with the men out of
their minds once more, waiters all in a most elegant restaurant,
trapped and racing through a silverware concerto in which chairs
floated about, shish-kebab skewers dueled one another, and stacks of
jellied dishes changed hands in the night. The moment peace was

restored, a pair of curtains parted and Miss Channing came down a
long stairway, red on red, to begin the evening's title song. It was the
beginning of a musical-comedy madness that threatened to linger
with you until your ears wore out. -

Miss Channing. Who *is* Miss Channing? Here, as she rocked her
way in rhythm across that circular ramp, crossing and recrossing her
leaping friends in the white spats, she was—she had to be—everything from Fay Templeton to *The Black Crook* to Little Nelly Kelly
and back again. With hair like orange seafoam, a contralto like a
horse's neigh, and a confidential swagger that promised to buy lottery
tickets for the entire house, she fulfilled for you a promise you made
yourself as a boy: to see, someday, a musical-comedy performer with
all the blowsy glamour of the girls on the sheet music of 1916.

Miss Channing had gone back for another look at that advertise-
ment labeled "His Master's Voice," and she had swallowed the
records, the Victrola, and quite possibly the dog. Glorious.

Eventually Pearl Bailey took over the role, and when—at the
matinee I attended—the orchestra struck up "Dancing," a child who
will never see two again simply sailed out of her seat in the very first
row and went winging up and down the aisle like a sea gull who'd
been sipping brandy. She couldn't help it.

Watching Miss Bailey, I knew what she'd found (the keys to the
city, the hearts of the town), but I didn't know what she was looking
for. She was always bent slightly forward, elbows raised, fingers
dripping from her wrists as though they'd been hung up for the
night, surveying the floor, the pit, the auditorium at her feet, clearly
expecting that in all that vast landscape she'd find someone or
something to tell her a secret. When she seemed to hear the secret
she cocked her head reflectively, in the manner of someone who's
checking her jaw to see if the Novocain has worn off, and decided
that yes, she'd got it and yes, she liked it. If she liked it a lot, she'd
sing a song, holding the song clamped between her hands in midair:
she appeared to be juggling a horizontal stack of books there, pressing
the melody tight so that nothing would fall. Nothing did. The stage
itself became a cool and confident smile, eternally rocking.

And I realized that sooner or later people would stop going back to
see *Hello, Dolly!* They'd just settle down and live there.

Dennis

Let me tell you about Sandy Dennis. There should be one in every home.

She's dangerous, of course. She's got the tongue of a delectable cobra (don't say there's no such thing, I've been there) and while she never uses it to strike dead anyone on stage, she can turn in a doorway, prepared to exit, and wipe out whole scenes with its adderlike leap.

In *Any Wednesday*, no explanation was ever offered for this peculiar conduct. Miss Dennis was not playing a *femme fatale*, or anything near it. She was playing an idiot child who claimed to be thirty (it was her birthday) and one who was described by one of the men in the company, in a wild overstatement, as looking about twelve (significantly, there was just one candle on her birthday cake, and my guess was that that was just about right).

She was also somebody's mistress, but she was mistress of nothing she surveyed. The apartment she kept had been put in the name of her paramour's holding company, to make her and it tax-deductible, and her paramour's wife was right now in the process of redecorating it to suit nobody's taste. As a kept woman she was a complete flop, never certain that the new diamond necklace she'd been given for her birthday wasn't going to be borrowed back tomorrow to be photographed for the company's sales promotion campaign, and she shouldn't, she shouldn't, have been as devastating as she was.

In the play she was a patsy, and it took quite a long time for her to see the light, the light being a nice boy from Akron, Ohio, if I've got my cities straight. But Miss Dennis had a very interesting idea about patsies. If they weren't so dumb, they'd be dynamite. "Patsies of the world, unite!" you could almost hear her crying, as she got rid of the dishes by simply hurling them through the doorway, as she got a champagne bottle to her lips virtually before it had been uncorked, as she strode up and down stage with her hands high in the air and the vast sleeves of her dressing gown cascading in Greek folds that might have made Margaret Anglin or even Florence Reed envious. (Could Miss Dennis play Electra? No, no, not until she's thirteen.)

Having cried havoc, she also cried tears. That was the trick. Behind all the cat-on-the-fence energy there was a faintly humiliated mouth, and behind all the haymakers there was a doll in bare feet who couldn't say anything angry without making it sound funny, and winsome to boot. Listening to her do a simple line, something like "I'm just so touched" or, with mournful pleasure, "I never had a pillbox," you got the combination. Dumb, knowing, injured, and outraged in seven syllables or less. The girl was enchanting.

Guinness

One went to see *Dylan* for the sorrow in Alec Guinness' face. This is not an ordinary reason for going to see a play, but this was not an ordinary sorrow. Nor any ordinary face.

Perhaps the first thing one noticed was Mr. Guinness' quaintly elongated nose, which seemed sorry that it had turned up rather than down, making him into such a clown. He was sitting huddled on a beach in Wales when we met, trading coarse and stinging flippantries with the wife he loved, and when he was tired of rubbing his knuckles against the arms of his dirty green sweater, he turned his head upward so that we could see his eyes. They were bleary with an old spark, like remote stars that have turned into little more than hazy horizontal and vertical crossed lines by the time they reach us—you know, the way children draw stars. Clowns paint their eyes in this way, too, though Mr. Guinness had not used paint.

He had used pain to get them set in this preposterous way, glistening, faraway, startled, thunderstruck with the hilarity of having come to nothing. As the poet Dylan Thomas, on the stairway to being dead, he had looked into himself and discovered that "all the best of him" was fifteen years old. He was going to grow older without singing anything new. Some malevolent hag had cursed him.

Well, so be it. With a little hop that had no heart in it he was on his feet to snuggle against his wife, bid her good-bye, and be off to America where he could "continue his lifelong search for naked women in wet mackintoshes." The leap was lively, the wit would flare, the women would come, and he would love every other living thing in this world. Only his smile would stay sober.

Mr. Guinness' portrait of the old artist as a young man, following his bright bow-tie up the thousand steps that lead to airports, rostrums, the third-floor parties of the very, very rich, and the pyramid of eighteen whiskies from which he would take ultimate flight, was mesmerizing. But I don't say "mesmerizing" casually, as though it were just another adjective and good enough for him. There was a still center in the actor, a coal in the ashes, that defied us to will our eyes away, whatever might be calling. Mr. Guinness giggled because his father liked Wordsworth; his breath left him because he had been all over America and had not a cent to show for it; he brayed the answer into a transatlantic telephone before his wife could ask the question; he smirked that he was not up to "having his trouser cuffs kissed." And all the time we saw the thought behind the indecent gesture, behind the small-boy uproar, behind the giggle—the thought that said "Isn't it too bad? I'm only me."

6

CHEKHOV AND OTHERS

THAT FURTIVE FELLOW CHEKHOV

I AM NOT going to tell you the story of my life, and I am certainly not going to tell you the story of Chekhov's, but I thought I might say a few words about our life together. We have been playing hide-and-seek for years.

When I was very young, I understood Chekhov, as indeed everyone did. He was a long neurasthenic sigh, accompanied by the flutter of falling leaves and rattled hands, by the night-music of imminent tears. His element was mood, and the mood was languid, an evocation of the inertia that suffocates. Poetic, of course, in the dapple of light from the trees that were doomed and in the ripple of unfocused conversation. But a still life, with everything in it already in the first faint brown stages of decay. If someone or something provoked a beginning smile now and again, it was not a smile that could delay the coroner; one knew that the servants were already storing the funeral baked meats in the hall. Actresses loved playing Chekhov for the limited time audiences would permit them to do so; actresses have always loved playing consumptives on couches, and *Camille* was getting a bit old-hat. Stanislavski had directed the plays as chords of despair and had, in the process, made Chekhov famous as a dramatist. Who would question the insight of Stanislavski, or the rectitude of his controlling hand? *Whack!* went the axes in the cherry orchard after all of us had wept to no purpose for three hours. This was the way to do the plays. We nodded and applauded, and nodded.

I first began not to understand Chekhov when, as a student, I came upon those curiously broad and vigorous and (shhh!) blatant little farces—*The Boor, The Marriage Proposal*, those things—which are still performed by amateurs when they think no one is looking.

I was baffled. How could a man who'd begun as a not very distant cousin of Molière have, the moment he wrote a longer play, put such a vast and bewildering distance between himself and his beginnings? It seemed unlikely to me that a man's temperament—whichever it was, essentially effervescent or essentially gloomy—could have erased itself entirely in one substantial phase of his work. But these were written as vaudevilles, I was told, and no doubt merely for money. And a man can, after all, live down his shameless past. The farces might be dismissed as a young man's folly, even if they were rather good.

I dismissed them and got on with the truth, only to have my nervous system seriously unsettled by seeing Ruth Gordon in a production of *The Three Sisters* which found stars of such eminence as Katharine Cornell and Judith Anderson behaving with a most exemplary sobriety. Miss Gordon did not behave with a most exemplary sobriety. She was extraordinarily funny. She wasn't farce-funny precisely: as the sister-in-law who was sweetly but firmly devouring all she surveyed she defined the dramatic purpose of the role with brutal clarity; but in the deviousness and the affability and the preposterous gentility of her brutality she let us look right through her into the cruel face of comedy, into the mask whose mouth explodes into a cackle that has something savage at its source but real hilarity in its ultimate knowledge. If I remember correctly, Miss Gordon was subjected to some reproof for having dared be entertaining while everyone else was at church. As for myself, I made a compromise: I cherished her memory while murmuring secret apologies to Chekhov.

But trouble struck again one Saturday matinee while I watched Joseph Schildkraut make the languid, incompetent, billiard-playing Gayev of *The Cherry Orchard* into a delightfully languid, incompe-

tent, billiard-playing Gayev. As Mr. Schildkraut practiced his hypothetical billiard-shots when he should have been noticing that the sky
was falling in, he became a richly styled and immensely attractive
fool. Not an object of pity; a likable, even an admirable, ass. And
trouble came on the double that day. I began hearing voices, which
is a dangerous thing to do; we all know what happened to St. Joan.
I began to hear voices that weren't there. The young actor who was
playing the student Trofimov was reading his earnest apostrophes to a
better future and his earnest condemnations of people "who do
nothing but talk" in complete earnestness. We were to believe
everything he said, take it at face value.

But I found myself disbelieving it. Knowing myself for an irresponsible turncoat, I kept hearing it all as wonderful wind, as sublime and
delicate fatuousness. Everything that came from the stage went in
one ear and came out the other hopelessly translated. I also noticed,
though only a sneak would do this, that the young student who
voiced such contempt for people who do nothing but talk was himself, and eternally, doing nothing but talk. I sniggered, but was
shushed by those around me. Afterward I spoke with the actor
playing Trofimov, who was and is a friend of mine in spite of the
harsh things said both ways over dinner; but the debate profited
neither of us. That could not have been Chekhov's voice I thought I
heard pleading to be released from such responsible sobriety. Later
on I heard from other sources that many members of the acting
company quite disapproved of Mr. Schildkraut's scene-stealing giddiness.

Well, that was the way matters stood with me until between five
and ten years ago when, no doubt as a result of full-scale biographies
that were beginning to appear, a rumor began to circulate that
Chekhov wrote comedy. Biographer David Magarshack seemed to be
telling his readers that Stanislavski had a terrible time trying to
persuade Chekhov that *The Cherry Orchard* was not the "gay
comedy" he thought, but a tragedy. And biographer Ernest Simmons
was loosing upon the world an even more appalling suggestion: that
Chekhov intended "a happy comedy" when he nervously offered the
world *The Three Sisters*. The one person who *did* question the insight of Stanislavski, it seems, was Chekhov. Nothing made Chekhov
more furious than all that moping.

The hint, in its first freshness, was not lost upon directors. David Ross mounted an off-Broadway *Uncle Vanya* which meant to be funny and was in fact funny. It was immediately criticized in some quarters for being too funny, which in a small way it may have been: Mr. Ross had to press a bit to make *anyone* see humor in what had always been a highly correct gloom. More importantly, a young translator named Alex Szogyi had picked up Chekhov's first and unproduced play, called here *A Country Scandal*, and found in it a brittle, deadly ironic, garishly fanciful humor. "I don't want happiness, I want *you!*" a husband cried to his wife. *A Country Scandal* seemed, in fact, the long-lost land mass that might bridge the world of the early farces and the infinitely subtler comedy—if we are to let Chekhov call it comedy—of the later plays.

But the story is not over and the comedy is not out. Director Ross retreated from his exposed position in later, drowsier, devoutly mournful productions. And one could always pretend to wonder if Mr. Szogyi, in culling a play from a mountain of manuscript, hadn't tipped the scales in favor of his own temperamental preferences. The genuinely funny productions *could* be explained away if anyone wanted to and if everyone was eager to get back to the black bat-wing silhouetted against a lowering moon.

It would seem that everyone *is* eager to forget that furtive fellow Chekhov, with his peculiar habit of complaining whenever his plays were tear-stained—at least if we are to judge by the Actors Studio revival of *The Three Sisters* and by the touring *Sea Gull* which Eva Le Gallienne brought us not long ago. In *The Three Sisters* the actors were making mood again. They did it slowly, patiently, occasionally even well—and they cried; oh, how they cried! It is true that a laugh escaped its keepers every now and again, perhaps twice an act; though the players responded strangely whenever one did. For instance, it is simply impossible not to see humor in the moment when a talkative military man has talked everyone in the room to sleep. But Kevin McCarthy, who played the military man on this occasion, was resourceful. The audience, noticing the omnipresent sleepers, had almost begun to laugh, had—shall we say?—half laughed. Mr. McCarthy raised his hands wistfully, shook his head, moved slowly away, and then, in a voice with much dream in it, sighed, "It looks like they're all asleep . . ." as though the situation were not comedy but reverie. He was doing his level best to absorb or even to silence humor with a slumbering sprinkle of stardust.

What was truly odd, though quite traditional, about the production, however, was its insistence that all of Chekhov's characters knew themselves. Nearly everyone who spoke spoke as though he were speaking intelligently, as though no one of these folk were in any way blind or foolish or self-deceiving. The actors seemed not to have considered that there might be anything the matter with the characters; these were offered us as true innocents, unlucky souls unjustly put upon. Yet Chekhov does, very frequently, make it perfectly clear that nothing his characters say can really be taken at face value. As a rule, what they say can almost be taken at reverse value.

If a character says of someone that he is "a rude, common man," we are clearly to understand that it is the speaker who is rude and common—and rather funny for being so obtuse about the matter. If a military man makes a considerable speech about the poor "local intellectuals" who can talk about nothing but their wives and their horses, you can be dead-certain that in one half minute the military man himself is going to be talking about his wife and his horses. And that is what he does.

But there was almost no sense of this inversion, this failure of perception that is essentially comic, anywhere in the Actors Studio's *The Three Sisters*. We tended to believe what we were told; and of course that wasn't funny. The fact that there is a profound undercurrent of sadness in the play should not be permitted to destroy its primary character. All comedy is sad at base, and only amusing and witty and wicked on top. Here there was no top, no target, no ultimate intention. Here there were no fools, no vain, self-dramatizing, quite helplessly wonderful fools. And, if I may be permitted to say so, no Ruth Gordon.

But if everyone was wistful on the Morosco stage, I was more wistful than they. For I should still, in my bafflement and in the derangement of mind which overtakes me whenever those unbidden voices begin intruding upon the lachrymose night, like to see Chekhov plain, if only to discover whether or not he knew what he was doing. If he wrote tragedies, or somber mood pieces, he didn't know what he was doing. And I refuse to believe that.

MOSCOW ART CHEKHOV

Now, here's a curious thing. *The Cherry Orchard*, perhaps all of Chekhov, cannot be truly sad *unless* it is funny.

I had never seen a Moscow Art Theater performance of *The Cherry Orchard* until the company paid a courteous visit to City Center, and I went with a half-dozen contending questions in my head. Chekhov had never liked what Stanislavski did with the play: the author insisted he had written a comedy and that the director had made tragedy of it. But the quarrel had ended in a terrible irony. Chekhov's comedy had apparently been scuttled, but Chekhov's reputation had been enormously enhanced. The production had been successful *against* its author. Why?

What comedy was missing? And what had Stanislavski put into its place with such authority that forever after the play would be seen as he saw it, would be duplicated and imitated time and time again until the entire world would think of Chekhov in terms that Chekhov himself detested?

I couldn't hope that a performance in 1965 would answer questions first raised in 1904. Though the physical staging might still be Stanislavski's—people might dance behind archways or nestle against haystacks as he had directed them to so long ago—at least two things were bound to have changed. New actors may try hard to echo a tradition of performance; but they cannot help bringing *themselves* into the tradition, which means they cannot help altering it in subtle ways. And the political and social changes in Russia since 1904 must, willy-nilly, have done something to the atmosphere. An institution may be revered and told to go on doing its work as before, no matter what aesthetic is being imposed upon newer playwrights and their playhouses. But what is happening on the street, or in an auditorium five blocks away, is bound to drift in through the stage doors, if only as an awareness. A change in the climate is noticed, and felt, even by an actor who is bundled protectively to his ears. Was there any chance at all now of estimating Stanislavski's original tone—and hence Chekhov's dismay with it?

In point of fact no one can be certain how much the interior intellectual life of *The Cherry Orchard* has changed color with regimes. One can suspect—but not prove—that the student Trofimov has gained earnestness with the years. Trofimov looks to a nobler future and makes impassioned speeches about it. He sees stupidity and corruption about him; he will have none of the old way of life; he expects that one day mankind will march boldly into a much purer dawn. Possibly the first actor who played the part saw some humor in it, as I now feel certain Chekhov did. Trofimov is, after all, as much a prattling dreamer as the sentimental, irresponsible, wool-gathering Gayev is. By the end of the third act he is going to look a good bit of a fool as he falls all over himself and tumbles downstairs in one of his temperamental fevers. But after a revolution any character who seems to have prophesied a revolution must inevitably acquire a small halo. The part is presently played as though Trofimov had spent time in the wilderness with John the Baptist and had come back clear-eyed, an accredited visionary. Has his stature as a seer grown week after week since 1917, without orders from above or without anyone's quite noticing it? The question is probably unanswerable, and must be passed.

But there was illumination aplenty, on other scores, in the production brought us. To begin with, the Moscow Art Theater feels its way toward rather more comedy in *The Cherry Orchard* than we who have heard Stanislavski's edict but seen little of his work are inclined to give it in our own performances. Indeed some of the comedy is surprisingly broad: the clerk Epikhodov is not merely accident-prone, breaking a billiard cue a moment after he has picked it up; he is a Dromio, unable to leave the stage without backing successively into three pieces of furniture which are by no means in his way.

There is comedy in the complacent money-grubbing of a corpulent neighbor, comedy in the way in which a servant who has risen above himself elegantly spits out his cigar ends, playful comedy in the determination of lovers not to be spied upon at sunset. The outer edges of the play are conceived lightly; not everyone anticipates doom.

But—and here no doubt is where Chekhov's blood pressure rose— there is no fatuity, no giddiness, no transparent thoughtlessness of a gently amusing sort at the center of the piece. When we come to the

brother and sister who own the estate that is to be lost, and above all
when the sister, Ranevskaya, lets her temper flare at the idealist
Trofimov, we come to something that is as hard and inflexible as
Medea's mighty will. In the Moscow Art production, Ranevskaya
does not let a world slip through her fingers out of flightiness, or
charming presumption, or a womanly affectation of being unable to
cope with figures. She stands sturdy as a rock, surveying her diminishing world with alarmed but far-seeing eyes, an intelligently tragic
figure who knows that she is about to be bent by the wind but is
ready for it. When she lashes out at Trofimov for his endless prating
of things to come, the scene is not a delightfully exasperated tussle of
cross-purposes, an explosion of misunderstandings. It is a showdown.
Willed death confronts willed hope, with countenances of granite.

Actually, there is nothing in the earlier portions of the play,
nothing in the texture of the play, to justify so rigid and inexorable a
duel. Ranevskaya is simply not a tragic figure. She has no purpose, no
intention, no passion to make her one. It is the very purposelessness
of her life, her ingratiating ability to circumvent decisions, that
defines her. The business of turning her into Brünnhilde, or into a
kind of dowager Prometheus, does not work. We look at her displaying so much keenness of mind and force of character and decide that
she would not only have accepted the peasant Lopakhin's offer for
the estate; she would have sat at the table with him and bargained
until she had forced the price higher. If the present interpretation of
the role is in the Stanislavski tradition, then this is the point at which
Stanislavski overreached himself and outraged his playwright.

But there is a further consequence that interests me more. As the
lady of the orchard becomes increasingly hardheaded, strong-willed,
tragic, we feel less and less for her. At the center of the Moscow
Art's *Cherry Orchard* there is little pity. The axes are closing in and
we feel no sorrow. Ranevskaya will be dispossessed; but her plight
will not move us.

It may be one of the distinguishing marks of Chekhov's work that
tears come only when they are not asked for, only, in fact, when there
is a sustained—if unrealistic—surface gaiety. The Ranevskaya who
touches us will most likely always be the woman who puts the
brightest, most impossible face on things, who dances and mothers

and cajoles when she should be taking stock, who flies into a tantrum with a talkative student because she is temperamentally incapable of listening to anyone. A charmer, an optimist, inadvertently a fool.

When we see that her silken, impulsive, endearing evasions are funny because they are hopelessly out of kilter with the facts, when we laugh because she is helplessly prisoner of a grace that is now irrelevant but still a grace, when we cannot help smiling that she should mismanage things so adroitly, then we will feel sorry for her, too. Pathos cannot be bought with long faces; it is a reflex from having noticed something absurd that cannot change itself. At least I think it is in Chekhov.

Why, then, was Stanislavski's *Cherry Orchard* so successful, so successful that its mood has been imposed upon most productions of Chekhov for sixty years? The Moscow Art Theater production seems to give us an answer to that, also. It is filled—even now—with a superb sense of continuing life, of dancers who go on dancing even after the ballroom doors are closed, of old servants who must surely be in the kitchen when they are not actually before our eyes, of restless footsteps going up and down stairs we never see and no doubt pacing the floor above us though we never hear a sound above. The people of the production are busy with themselves. They leave the scene with something in mind; when they return, their eyes have changed as eyes do when something that needed doing has been done. Nothing is ever forgotten. The probabilities of the day behind and the night ahead are constantly in mind; they fill the personalities we learn to recognize with a twenty-four-hour history. No actor seems to reflect on anything that is not in the play. The play fully occupies its residents. They are never going to be anywhere but in it.

The physical, visual, aural, tactile echoes are overwhelmingly dimensional. You could walk with Varya, in her black dress and with the keys at her belt, throughout the house and never see her work finished. The stage is composed of planes, receding infinitely. There is no corner you could look around and see only scenery. I don't think I have ever attended a production in which the naturalistic flow of event was so matter-of-fact that there was no event at all, only the indisputable comings and goings of the of-course people, the people who of course live there, always have. Where else should they be? How else should they dispose themselves?

Chekhov ought to have complained. And the production ought to have been as successful as it was.

The theater plays tricks like that.

THE COMIC COUNTRY OF THE BLIND

Chekhov's position in the theater of our time is a peculiar one: he is intensely admired for reasons which would have appalled him, which did in fact appall him. "Is this really my *Cherry Orchard?*" he cried after he had seen an early production of the play. "Are these my types? . . . I describe life. It is a dull, philistine life. But it is not a tedious, whimpering life. First they turn me into a weeper and then into a simply boring writer . . . criticism has tricked me out in the guise of some kind of mourner or other."

But *The Cherry Orchard is* about dull, philistine life, and it does record the failure of Russian society at the turn of the century to adapt itself to changing conditions. The Ranevsky household is helplessly caught between the oncoming rise of the lower classes and its own aristocratic inertia. The peasant, Lopakhin, is reaching for power, and he is certainly going to seize it: the world is turning in his favor. In the act of reaching, he would like to do a little something to help this faltering family he has always admired. But the dreamers cannot be helped; they are prisoners of the past and victims of the future. They behave as they have always behaved, which is no longer good enough. The play ends with these attractive, incompetent people being dispossessed, sent bag and baggage out of the only home they have ever known into a world that promises them nothing. How, then, is this play a comedy?

Well, it is a comedy in certain of its secondary effects. Lopakhin sticks his head in at the door to moo like a cow at the very moment bad news is received; the juxtaposition of these two moods is meant to be funny—in a macabre way, perhaps, but funny. The odd way in which all conversations bump into each other, nearly running each other off the rails in a succession of emotional non sequiturs, is funny in its confusion, too. The confusion has something to do with the incompetence and failure of these people, but it is a comic confusion nonetheless. There are broader things still: deaf Firs giving the wrong answer to a question, Gayev noisily sucking candy while speaking of death, Pishchik going to sleep and snoring in the middle of his own sentence, Trofimov insisting that he holds the key to the future of mankind while being hopelessly unable to find his own rubbers.

Do these things make the entire play comic, or account for Chekhov's peculiar insistence that its fundamental tone had been got wrong? No, not quite. There is the sad heart of the play to be accounted for and dealt with. The principals are really most pleasant; why should they have to suffer so? They are lifelike and they do suffer; doesn't that qualify them for our tears? Line by line, they are deeply natural; how do we dare call them fools? To call the whole play comic, comic in *essence*, I think we should have to conceive it as comedy taking place in the Country of the Blind. Most of its characters—above all, its doomed principals—are truly sightless: they cannot, will not, see what stares them in the face.

How and when do we dare to regard a blind man as funny? It would be unfeeling of us, hideous even, to stop on a sidewalk and laugh mercilessly at someone who was trying to negotiate a curbstone, in heavy traffic and bad weather, with a tapping cane. The notion revolts us, or at least disturbs us; we can't get used to it as an attitude.

Ah, but suppose the blind man came into your own kitchen and absolutely insisted that he could see as well as you could. Suppose, in his determination to behave exactly as he had always behaved when he had his sight, he also insisted upon making dinner. Suppose no one could talk him out of it. Suppose he insisted upon serving the dinner, too, with a great air of elegance about him as he spilled the soup down your back. Would the mess in the kitchen, and the catastrophe in the dining room, be funny?

It would. The man is a fool and deserves to be laughed at, not because he is blind but because he so stubbornly persists in pretending not to be. He wants to go on behaving just as he used to, as though nothing at all had happened to him. Tell him anything to the contrary, try to help him out a bit with the soufflé, and you're liable to get your fingers slapped. He is in charge, thank you.

The mess is of his own making. And there is that lemon-cream pie all over the floor.

Of course, even as we laugh, or perhaps try to suppress an instinctive giggle so as not to discomfit him further, we are aware of the disability he refuses to acknowledge. Behind the muddle of the moment, which is funny because it is a muddle, lies something more serious, though not necessarily as fatal as this dinner party has turned out to be. Behind what is now preposterous lies something we must pity. The two moods exist together: the preposterousness stands to the forefront because of what is happening right now; the pity stands a little bit back, in the shadows. It is a shadow.

This is the kind of comedy Chekhov wrote: people who are actually pitiable behave so preposterously that we are forced to see them as crippled clowns. "I can't approve of our climate," says Epikhodov, as though the climate had asked him to. "It hasn't a soul of its own," says Gayev of a cupboard, "but still, say what you will, it's a fine piece of furniture." Since a cupboard *hasn't* a soul of its own, Gayev has said exactly nothing, profoundly. When Lopakhin is asked if he has been hurt by Varya's stick, he answers, all in a breath, "No, not at all. There'll be a huge bump, no more." Lopakhin is being brave and having his bump at one and the same time. We all do that, sooner or later. When we do—even if the bump is real and hurts—aren't we being absurd in dismissing it generously while making sure that we get credit for it?

Things are against Epikhodov. No matter what he turns his hand to, no matter how much sober industry he brings to the matter, a wicked spirit in the universe will trip him up. He tells us so. Finally we see him at work. In the last act, when the house is being cleared, he carries a trunk onto the stage and sets it down on top of a hatbox. The hatbox crumples beneath the weight of the trunk. "Well, of course, I thought so" is what he says to himself as he walks away, resigned to the tricks a hostile world is always playing on him. If life is going to do things like that to a man, what chance has he? (The moment is an understated fragment of comic genius if ever I saw one.)

Trofimov is a trap for the unwary. We are quick to suppose that Chekhov was utterly serious in writing this young man's robust calls to a nobler future. And of course Chekhov was partly serious, as always; that is to say, he began by knowing that there was an actual need for social change and that some young men were in deadly earnest about achieving it.

But beware. This young man's earnestness is deadly, indeed. He is so passionate about the future that he is going to stay right where he is, in school, forever. He is so convinced that the millennium is going to be brought about by hard work that he refrains from doing any. ("You don't do anything; only fate tosses you about from place to place; it's so strange. . . . Isn't it true?" cries Mme. Ranevsky in her strange burst of clarity and candor.) Trofimov's ideals are lofty and he can honestly say that he is remote from triviality, but people who talk about how untrivial they are usually make a man wonder. Indeed, Trofimov's loftiness places him quite "above love," a position from which he may very well fall down the stairs with our gleeful approval.

Perhaps Mme. Ranevsky's outcry against Trofimov should not be held as comic evidence against him; after all, the lady is a dreamer herself. But these people do really very often see one another accurately, as though there were occasional patches in the fog through which truths were suddenly visible: everyone tells Gayev he talks too much, and Lopakhin's exasperation with the lady who will not listen to him is real and justified. Each of them knows, from time to time, what is wrong with the others. What they cannot see, or get right, is what is wrong with themselves.

Now, if the self-deluded are bound to be amusing, Chekhov's amusement is always considerate. Chekhov pays his people the compliment of not exaggerating them—much. He does like them, and so tries to be faithful to them. He does, in his rueful and de-tached way, feel for them, idiots that they are; and so he does not throw them downstairs or beat them with sticks or make them moo too often. He suggests, perhaps, that there is very little he needs to do to them to accent their follies. If he simply lets them loose and keeps close to the truth, they will take care of themselves, making their own comedy as they rush or drift or skitter from mood to mood.

Most comedy, nearly all that we are familiar with, arrives at its effect through exaggeration. A miser becomes monstrously greedy; a drinker becomes roaringly drunk; a hesitant man stammers and sputters until we can hear nothing else. Each of these things is, deep down, somewhat tragic or pathetic. But we are not permitted to see what is deep down because the surface is wrenched so wildly out of shape; the disproportion at the top is so emphatic that it seems, in its fantastic grossness, only funny.

Chekhov's comedy is too considerate, too kindly, too honest in a way, for this sort of grossness. Chekhov has deflated the comic balloon somewhat and brought it back to a shape that is *almost* normal. Because he has done this, it is easy for us to mistake what he has done, to confuse a very delicate and controlled comic highlighting with the lifelike and somewhat more serious subject matter he means to be comic about. He has narrowed the gap between the preposterous and the pathetic; but he has made it perfectly clear to us which side of the gap he stands on.

Standing there and smiling all the while, he reminds us of a truth; if you do not exaggerate comedy, you will see how sad it is.

THE RUIN OF A RUIN

When I was about seventeen a large apartment building began to go up across the street from where I lived, and, within a month or two, the Depression struck. Halfway up its promised six or seven stories, with brickwork rising at irregular heights and with windows marked out like the teeth in a jack-o'-lantern, the building stopped. No man came back to work, no money was ever found to put flooring into the vast cavity, and every day I passed newness that was turning into oldness without once having been used. In due time, three or four years later, the world began to move again and with its movement came the wreckers. Nothing could be salvaged: not the wings that met at rectangles, not the stone that framed a courtyard, not the blind intricate foundations that scurried mazelike, unidentified and uncrowned, inside the shell. I always felt wistful about that building.

I felt very much the same about *More Stately Mansions*, Eugene O'Neill's last surviving unfinished play, which finally had its cross-beams and its mortar thrown up on Broadway so that we could see what it looked like before we were forced to tear it down. The play was born a ruin: a great architectural emptiness derived from slaved-over blueprints, an eyeless, topless tower that could not escape the earth in which it was so deeply imbedded. The draftsmanship was finished. The earth had been dug. No one would ever live there.

Strangest of all, it was a ruin meant to describe a ruin. O'Neill was here concerned with the wracking and the wrecking of the American heart as it turned, so soon after its appearance on the face of the earth, in two contrary directions, committing itself to neither. Ingrid Bergman was the mother image in this production of the play, a lingering porcelain shepherdess in a garden imagined by Rousseau, a creature clinging with passion and baffled purpose to the poetry of living in an uncorrupted, beautifully mannered, temple-haunted world carved out of virgin wilderness. The first American Daydream was hers. She was half mad trying to hold it in her head, and to hold her eldest son in it, while the second American Daydream, robust and rapacious, took over.

Colleen Dewhurst, with an Irish immigrant's lilt and an upstart's unsparing eye, was the new breed, the new threat, the new promise. Using her brain and her body with pragmatic energy and utter candor, she was out to remake the world so that it would serve rather than restrain her, salute rather than despise her. Hers was the long reach, the capacity to uproot and to devour—and to grow. Acknowledging her lusts and as readily realizing them, she was prepared to do battle for Miss Bergman's prized son and for all the children that might come of their union.

The son, Arthur Hill, was the ravaged man in the middle, bound to both promises, in love with both women, eternally drained by his eternally unresolved allegiance to two forces that could, in the end, only show one another their teeth. He was himself the duality the women separately represented, slaving over a book filled with utopian hope by night and savagely beating down his business competition by day, burning the book in self-disgust but unable to resist the cool, primitive lure of his mother's garden, his mother's remembered milk-white skin. He was pioneer-brute and pioneer-believer at once, torn to shreds by "the conflicting selves within a man," angrily and in anguish determined to make a choice between the two bids for his soul. "But what if they won't let you choose?" Miss Dewhurst asked him, patiently, mercilessly.

The master plan of the play, then, was not tendentious, not

moralizing. O'Neill wasn't saying that greed and industrial growth killed the philosopher-poet in the American, and that the death was wrong. He opted neither for the Rousseauish idyll—a tiny Versailles hacked out of the forest—nor for banks and railroads bought with blood money. He was saying that the American wanted both all the time, still wants them; and the double want that can never be satisfied, never come to rest, is a lasting crucifixion. The nails that continue to gnaw at the flesh are inside the man; the self-destruction is self-generating; the rip in the fabric is not a thing that can be mended—it can only be known, accepted, perhaps survived in some unimaginable transcendence.

Thus, inside the play's architecture where busy people came and went about their chores, Mr. Hill had to put his hands to his eyes to hide the blur. He could not tell his mother and his wife apart; they were maddeningly the same woman to him. Try as he might, he could not isolate them: though he installed his wife in his office as secretary and afternoon mistress, he could never be certain that she wasn't secretly in league with his mother to possess and destroy him. There was a continuing battle over the disposition of the children: they were given to the mother to care for, they were snatched back in fear and rage. A harmony of hate developed between Irish wife and Yankee mother: they had to be in league together because they were indissoluble desires in the blood and bone of the man who lived with them and nearly died of them.

Alas, it was just at this juncture—the point at which the master plan was meant to meet and be filled by believable, tangible, domesticated creatures who had private as well as archetypal lives to lead—that the play, being unfinished, fell apart. The blueprint could more or less be read. But the emotional body of the play—the small personal truths that had to be felt and followed and understood as truly personal if the great shell was to contain life—would not function. Arthur Hill might decide, in sudden waspishness, to snatch the children from his mother's garden; but it was a dictated decision, arbitrary and half absurd; it hadn't come from a need in his nerves. Ingrid Bergman might languish in her private retreat, playing nostalgic games with the son she had lured there; she could not make the image a dramatically possible one, for no person had been written yet, only a prospectus.

Neither Miss Bergman nor Miss Dewhurst was in any way at fault. Both were excellent, given the fact that so little flooring had been laid at their feet. Miss Bergman, a luminous Lady of the Camellias whose only sickness was in her head, rapped out a bristling retort with knife-quick precision (her priggish younger son was "God's most successful effort at taxidermy"), softly inserted a verbal dagger where it would do most harm (sending the son she loved back to his wife, she concluded, "Write me frankly of your discomfort"), moved and spoke with infinite composure, unerring grace. Miss Dewhurst, in a more bluntly defined role, used her husky, warm, belligerent voice and her wolverine laugh to call bluff upon bluff, seductively, arrogantly, contentedly. Only Mr. Hill was wildly off form, strangling on his abrupt transitions, gasping after meaning as though it were a runaway horse. Because we know him for a first-rate actor, responsibility had to be passed on to director José Quintero, who had really helped no one. Having made his own cutting of the text, and having asked designer Ben Edwards for the gloomy reaches and voidlike portals of the settings, Mr. Quintero seemed determined to reinforce what was already wrong: instead of making the day-by-day life of reading newspapers, baiting bankers, and doing the evening sewing genuinely intimate, plausible, concrete in its detail, he had urged everyone toward overinflated melodrama, arranging them again and again like so many self-important statues in the moonlight.

Nor was the ultimate failure due to those familiar demons that had dogged O'Neill throughout his creative life: the inexplicably flat prose ("The company stands on the brink of bankruptcy"), the obvious overambition. It was due, as things stood, to the fact that the play *was* unfinished. O'Neill had never completed the necessary business of relating dimensional people to the implied dimensions of his panoramic scheme. The characters were still rather naughty and disobedient children squabbling among themselves, and over little more than mud pies, beneath a vault that overshadowed and outweighed them. He might possibly, at the height of his powers, have made the two grow together, become adequate supports for one another, interchangeable parts. He knew that he hadn't and he'd torn up the play.

Should it, then, have been produced? I think so. It exists. Not all copies of the manuscript were destroyed. Now they never will be. Because the work exists and because it was a project for the stage, our information about it can only be increased by seeing it on the stage. In the same way that an important playwright's very earliest works are mounted out of curiosity about, and respect for, a career as a whole, an aborted major play may very well be studied—and indeed respected—for what it has to tell us about a man's mind, his habits of work (while the work was only in progress), his unrealized intentions. The intentions cannot be concealed; since we are going to know them anyway, they had best be known in the medium for which they were formed. Politeness has never kept us from producing either *Titus Andronicus* or *King Henry VIII*. And there is always the further chance that out of what seems an inchoate abandoned manuscript we might, with the right cutting, get something as gratifying as Chekhov's *A Country Scandal*.

Even if this production suggested we can have no such thing, it still may be fairer to O'Neill to let us see him struggle in the open than to hide the play away as though no one of his stature could conceivably have tried to write it. The struggle was—is—a massive one. We watch him contending with stresses, straining to heave into place granitelike blocks of material as unwieldy and oppressive as the stones of Easter Island. What is astonishing is the resolution, the energy, the near-demented but still orderly and imaginative passion that went into the intolerable contest. Time won. But the contest itself is extraordinarily impressive. Even assisting at a stillbirth must have some mystery about it.

I shall remember the play as I remember my desolate building— not with contempt but with regret and a kind of longing.

IN AND OUT OF THE MIRROR

Shakespeare was always toying with the fact that the stage is a stage is a stage, though I hadn't noticed how thoroughly make-believe *Antony and Cleopatra* was meant to be until I saw Michael Langham's production of it at Stratford, Ontario.

There's a passage toward the end of the play, while Cleopatra is exquisitely stage-managing her own death, that gives the whole show away—or, rather, thrusts the show as *show* full into our faces. Cleopatra, incorrigible minx that she is, has a variety of reasons for wishing to die, among them the certainty that Antony and Iras are both already dead and the possibility that the two of them will be up to some hanky-panky in the netherworld before she can catch up with them. But there's a special reason. If she lives, Cleopatra will be carried back to Rome, Octavius' prisoner, there to be made a show of. Worse, she will be forced to look at shows *about* her.

> The quick comedians
> Extemporally will stage us and present
> Our Alexandrian revels; Antony
> Shall be brought drunken forth, and I shall see
> Some squeaking Cleopatra boy my greatness
> I' th' posture of a whore.

Recall, for just one moment, that the performer who read these lines in Shakespeare's time was actually a squeaking boy, and your eyes are apt to begin doing double somersaults. We are—now—looking at the very play that Cleopatra is killing herself to avoid seeing. She is already an actress playing herself, expressing the hope that she will never see herself played. Shakespeare wants us to know that the stage is an artifice, and so—begging your pardon—is the illusion we call life. The two are interchangeable because neither of them is entirely real.

The special interest of Mr. Langham's production, with Christopher Plummer shaking his bewildered head as Antony and Zoe Caldwell curling her lip in mock surprise as Cleopatra, lay in its constant underscoring of the proposition that gestures are only gestures and not one of them is trustworthy.

Miss Caldwell, ever-ready with a quick posture, swooned elegantly for Antony's benefit. "Dearest queen, what's the matter?" Mr. Plummer promptly asked, with an edge to the "dearest" and a faint weariness in the "what's the matter?" which patiently, though wryly, suggested that she'd better snap out of the pretty coma and perhaps explain herself. He didn't believe in her vapors, and neither did she. They were acting for one another, sometimes sportively, sometimes strategically, sometimes to hurt.

They both enjoyed and detested what was spurious in themselves. Mr. Plummer was nowhere better than in a confrontation with an angry Octavius whom he somehow had to placate if he was to retain his power in Rome. He'd been a bad boy. He was candid about that. He was determined to reform, confident that he could. An open manliness in his face and bearing said so. He would marry Octavius' sister without hesitation to prove his sincerity. It would have been very difficult to distrust this man; he wore simplicity and truth on his shoulders like epaulets.

Yet during the entire scene our strongest impression was of a man giving the most earnest performance of his life, a performance so well rehearsed that there were almost no traces of technique left in it. It seemed life to the bone, and it was almost less than skin-deep. Mr. Plummer had perfectly shown us how persuasively solid, and at the same time how thin, a shell can be.

We knew that this shell would crack the moment it was safely out of Octavius' presence. For the moment, though, a convincing stance had to be adopted. If, for that moment, Mr. Plummer seemed half to believe in the stance himself, we knew why. He had stopped thinking. He had stepped onto a platform and done what was expected of him. Thought, self-knowledge, truth would return to him when he was next in Cleopatra's chambers, or perhaps in his own dressing room. The actor played an actor beautifully, retaining the real nature of the man only as invisible undertow.

Miss Caldwell's success could be measured by the single criticism that was sometimes made of her. "But she's not *regal!*" I heard a woman on the lawn exclaiming at intermission, and the objection had been voiced before. It was a real tribute to the actress' cunning that she had not been trapped into the velveteen languors and imperious self-control that have cushioned and concealed Shakespeare's mercurial wench (write "witch" if you like) in our time. We are accustomed to *grandes dames* in the role; kittens with claws are reserved for Bernard Shaw. But Miss Caldwell has a nasty eye and a lizard's tongue: she saw all that is coy and funny and feminine and cruel in the magnificently contrary queen Shakespeare did write.

She was happiest when, before really planning her death, she spread rumors of her death—so that she could be told precisely how Antony took the news. Antony was her audience, even more than he was her lover. And she, like any actress worth her salt, felt the need to bend her audience to her will: by cajoling, by commanding, by cheating. Her ears were alert for applause, for the effect she was having. She tasted each new effect as though it were a wine sauce, salve to her soul. And then arranged a new one.

The performance permitted an interesting new reading for Eno-barbus' celebrated "Age cannot wither her nor custom stale her infinite variety." Most Enobarbuses shudder, I imagine, as they approach the line nowadays; quotations that have become chestnuts are hard to turn back into speech. William Hutt, the Enobarbus at Stratford, had no need to shudder. He'd been watching this queen, closely, and knew what a performer she was. Just before the word "infinite," he paused. Then he inflected "infinite" in such a way as to suggest that he had had the whole bit, that he had seen the repertoire of moods and despaired of ever seeing the end of it, that Cleopatra was a con queen who would never run out of fraudulent, if admit-tedly fetching, little tricks. The line wasn't praise. It was despair.

To the bitter end, the gestures were Games People Play, substi-tutes for the emotions that were really being felt, attitudes adopted out of romantic, political, or perverse dramatic necessity. "Come on!" cried Antony as he tried to whip up some enthusiasm for one more battle, sounding for all the world like Charlie Brown urging his base-ball team into a last inning he knows he will lose. He wasn't leading. He was begging. And there was pain in the posture, in the rather pitiful and childlike carrying on with what was essentially charade, action without core. The tone was a dangerous one to use in the theater; Mr. Plummer managed it splendidly.

Good as production and performances were, Mr. Plummer and Miss Caldwell did not yet quite make a great Antony and Cleopatra. Very good, not great. One undertow was missing: the threatening tide of actual sensuality that drives these two into so many artifices. I don't know why this was missing. It was almost as though, in acting so much, they had forgotten the first sting of flesh that set all the teasing and distrust and elaborate deception in motion. Or as though the two players had developed such a healthy, wary respect for one another as professionals that they tended to stand apart from one another, spiritually, each cagily measuring and admiring and studying the other's work. It is one thing to notice and make the most of the sense of playing within a play. It is another to remain a wee bit outside it, as both were still doing.

But this *Antony and Cleopatra* made its particular, and rather original, point. If the stage holds a mirror up to nature, the mirror itself is a peculiar Alice in Wonderland sort of contraption. It can be stepped in and out of, almost at will.

SHYLOCK

Shakespeare is honored in many ways, but the most striking tribute we pay him today is in continuing to produce *The Merchant of Venice*.

Each production is, really, an act of faith, made in the face of the evidence. Every time anyone decides to mount the play, he is saying, in effect, that Shakespeare cannot possibly have meant what he seems to mean, that the humane and penetrating intelligence we have come to know so well through thirty-six other plays could never have been capable of the unthinking, unfeeling anti-Semitism that poisons the portrait of Shylock.

The evidence to the contrary is formidable, both inside and outside the play. Within the fairy-tale structure of the piece, Shylock is most certainly the villain, a scoundrel whose harsh terms and ready knife constitute the only threat to the happiness of some of the nicest people who never lived. Shylock starves his servants, loves his ducats more than his daughter, and is altogether incapable of mercy. In addition to what Shakespeare has written there is the atmosphere in which he wrote: we know that the Jewish physician Lopez had just been executed for treason, that Marlowe's monstrous *Jew of Malta* had been making money in a rival playhouse, that the mood of the moment may very well have equated Jewishness with villainy. Shakespeare, great as he was, was also a man of his time: how can we be sure that *The Merchant of Venice* isn't an unconscious lapse on the part of a first-rate mind brought about by an error that was simply in the air, too much a commonplace to be questioned?

Receuil de Plusieurs Fragments des Premières Comédies Italiennes, 1928
from NATIONAL MUSEUM, STOCKHOLM

Stubbornly, and with a dogged intuition that there must *some-where* be an explanation that will confound the plot of the play and the facts of Elizabethan life, we keep plunging into the embarrassments of the work in the hope that, one time or another, an actor's or director's inspiration will penetrate the mystery at its heart. There are clues that actors and directors have made much of. The "Hath not a Jew eyes?" speech stands there, a sudden and puzzling invitation to sympathy. This hated Jew may yet be a man. Shylock, mourning the theft of his turquoise, pauses to remember that "I had it of Leah when I was a bachelor." This widower is clearly no monster. And, technically speaking, is Shylock ever wholly in the wrong? Antonio has understood and accepted the terms of the bond; no one has deceived him. Shylock never demands more than the terms of the bond; he is within his rights. The defeat of Shylock is not accomplished by strict justice, but by a trick. Isn't the Jew more sinned against than sinning?

The possibility that Shylock is as much a victim of Venetian society as certain improvident Venetians are the victims of his malice is the hint that has been most exhaustively explored in our time. The text has been all but X-rayed in the search for lines, phrases, hitherto unimagined attitudes that might help to justify Shylock and so acquit Shakespeare of the charge that is implicitly brought against him. In performance, all such lines, phrases, and attitudes have been carefully stressed; perhaps our commonest experience of the play in the theater is that of watching an edgy actor approach an uncomfortable passage with the thought "How am I going to twist *this* scene so as to avoid offense and gain a little respect?" plainly written on his face. The other principals have been freshly reexamined. How admirable is this Antonio, who can barely refrain from spitting on a Jew while arrogantly taking his money? What sort of sponging fortune-hunter is Bassanio, anyway? Can a more cold-blooded package than Jessica be imagined—a girl who abandons her father, steals his treasure, and turns Christian on demand?

From so much earnest inquiry has emerged a by now familiar Shylock: a man who is at the very least a dignified representative of an oppressed race and whose vigorous insistence upon his pound of flesh is the direct result of renewed insult, evasion, and betrayal by the Christian community; and a man who may, in the hands of a genuinely gifted actor, acquire something of the stature of a tragic hero, moving us to compassion and benediction as he stumbles brokenly from the courtroom.

Around him, the Venetian butterflies who pass their time in planning masked revels, marriages by guessing games, playful boy-girl disguises, and coy exchanges of rings, dance out their ephemeral lives under varying shades of light. In one production they become a tinseled, irresponsibly charming counterpoint to the main, more sober business of the evening. In another, they become a faintly melancholy echo of a romantic world that is vanishing under the burden of Venetian commerce and business-by-bond. In the production that may have brought every facet of our contemporary reinterpretation of the play into an ultimate balance—Tyrone Guthrie's staging for star Frederick Valk at Stratford, Ontario, in 1955—the sporting bloods of the Rialto were, for the most part, decadent bigots, Antonio and Bassanio were latent homosexuals, Belmont was peopled with opportunists, and the entire company joined forces in hissing, hooting, and spitting a stricken woolly bear of a Shylock out of the play. If this last series of images seems in any way excessive, it must also be said that Mr. Guthrie has given us the only recent mounting of the play that treated the play as though it were all of a piece. If Shylock is the hero, then the Venetians must be villains. And so they were.

But we are confronted now with the most disturbing evidence of all: that the persistent, humane effort to read sentiment into Shylock, even when that sentiment is actually achieved, does nothing to stabilize or illuminate the play as a whole; it merely succeeds in turning it upside down.

The late Frederick Valk, for instance, created a moneylender who was expansive, genial, even generous, and he was both believable and moving so long as the rest of Tyrone Guthrie's Venice was plainly in the wrong. The fact that Antonio, Bassanio, Portia, Lorenzo, and Jessica were in the wrong, however, effectively robbed us of any interest in their love affairs. Having watched them revile a decent man and drive him sobbing from the stage, we were disinclined to indulge them their lyrical fifth act; little patience was left for polite prattle about starry nights, forfeited rings, and the conjugal bed. Shylock appears in only five of the play's twenty scenes, with a sixth devoted exclusively to conversation about him. Three-fourths of the evening, then, and all of the major characters but one, had turned slightly sour.

This new, nervous imbalance—both of structure and of sympathy for the people at hand—is not always so marked as it was in Guthrie's uncompromising production. Most productions compromise, straining for the maximum dignity and tragic emotion in Shylock while straining for the maximum gaiety in the revels of his enemies. The effect—and we have been able to see at least six such *Merchants* in the past ten years—is always disturbing. Shylock may have seemed dignified indeed in his exchange with the judge, only to flounder miserably, immediately thereafter, in the necessary but extremely undignified business of whetting his knife on his shoe. The line "I had it of Leah . . ." may have bolted from its context with stunning sentiment; but we are fretfully aware that the line has been isolated from its context, that the actor has most carefully suppressed the frighteningly comic touches on either side of it. Even in his own scenes, quite apart from his relationship to the light nonsense at Belmont, Shylock is inconsistent, unsettling. We come away complaining of one thing or another: the actor has not been able to sustain Shylock's tragic greatness; the other players have not been adroit enough to hoist the light scenes into the air; the director has failed to pull the "two tones" of the play into satisfactory balance. After three or six or a dozen such productions, we reluctantly come to one of two possible conclusions: either Shakespeare never meant Shylock to be played so sympathetically, in which case he probably *was* anti-Semitic; or he did mean him to be sympathetic in the midst of all this foolery, in which case he was quite a clumsy playwright.

Both views, in effect, abandon the play. Those who come to the former conclusion simply refuse it performance, as certain high-school and community theaters have done in recent years. Those who arrive at the latter conclusion go on patiently waiting for the superbly serious Shylock who is sure to come, while granting that, in the overall management of the play, Shakespeare had temporarily lost command of his craft.

Since most of us are not quite willing to surrender the work, since there is so much in it that is irresistibly appealing, since Shylock himself will never stop teasing us, it is surprising that we have not had the energy to cast about for still another alternative—especially since one exists. There is always the hypothetical possibility that Shakespeare knew what he was doing, that what he was doing was writing a true comedy, and that he was able to sustain his single tone perfectly because in Shylock he had drawn neither a melodramatic villain nor a tragic hero but a true comic giant.

That the alternative exists, and ought to tempt us to experimentation, is plain enough. The play has always been called a comedy: it is so listed in the First Folio and in Francis Meres' catalogue of 1598. It was written *circa* 1596, not during the later period that produced the mixed tone of the "dark comedies" but somewhere between *A Midsummer Night's Dream* and *Much Ado About Nothing*. The oldest acting tradition has always held that, as John Munro reminds us in *The London Shakespeare*, "Shylock was apparently meant originally to be a ludicrous figure with a large nose and odd gestures which were mimicked by Launcelot." The tradition extended beyond Shakespeare's time: in his *Comic Characters of Shakespeare*, John Palmer insists that "Shylock as a comic character held the stage for over a century." The first known production after the Restoration, in 1701, featured the best-known comedian of the day, Thomas Doggett, in the role.

Indeed, there is no indication that Shylock was ever imagined as other than a comic figure until the revolutionary performance given by Charles Macklin in 1741. Whether Macklin made him a blood-curdling villain (during the knife-whetting scene, reported a member of the audience, "Mr. Macklin was so highly characteristic in the part, that a young man who was in the pit fainted away") or a mixture of melodrama and pathos ("This is the Jew/That Shakespeare drew," enthused Pope) is not certain. What is certain is that Macklin shattered the earlier tradition and paved the way for the somber, or at least sober, Shylock we elaborate today. Macklin "rescued Shylock from the crudities of the low comedian" is Phyllis Hartnoll's verdict in *The Oxford Companion to the Theatre*.

Perhaps so. But there is something faulty in the rescue work: both character and play continue to prove troublesome and unresolved. Is it possible that the way Shylock was played in Shakespeare's time, and for nearly one hundred and fifty years thereafter, is the right way, the only practical way if the piece as a whole is to prove satisfying?

The thought horrifies us. Are we going to make Shylock a villain again and poke crude fun at him besides? Are we really prepared to double the offense we may give to Jews in the audience, while we confirm, in spades, Shakespeare's suspected anti-Semitism? The promised spectacle of a "ludicrous figure with a large nose" dancing grotesquely about the stage so that Portia and Antonio can go scot-free and the play become a unified piece of comic writing so revolts us that we avert our eyes and cut our contemplation short.

But we have, in our quick dismay, neglected to ask certain obvious questions. What makes us think that the original comedy performance was a *low*-comedy performance? Who played the part?

Not one of the low comedians, if the conjectural cast lists worked out by T. W. Baldwin can be accepted as reasonably accurate. The company's principal clowns—Kempe and Cowley—were occupied elsewhere: Kempe as Launcelot, Cowley as Old Gobbo. What sort of actor was left, then, for a funny Shylock? Apparently our Jew was the property of one Thomas Pope, creator of a quite different species of fool: Falstaff, Sir Toby Belch, Jaques, Benedick, Mercutio.

The line of parts is interesting. Thomas Pope would seem, on the face of it, to have been a comedian, most probably a superb one; and his particular humorous vein must have been capable of absorbing some fascinating complexities: a streak of knavery, a streak of melancholy, a flash of fire. One other quality leaps out of the line: the parts are one and all, no matter what skulduggery they may embrace, sympathetic. In these hands Shylock is not likely ever to have been a simple, despicable buffoon.

Even so, the likelihood that Shylock was once one of a certain brotherhood of outsize, attractive rogues does not wholly clarify the man for us. Neither Falstaff nor Jaques is really Shylock; we still lack a precise, practical, playable image, the sort of image that might have come into Shakespeare's head through a hint in his sources or in one or another comic convention of the Elizabethan stage.

The supposed sources for the play suggest very little along this line.

The story of the bond appears in very early folklore, when the holder of the bond was not yet a Jew, but the atmosphere of the legends is essentially melodramatic. The Jew, the bond, the passionate love for a lady of Belmont, the lady's disguise in a court of law, and the forfeited betrothal ring are found in combination as early as 1378, in Fiorentino's *Il Pecorone*; but a translation of this work was probably not available to Shakespeare, and he is thought to have picked up the outline by hearsay, without a specific tone attached. The commercial popularity of Marlowe's *Jew of Malta* may have induced Shakespeare to write his play; but the play he wrote and the Jew he created bear only the most superficial resemblance to Marlowe's savage inventions.

These sources, which Shakespeare may have carved up and recombined in his characteristic fashion, might very well lead us to a violent Jew, a voracious Jew—but not to any comic Jew that Thomas Pope is apt to have played. Was there no familiar image, no elderly, moneygrubbing, fantastically funny fellow, *anywhere* in the Elizabethan storehouse to help set Shakespeare in motion and the rest of us on a likely scent?

There was such an image, just such a fellow. His name was Pantalone, and he appeared endlessly, with many droll variations but with a few indispensable comic trademarks, in the improvised performances of the Italian *commedia dell'arte*. (The players improvised from standard scenarios, many of which survive.) That Shakespeare and his associates knew Pantalone and his retinue is quite clear. *Commedia* troupes began visiting London as early as 1574. Companies returned at intervals thereafter; one is thought to have spent the entire season in London during the year of Shakespeare's arrival from Stratford. Playwrights Thomas Heywood, Thomas Kyd, and Ben Jonson all mention these *farceurs*, with their repertory of Harlequins, Dottores, and—in the Anglicized spelling—Pantaloons. Among the papers left by Burbage's greatest actor-rival, Edward Alleyn, were four *commedia* scenarios, in the oldest of which "Panteloun" appears. Shakespeare himself, of course, made reference to this salty, drooling, somehow venerable figure in *As You Like It*, and elsewhere came to call his own fools "zanies," after the *zanni* of the Italian travelers. Pantalone was, as a suggestive theatrical image, available.

Who was he, what was he like? To begin with, he was a merchant of Venice. He was old, wealthy, and had his fortune tied up in shipping. When one of his cargoes was destroyed by storm or pirates, he tore his beard and spat into the sea in impotent rage. He was a miser.

"All his life long," as Pierre Louis Duchartre reconstructs him for us, "he has been engaged in trade, and he has become so sensitive to the value of money that he is an abject slave to it." His precious ducats are eternally on his mind. He is swiftly suspicious, sure that someone is going to swindle him. To help save ducats, he starves his servants. His hungry valet frequently threatens to leave him. The old father of the hungry valet sometimes comes to intercede for his son. The valet invariably mimics his master's speech, behind his back.

Pantalone has a daughter, with whom he is severe. She is an ingenue in love, eager for marriage, more eager still to be out of her father's tyrannically run household. Secretly she makes arrangements to meet her lover, usually by means of letters smuggled out by the friendly, conniving servant. When the chance comes, she elopes, often taking a supply of ducats along with her. Pantalone boils in rage, driven nearly out of his wits by his daughter's behavior. Others are delighted to see him so beset, he is such a "skinflint" and "calamity-howler."

At the last, Pantalone is the butt of the joke—robbed of his ducats, deceived by his daughter, the sputtering, breast-beating, hair-tearing victim of his own greed.

He carries, of course, a large purse at his belt. He also carries a sizable dagger. He is quick to draw and brandish the dagger when outraged, which is rather often; somehow or other, though, he is never permitted to use it. Vocally, to take a cue directly from Shakespeare, "his big manly voice, turning again toward childish treble, pipes and whistles in his sound." This shrill, shuffling, furiously gesticulating patriarch is only an inch or two shy of senility. For clothing, he wears a long black cloak, a rounded black cap, and either soft slippers or Turkish sandals. He has a prominent hooked nose.

In the *commedia* scenarios and eyewitness reports that survive, Pantalone has still other characteristics. Sometimes, for instance, he is an amorous old fool bent on marrying again, a trait that Molière took hold of and elaborated brilliantly in several of his finest comedies. In the process of making varied use of the Pantalone figure, however, Molière did not neglect the particular bundle of crotchets, nor the precise story line, we have just been describing. One of his masterpieces, *The Miser*, presents us with a greedy, near-senile Pantalone (Harpagon) whose daughter deceives him, whose servants groan over the food allotted them and helpfully conspire with the daughter, whose money is stolen, and whose comeuppance is the result of his own greed. No one questions the derivation of Harpagon from Pantalone; we have simply neglected, I think, to draw the same conclusions from the same materials in the case of Shylock.

While it is unlikely now that anyone will ever be able to *prove* that Shakespeare took his Shylock from his memory of Pantalone, the catalogue of similarities is too striking to be dismissed. As will be obvious, each item in the catalogue appears—with a surprising minimum of alteration—in *The Merchant of Venice*. Nor do the resemblances end with the character of Shylock; through Jessica, Launcelot, Old Gobbo, and possibly Tubal, they extend to the general personnel, the incidental comic episodes, and the romantic story line of the play. When bound with the casket sequences and the lyric fifth act, these touches become part of a consistent light-comedy pattern, notes struck in a single true chord.

We might add, speculatively, that the chord itself—Shakespeare's image of Venice and all that might pass in it—may have come from his experience of watching the Italian troupes play; these *were* Italian, they *knew* Venice, they exuded its spirit in a style that was both mocking and accurate; they constituted Shakespeare's most intimate, direct, and reliable sense of the atmosphere of the Rialto.

Pantalone does suggest Shylock, just as the standard *commedia* story of a charming ingenue who outwits her foolish, niggardly father suggests at least one of the plot lines and much of the atmosphere of the play as a whole. But does Shylock suggest Pantalone? Going back to the text with these performance images in mind, does Shylock *read* as a comic, garrulous, sputtering, excitable, stingy old goat?

We have tried so hard to read the lines in every other conceivable way that fresh hearing, uncluttered by prejudicial associations, is next to impossible. But let's make the effort. Shylock is introduced this way:

SHYLOCK.   Three thousand ducats: well.
BASSANIO.   Ay, sir, for three months.
SHYLOCK.   For three months: well.
BASSANIO.   For the which, as I told you, Antonio shall be bound.
SHYLOCK.   Antonio shall become bound: well.

What are those repetitions all about? What is that rhythmic "well" doing there? Don't they sound, on quick acquaintance, like the mumbling, lip-smacking, beard-moistening reiterations of the amusingly aged? Abstracted from their context they might do as a pattern for a vaudeville routine, that familiar one in which the blear-eyed comic gropingly reiterates the instructions his straight man is giving him until he is ready for the surprise switch. In the context of the play, they create precisely the kind of comic rhythm that lends itself to burlesque imitation by one of the secondary fools—which, of course, is what Launcelot Gobbo takes advantage of a little later in the evening. Indeed, if Launcelot's mimicry is to be effective, the initial rhythm—and the actor's management of it—must be inherently funny.

The longer speeches into which Shylock soon plunges are marked by absurd pedantry (he is constantly explaining what is already clear), further chatterbox repetition, and the device of a long list of negatives swiftly followed by a simple, complacent positive. The devices are all stock equipment for the comedian. Shylock has, in addition, a leering sense of humor of his own; he rather fancies himself as a jokester, doing his best to make a merry jest of the bond itself and indulging himself in casual throwaways (asked if his money has the potency of ewes and rams, he murmurs, "I cannot tell. I make it breed as fast"). It is not difficult, here, to recognize the bland, obsequious humor of the man who thinks himself cleverer than anyone else, who rubs his palms and chuckles happily as he spreads molasses for the flies and thinks lovingly of the future; he is at once crafty and transparent, a combination calculated to make him comic.

The next we hear of Shylock we hear from his hungry servant Launcelot ("I am famished in his service. You may tell every finger I have with my ribs") and from his put-upon daughter ("Our house is hell"). The material is unmistakably giddy, topped by a romantic letter secretly delivered by the conniving servant; Shylock's household is established by a stand-up clown improvising pure nonsense.

When Shylock himself appears a scene later, the Pantalone-like stinginess recurs as he washes his hands of his servant (who was a "huge feeder"), the senile pedantry returns as he gives Jessica instructions for the night ("stop my house's ears, I mean my casements"). The phrase "I did dream of money-bags tonight" is so blatantly grotesque in its wording that it cannot be anything other than a cartoon of avarice. There are also three basic comedy bits in the scene: the business of Shylock's being of two minds, shouting for Jessica below a window and pursuing a completely different thought at the same time; the business of the shout's being echoed, unexpectedly, by a too-helpful servant, startling Shylock and causing him to turn on the servant; the business of Shylock's not quite hearing a sly exchange between the servant and his daughter, leading Shylock to ask what was said and Jessica to misreport it. Add to this the fact that Launcelot and Jessica are, throughout the scene, playing *against* Shylock's abstracted, slightly frantic mood, punctuating his scattered instructions with puns, irrelevancies, malapropisms, and—we may suppose—sly winks.

Once Jessica and the ducats are gone, we do not immediately see Shylock in his anguish. The anguish is reported to us—in itself a suggestion that it is going to be humorously handled—and reported to us not by fellow Jews who might view Shylock's plight sympathetically but by friends of Bassanio's who can view it only with comic relish. Is the report truly comic? Why does it not strike all actors—as it does almost all audiences—that "my ducats, and my daughter!" is a roaring incongruity, a pairing of values so mismatched that their juxtaposition seems the very soul of comedy? If one or another value gains a little edge in importance as the harangue goes on, it is the ducats and not the daughter—the scales fall not toward sentiment but toward the absurd. And the incongruity is stressed in that splendid burst of incoherence, "O my Christian ducats!" As Salanio says of it, "I never heard a passion so confused."

What of the scene in which we *do* meet the ravaged Shylock? Its structure, after the introductory exchange between Shylock and Bassanio's friends, is completely, explicitly comic. Even the introductory passage has its familiar echoes, the obtuse and literal over-explanation ("I say, my daughter is my flesh and my blood"), the monomaniac repetitions ("Let him look to his bond"); even the "Hath not a Jew eyes?" speech begins with one of Shylock's snappish jokes (asked what Antonio's flesh is good for, he raps out "To bait fish withal"). But here is what happens in the scene proper. Tubal informs Shylock that Jessica cannot be found. Shylock is at once in the abyss, wallowing in those same comic incongruities Salanio found so "outrageous" ("I would my daughter were dead at my foot, and the jewels in her ear!"). Tubal next reports that Antonio has had ill luck. Shylock ("What, what, what?") is swiftly transported to seventh heaven ("Good news, good news! Ha, ha!"). Tubal mentions that Jessica is thought to have spent fourscore ducats in one night. Shylock dives to despair. Tubal speaks of a ring Jessica has traded for a monkey. Shylock writhes in torment. Tubal remarks that Antonio is undone. Shylock bursts into a fever of delighted activity.

Up, down, up, down, with the sentences growing tighter, the exhilaration and the agony coming closer together, Shylock is alternately sobbing and gleeful in ever-faster reversals until he is all but spun off the stage. The trick remains, of course, standard property among comedians today.

As we move toward the courtroom, Shylock's frenzied bout with Antonio and his jailer is a sputtering summary of all the repetitions, rationalizations, and caterwaulings we've by now become accustomed to. And, in briefly renewing our acquaintance with Jessica, we are given a significant scene which is now most often omitted in production: a lively, witty, playful, extraordinarily candid passage in which the entire Jewish-Christian theme is made lighthearted sport of ("This making of Christians will raise the price of hogs"). The scene is delightfully in keeping so long as the play is regarded as a thoroughgoing comedy; it is normally abandoned in our own mountings, I suppose, because the mountings themselves make it inexplicable.

In the courtroom Shylock is impudent to the judge, fawning with Portia, shrill in his glee over "A Daniel come to judgment," filled with a wonderfully pious righteousness ("Shall I lay perjury upon my soul? No, not for Venice"), whimpering when defeated ("Shall I not have barely my principal?"), and protected in tone at every turn by Portia's own little jokes and Gratiano's ebullience. Through it all, he whets his knife on his shoe, gleefully anticipating the victory to come, sassing the Duke who bids him to desist. That this business is irretrievably funny may be best attested to by every actor who has tried to play it as though it were not. The image is, simply as an image, outrageously, preposterously ludicrous; in ever so sober a production the snickers cannot be stilled. It is possible that Shakespeare, who knew a comedy bit when he saw one, did not intend embarrassed snickers but wholehearted belly-laughs.

These are the devices that the part and the play are made of, the comic carpentry on which both structures rest. Let us suppose that Shylock *could* be played as a delightful dervish of a Pantalone, and that the comedy as a whole would profit by the vision. Clearly, we have not yet accounted for everything. Though the "Hath not a Jew eyes?" passage begins in a joke, it moves on to something else: to a quite firm defense of Jewishness and the common humanity of Jews and Christians. Though the "Leah" line is surrounded by comic images, it is in itself instantly moving, a catch of breath in the middle of a laugh. If Shylock is the English cousin of an Italian vaudevillian, where does that pathos come from? Precisely where it has always come from, I think: from that unexpected stab of sorrow that so often accompanies the comic image when it is raised to its highest power.

The likelihood that pathos will emerge from the most outlandishly, even grotesquely, conceived cartoon stems from a very simple principle: all truly funny figures are necessarily sympathetic figures. If a man makes us laugh, we like him. He may do quite terrible things in pursuit of the objects of his lust, his avarice, or his spite; because he delights us in his outlandishness, in his methods, in his mania—and because we are quite sure he is going to be as delightfully discomfited—we feel no emotional revulsion for the things he does, or for his person. We secretly admire him; we look forward eagerly to his next appearance onstage; in an oddly inverted but very understanding way, we feel for him. And because we feel for this enchanted buffoon, we can always be, delicately, touched by him. It is perfectly clear to us that Chaplin can kick a child at one moment and involve us emotionally at the next. (I recently took my wife to a revival of an early Chaplin film; her response at the end was "Why do you say it's funny? I cried!") Yet the dominant Chaplin image is funny; the pathos wouldn't stir if it weren't.

A considerable complexity is required of any comic figure if so sobering a note is to be embraced, and to be embraced without destroying the dominant image. That the original Pantalone is capable of nearly infinite extension and very rich variation is amply demonstrated by Molière; we do not have to look to Shakespeare to find it. Molière's Harpagon (*The Miser*) and Arnolphe (*The School for Wives*) are both Pantalones, closely derived from the *commedia* form; and they are both, in Molière's hands, men of vast stature and psychological subtlety. Nor can any villainy they may do force us to despise them. Indeed Arnolphe comes at last, in *his* up-and-down torment between raging anger and tender devotion, to a note of brokenhearted submission:

> You want to see me weep? And beat my breast?
> You want to have me tear out half my hair?
> Or shall I kill myself? Is that what you want?
> Oh, cruel girl, I'm ready to prove it so.

That last line is no longer quite comedy; it is Arnolphe's way of saying "Hath not an old, ugly man the power to love?" But Molière pulls him back quickly from this hint of a heart; the note is only faintly struck; Molière's characteristic tone, even when his characters are at their most complex, is one of detachment.

Not so Shakespeare's. Shakespeare is at his most characteristic, in dealing with outsize buffoons, in his management of Falstaff. Falstaff is a coward, a bully, a liar, a lecher, a tosspot. And he can be hurt, hurt so badly that it hastens his death. When we at last ask what was the special contribution of Shakespeare's genius to the tangle of sources that might have given birth to any such character, we can answer: the power of introducing strong feeling into the most Rabelaisian of rogues without breaking the mold that made him essentially merry. There is no reason to suppose that he might not have been able to do the same thing, with the assistance of the same actor, for Shylock.

If we are to imagine Pantalone as a playing model for Shylock, then we are not obliged to stop at the simple, playful level of senile rhythms and servant-slapping horseplay; we are free to imagine Pantalone risen to the complex comic stature and psychological brilliance of the best worst man in Molière; and we are further free to see in him the levels of sentiment that Shakespeare divined in the biggest boozers and most brazen scalawags he knew. It's a tall order, and one that has not been delivered in more than two hundred years. Ralph Richardson might bring it off. The Bert Lahr of *Waiting for Godot* might just possibly have made it stick.

What of the Jewishness? Pantalone, with his black cloak, black cap, and exceedingly prominent nose, was not Jewish. In the process of dovetailing sources, Shakespeare can have taken the Jewishness from the *Il Pecorone* tradition, from the commercial popularity of Marlowe's play, from the talk current in London after Lopez' execution. Wherever he took it, what he took was a stereotype: the medieval stereotype of the Jew as avaricious. He took it *as* a stereotype; there were too few Jews then living in England for Shakespeare to have had extensive personal knowledge of the race. Insofar as he borrowed the stereotype at all, and he probably borrowed it for commercial reasons, he cannot be absolved of a certain opportunism, of having lent himself to the exploitation and perpetuation of a disparaging legend. (He behaved even more badly, and for just as poor reasons, toward Richard III.) The fact in itself is unpleasant, and we will have to live with it.

We had best, however, not be smug about the matter. It should first be remembered that Shakespeare would have employed the stereotype as matter-of-factly, and with as little malice, as an American playwright of the early twentieth century making uncritical and even affectionate use of those other stereotypes, the superstitious Negro and the drunken Irishman. Furthermore, Shakespeare might have treated his borrowed equation in one of two ways. He might have made the Jew a bloodcurdling melodramatic villain, as most of his sources had done. Or he might have taken the kinder course and made him comic, which is what I think he did do. In the public mind, the progress of social adjustment moves something like this: from the alien as menace to the alien as buffoon to the alien as human being. It is quite conceivable that Shakespeare actually furthered understanding by nudging this process into its second stage. I do not say that he did this deliberately; but he had noticed that a Jew—and especially a funny Jew—had eyes. If we can imagine an accepted stereotype slowly and mysteriously taking on, under its manipulator's instincts, a broad and rather affectionate grin—as the superstitious Negro did when Mark Twain got around to Nigger Jim, or, more pertinently, as the drunken Irishman did when Sean O'Casey decided to make us fond of the loutish Captain Boyle—we may have come closer to measuring Shakespeare's peculiar achievement, and to the image in his mind as well. The Shylock we find on our stages is ambiguous, nervous, not very attractive in spite of his tears; Shakespeare's Shylock—if he was as funny as the earliest tradition tells us he was and as Thomas Pope might well have made him—may easily have been more likable.

The illustration at the beginning of these remarks, by the way, is not a drawing of Shylock, but of Pantalone.

7

THE PLOT AGAINST MUSICALS

THE NIGHT THE DANCING STOPPED

Oklahoma! is now more than twenty-five years old. That's strange. Most of our new musicals are still children of *Oklahoma!* and most of our new musicals look fifty.

Something's backwards here. Since when do the sprigs feel older than the grandfather oak? Why should the second generation get the backache? Oh, we all know about impulses running dry, and styles going stale, and composers who don't happen to turn up when you need them. That would account for imitativeness. But it doesn't account for the ague.

And this is the time of the ague, the time in which musicals can scarcely bring themselves off the drawing board, scarcely drag themselves in from out of town, scarcely survive the rude winter of Broadway when they do come. Snail-slow and gasping, they shuffle through the city, obviously elderly but without old-age insurance, newborn and born tired. Indeed a recent venture which lasted exactly one night in New York and was clearly intended to mine the *Oklahoma!* tradition had a stroke right on stage.

It wasn't the show that had the stroke, to be sure. It was an actor named Paul Rogers, stumping about the woodland stage on a handy crooked cane, pursuing a plot based on John Steinbeck's *East of Eden* as fast as his failing legs could carry him. Mr. Rogers was, at the time, either fretting about carloads of frozen lettuce that might never reach their destination, or about how many soldier boys would be lost in World War I, or about his own wild son Caleb who had probably gone where the whores are. Whatever pressure may have been uppermost in his weary mind, there was a sudden tremor, a startling slackness in his good right hand, and then the cane he was leaning on slipped out of control. Face ashen, he cried out, "What's happening to me?" And I thought on the spot it might have been *Oklahoma!* crying out.

For the last thing *Oklahoma!* would ever recognize is the revolution it began, or the backache it's come to. We do still date our current musical-comedy form from the arrival of that Rodgers-Hammerstein-Mamoulian-De Mille inspiration, from the sunny surprising night the book made sense, the songs fitted in, the dances expressed emotional states instead of Rockette mathematics, and Pore Jud in the smokehouse began to worry about being Daid. *Oklahoma!* was based on a substantial play, it had real characters, it developed its story logically, it had a flash of menace instead of comedy routines, it held its head high as an elephant's eye over all that had been corn before. It had a coherent structure. It could be taken seriously. And now we are so burdened with substance and shackled to seriousness that we groan as we move, prematurely gray.

I don't think we can quite understand what's happened—or at least one important thing that's happened—unless we look back at *Oklahoma!* itself. Look at the show as it was, not at the smash it turned out to be. *Oklahoma!* ballooned very rapidly. From a modest opening, and what might be called friendly reviews, it expanded in no time at all into the success of the century, not only the hottest ticket in town but the biggest deal. Its success determined its proportions in our mind's eye; thinking back, trying hard to remember, we're still conditioned by our own excitement. That wonderful show we finally got into had the size of the Hippodrome and the impact of a howitzer, didn't it?

No, of course it didn't. Nothing like it. The one thing we should never let ourselves forget about *Oklahoma!* is that it was an extraordinarily simple evening in the theater. That *was* its impact. The curtain went up on a wide-open backdrop and a fellow came in and leaned on a fence and after a while started to sing a song. He stayed there until he'd finished it, while a lady churning butter rocked in a rocking chair and listened to him. A girl who couldn't say no walked over toward the side of a shanty—left stage, slightly up, not very near the audience at all—and went right through *her* song without budging an inch. I suppose something busy did happen. A buggy was pushed out on stage and various cowhands who had no work to do sang fondly about its decor, beginning at a whisper.

Oklahoma! had a plot. It had to do with whether a boy would succeed in taking a girl to a picnic lunch. At the end of the first half this great issue was still unresolved, so unresolved that its emotional implications had to be danced out at great length in what remains the most exhilarating dancing—and, for that matter, the sexiest—ever devised for the American musical-comedy stage. Girl and boy did manage to settle things up between them by eleven o'clock.

If *Oklahoma!* was a straw in the wind, it was light as a straw. The wind lifted it into the air nightly. No canes, no arthritis, no crawling off to bed for a death scene. The show could lift because it had freedom, and it had freedom *because* it was simple. The plot left room to breathe. Room for the choreographer to invent and play and skip and not fuss about mighty issues, room for the composer to say what a nice day it was, room for the designer to splash paint—very sunny paint—over an uncrowded sky. The horizon was open. Not the Oklahoma horizon, the musical-comedy horizon. The so-called "substantial" story was no more than a couple of telephone poles leaning lazily in the distance. And, with so little hard work to do, a show could get on with its natural, buoyant business of exploring melody and movement, raising its face to the breeze. What was there to stop it, or cramp its joints?

But, next year, then the year after that, the problem. How do you top *Oklahoma!?* You can get a bigger success only by building up a bigger show. Bigger in what way? Not musically, for heaven's sake: you can't hope to have more songs, or better songs, than *Oklahoma!* had. Not choreographically, either: within a year or two everyone was saying there was *too* much dancing around, and by the time Rodgers and Hammerstein got to *South Pacific* they'd dropped the dancing altogether. But if you can't expand on song or dance, and you still want to be bigger than ever before, there's only one place to go: to more and more Story with more and more Substance.

The reach was upward, toward the library shelf, and after a while nothing but a Modern Library Giant would do. Slender volumes were obviously lightweight: no significant advance there. What everyone was really after was *Gone With the Wind,* and if that wasn't available then *How Green Was My Valley* would have to make do. Rodgers and Hammerstein themselves escalated quickly: *Carousel* was bigger than *Oklahoma!* and *South Pacific* was bigger than both of them. For a while the inflation was exhilarating: the steam was still up, the extended arm confident, the bubble of melody uncompromised.

But all the time there was an obstruction in the making. Like the ever-swelling corpse of Ionesco's *Amédée,* one musical-comedy ingredient was overwhelming the house, filling up all the living spaces. Multiplot was pushing its way into every nook and cranny, and doing more than eat away dance time. If, for instance, an actor has to sing "The times were restless then, You'd work a place awhile and then hop a train," he has clearly stopped thinking about what a beautiful morning it is and begun punching a time clock. The necessary narrative is getting rammed into the lyrics, all right; but the lyrics are no longer very lyrical.

Melody is robbed, too, surreptitiously. If the source material is so complex that a good actor must be hired to act it out, that actor probably won't sing as well as a singer. A composer may still write melodically; but he may never hear what he wrote.

With dance, lyrics, and melody all backed breathless against the wall, center stage is promptly choked with double-decked scenery: there must be three or four flights of windows for the subplots to look out of. *War and Peace* is a pretty busy novel; we may be ready for it.

If we weren't ready for *East of Eden* when it came (under the new title of "Here's Where I Belong"), the evening was still, for us, a *typical* failure. Its long arm went out to span the histories of a defeated father (now on the rise, now on the downgrade, then rise and downgrade all over again), a mother who'd wandered off seventeen years earlier ("You couldn't keep away, could you?" she said to her husband when he knocked on her door for the first time in seventeen years), a wild son, a bookish son, World War I, the development of refrigeration in the Salinas Valley, the morals of profiteering, the horrors of prostitution, a double love story and a father-son relationship complex enough to have gobbled up *I Never Sang for My Father* for breakfast. Small wonder that father Paul Rogers—a sturdy actor and sort-of-singing member of the Royal Shakespeare Company—began to feel poorly rather early in Act Two. It would have been less work playing *Macbeth*.

Miraculously, choreographer Tony Mordente did manage to make space for one sinuously staged dance. But do you know *what* was being danced? The problem of getting crates of lettuce into boxcars before the lettuce wilted.

All powers wilt under the burdens we assume in the interests of ever richer substance. Yet that isn't the sort of substance *Oklahoma!* first invited us to toy with. Nor, if anyone cares to count, is it the sort of substance the most resoundingly successful musicals since *Oklahoma!* have staked their lives on. *Guys and Dolls* was a short story, *Hello, Dolly!* a lovely, spindly farce. *How to Succeed* was a joke, *The Music Man* took up the staggering problem of whether the children of River City would ever learn to play musical instruments, and *My Fair Lady* was about teaching a girl to pronounce words. A few of the smashes have been massive, yes: *South Pacific, West Side Story*. Most have found something to sing about in relative lightness and slightness; they were girls of slender means.

If there's a handy rule to be concocted here, it might be this: when materials must be contracted into music, they're probably going to crowd the music, maybe cramp it; when they can be expanded into music, the dance is on.

SOBRIETY IN VENICE

Everyone who has ever been to Venice knows that no matter when you arrive you have always just missed the concert in the courtyard of the Doge's Palace. It took place last night, while you were packing your bags somewhere else. Now you can go watch the bandstand being dismantled and the chairs stacked away, wondering wistfully just what it was you were late for.

That happened to Leona Samish, the doomed-to-be-frustrated heroine of *Do I Hear a Waltz?*, and it may have been the truest thing that did happen in a musical determined to be true. True to itself, that is—rigid in its adherence to the Spartan outlines of Arthur Laurents' source play, *The Time of the Cuckoo*, firm in its resistance to all the ordinary blandishments of color, dance, and massed choral voices with which most musicals struggle to make themselves ample and merry and by means of which some musicals betray themselves.

There was to be no betrayal here. Mr. Laurents meant to look head on at the unlovely inhibitions Americans of Puritan stock take with them when they go abroad and he intended to sentimentalize nothing. Leona was going to miss more than the band concert. She was going to miss going to Harry's Bar because no one really wanted her along. Attractive as she was, there was something clammy about her rectitude. She was going to miss having so much as coffee with a shopkeeper who took a fancy to her. She could not conceive of coffee without a long-range commitment first. And she was going to miss whatever pleasure she might have taken in her long-delayed and reluctant surrender to the shopkeeper. Afterwards she would ask so many questions and make so many emotional demands—and she would do these things so publicly—that humiliation awaited her admirer and embarrassment her "friends" at the *pensione*. She would go home a shade wiser, but without much in the way of happiness stored up. Thus the narrative.

The production was wholly commited to Mr. Laurents' astringent vision. Even the color blue had been banished from Venice. In a series of very strict washes, designer Beni Montresor had bronzed the lagoons and the latticework, the bridges and domes, until they were uniformly autumnal, spinster-dry. "Look, they even painted the damn sky!" cried Leona in her first burst of exuberance. But they had painted it the color of her locked-up heart, as a warning.

Choreographer Herbert Ross was not asked to display abandon where there could be none. In his few moments of dance he confined himself, chastely, to the invitations a few boys extended to the few girls who would link arms with them, or to the reshuffling of couples who weren't certain they were properly mated or ever would be. Richard Rodgers' songs, careful to preserve the quality of fundamental reserve, were offered singly to principals who were forced to keep their distance from one another or to groups of four or five who might wish to compare travel notes. No orchestrated ensemble disturbed the lonely night.

Admirable? In intention, yes. Mr. Rodgers in particular was to be congratulated upon his restiveness, his continued unwillingness to redo the last show that had succeeded, his voluntary surrender of the devices traditionally used to wake customers up—though he may have been placing too great a burden upon his own gift for melody in demanding that it walk alone. Lyricist Stephen Sondheim had here and there given him some pleasantly compressed rhymes, if no very touching ones.

But an intention pursued as severely as this one must be prepared to offer its own compensations. What reward might we look for, with color and dances and the hurly-burly gone? Why, the rewards of seriousness, I suppose: character complexity, emotional involvement of however disturbing a kind, weight, wisdom, a piercing of once-showy surfaces.

Mr. Laurents could not or did not give us these things. His libretto, necessarily no doubt, was thinner again than the play on which it had been based. Leona and her tourist acquaintances had to be sketched in swiftly if there was to be time left for songs. Sketchiness, however, was very hard upon all of them. Because they were frigid or frustrated or otherwise dissatisfied people—causing the Italians they met to become distressed or disgruntled people—economy of line made them come out all the colder. We felt very little for figures whose inadequacies were reduced to flat statements, whose obtuse and fumbling gestures were recorded in two dimensions. When the Italian shopkeeper announced to Leona that he was sufficiently drawn to her to entertain the thought of an affair, we didn't feel that we had been caught up in an intricate contest between temperaments and cultures; we only felt that a standard musical-comedy leading man was being oddly blunt about matters. We hadn't noticed, while he was singing a song in praise of Venetian glass, that he was that much attracted to Leona. And when Leona was making so much fuss about whether she would or wouldn't accept a first casual invitation to coffee, she did not seem unduly virginal; she seemed merely to have a thing about coffee.

The problem of the straight-faced musical and its "purity" of execution went deeper still in this instance. For, after having shorn away from the surrounding production every last trace of gaudiness, Mr. Laurents had not kept his own sober text "pure." In a pinch, he was as ready to write sentimentally as the next man. "You make many jokes," the shopkeeper said to the flustered girl who was evading him, "but—inside—I think you cry." That is a line that would normally be accompanied by a throb of violins from the pit, if not a flight of choral voices from the wings. To attend to it seriously, and without its usual blanket of appurtenances, was like listening to *Blossom Time* raw. The narrative was newly sober and ascetic; but the lines were often like last week's, or last year's.

Nor in his dismissal of the kind of open comedy that helps most musicals become infectious had Mr. Laurents been consistent. Trying to persuade Leona to come lie with him, the shopkeeper reminded her that "Your friends would have done the same things in Kansas City." "Not in a gondola," she quipped. The quip may perhaps have been offered as one more example of Leona's foolish evasiveness; it came out as a routine musical-comedy snapback, and a lame one. The texture of the language was decidedly variable, and it was often at variance with the analytical earnestness of the master plan.

In the end, there was only one conclusion to be reached: if a musical is going to be as serious as *Do I Hear a Waltz?* it has got to be more serious than *Do I Hear a Waltz?*—still richer in its insights, still more uncompromising in its way with words. Conceivably this applies to the score as well. The songs here were musical-comedy songs, generally of a high order. But will musical-comedy songs carry the evening when the evening isn't a musical comedy? The materials in this instance might have been abrasive even for light opera—certainly they did not seem to suggest such treatment.

What, then? I don't know the answer, short of intimate opera itself. But there is a great yearning in the playhouse for the entertainment to turn one way or another, to dress itself more charmingly or to stir up a stronger fire. Half measures taken toward sobriety tend to leave us all halfhearted, torn between an elusive passion on the one hand and a lost playfulness on the other.

A LINE I'D CALL PRETTY

Having been rash enough to write a piece deploring the prevailing custom of basing all musical comedies on old movies or old plays, I now want to modify my position. In fact, I want to admit I was wrong. Wrong.

My confession comes not as a result of certain angry letters from composers and librettists who continue to display an exemplary loyalty to the movies they saw when they were in college. Loyalty is a quality I like in a man, but it is not what has persuaded me. Neither can I claim to have retired to my study prepared to rethink my position, retracing the progress of my error step by step. Thought had nothing to do with it.

I just happened to see a revival of *The Boys from Syracuse*. Reviewers rarely "just happen" to see things; mostly they go to the theater because dictatorial newspaper managements expect them to. But one or another conflict of obligations kept me from reviewing *The Boys from Syracuse* in the first case (I was probably off seeing some play that failed to communicate our failure to communicate), and I came to it carelessly and carefree, as well as late.

It was like the gentle rain from heaven, that show. All you had to do was sit there and let the lyrics kick their syllables. "I am sinless," sang the condemned old man who is also father to those identical

Antipholi, "I am twinless!" and you sank back in your seat in ecstatic relief that someone had remembered—some kind, kind soul had remembered—the pleasures to be wrought from compactness, from comic aptness, from the deft and daffy mating of the dead pan and the impertinent mind.

As we've said, most lyrics nowadays perform the functions of slave labor. They are always pushing something—the plot, or character, or whatever else the authors have not been able to get into the dialogue. Almost never do we hear a lyric with a leap in its heart, with a slyness in its condescension to the music, or even with an unlikely rhyme.

"This is a terrible city," began the jaunty-voiced hero of the Rodgers and Hart word-game as he contemplated manfully, and metrically, the unfriendly landscape he'd landed in. He wasn't being significant, mind you. There was nothing wrong with the city. He wasn't doing exposition, either, or recitative, in the manner of imitation Menotti. The tune was not a wail, the phrase was neither broken nor heartbroken. He was really getting ready for an impishly transplanted parody of all those hometown songs that used to keep people steadily moving into the big cities (here, it was called "Dear Old Syracuse") and he was being blunt, brassy, and right on beat about it:

> This is a terrible city,
> The people are cattle and swine,
> There isn't a girl I'd call pretty
> Nor a friend that I'd call mine. . . .

If your ear just happened to be pleased by the conversational suddenness of "a girl I'd call pretty," you were going to be pleased again later, even in the ballads, where the mockery was kept—oh, three or four millimeters away:

> It rained the day before we met,
> Then came three days that I forget. . . .

And if the jubilantly composed performers in the off-Broadway revival all seemed to be taking a special, most precise delight in making certain that you heard each pleasant, pointedly spaced word, it was no doubt because the lyricist's attitude of mind—cool but secretly confiding, ironic in the presence of poetry but not unaware that the poetry was there—was a comfort to them, too. The women of the house, busy at their sewing because their men gave them nothing else to be busy about, seemed truly content so long as they could sing:

> I weave with brightly colored strings
> To keep my mind off other things,
> So, ladies, let your fingers dance
> And keep your hands out of romance.
> Lovely witches, let the stitches
> Keep your fingers under control.
> Cut the thread, but
> Leave the whole heart whole.

The lyrics that were still so effortless in Ephesus were, of course, Larry Hart's, and Mr. Hart has been sufficiently praised since he left us. One of the troubles with posthumous praise, though, is that it tends to assume that the kind of thing a man did died with him and can never be recaptured, dare never be tried again. I think somebody *should* try. They might not get the hang of it right off, and people might say that though the lyrics were in Larry Hart's vein they weren't as good as Larry Hart's, but how about if they came out *half* as good? I mean half as crisp, half as witty in stealing a note from what ought to be the next line. I'd settle.

No need here to dwell on Richard Rodgers, either, the Richard Rodgers who is so adaptable that, after having buttoned his tunes so snugly to Mr. Hart's fit, he was able to unbutton them without thrashing and write just as good music for an altogether different kind of lyricist. When I say "just as good music," I hear a wrinkling of noses. Surely, everyone will say, "better" is the word for what came out of *Oklahoma!* and *Carousel* and *South Pacific*. And perhaps it is. But I'm not going to commit myself. I don't know that anyone has written more melodic surprise into what was meant to be a conventional musical comedy than Mr. Rodgers did for *The Boys from Syracuse*, and to hear the unexpected modulations of "The Shortest Day of the Year" or "You Have Cast Your Shadow on the Sea" is, today as twenty-five years ago, a shocker. Mr. Rodgers never did live along Tin Pan Alley; he was lost at sea as a boy and, when rescued, kept hearing inappropriate sounds. They remain inappropriately perfect. I've decided that I never *will* expect the modulations in "The Shortest Day of the Year," and I'm not going to try.

But what I started out to say was that *The Boys from Syracuse* is, as everyone has always known, based on a play, on two plays, perhaps on three or four plays. Its plot is borrowed, with due credit and a certain pride of race, from Shakespeare's *The Comedy of Errors*, which was borrowed from the *Menaechmi* of Plautus, which in turn may have been borrowed from a couple of oldies by Menander. And it does make hash of my earlier, querulous remarks.

It may not *seem* quite as sober and plodding and sentimental and earnest as so many of the musicals we now borrow from Loew's, Inc., or from *The Best Plays of 1947*. It may even seem somewhat slap-dash, cocky, improvised, and unrestrained. But we must mind our manners and remember our sources with respect. A play is a play is a play, and a play by Shakespeare is a play like anything. I am using the phrase "like anything" in the sense in which Gertrude Stein used it:

> I am Rose, and when I sing
> I am Rose like anything.

Perhaps it is too bad that Miss Stein did not devote more of her time to the musical theater. Anyway, the situation now calls for an apology, and a revised attitude, on my part, and I do oblige. I wish to revise my earlier statement and say that it is perfectly all right for musicals to borrow their stories from plays that are between four hundred and three thousand years old.

WHEN THE SHOE DOESN'T FIT

Anyone who has managed to get through the past few years is well aware of how fast history can move. Sometimes, though, we don't notice it moving—until we sit down before an image of ourselves (a poster, a piece of architecture, a play) that has always been accepted as standard and just isn't any more. We blink and realize that a skin has been shed.

It happened, I think, with *Hallelujah, Baby!* The Negro gains that that show contented itself with describing no longer seemed real gains at all, certainly nothing worth singing and dancing about. There we were up on stage, in the comfortable liberal postures we'd grown so used to—patting Negroes on the head as we tried to get them up front on the buses. And instantly we knew that paternalism was dead, had been killed inside us while we were scarcely looking. With so much more at stake in the air that we couldn't help breathing, our posture had changed before our eyes had.

In a quite different way, *The Education of H*y*m*a*n K*a*p*l*a*n* backed into us hard enough to make us realize we hadn't been standing still. When, some twenty-five years earlier, Leo Rosten had first written his charming stories about an exuberant Jewish immigrant who hit night school like a ten-strike, they had seemed apt. In another twenty-five years they will probably seem truly quaint. In 1968 they simply seemed false.

Now, this was a spot of bad luck for a well-meaning musical to run into. The entertainment had been tidily—if rather solemnly—put together by George Abbott. It had Tom Bosley, the Fiorello of old, to splash proud asterisks between the letters of his name—in living color, hurled at a banner from a paint bucket, the asterisks came out green—and then to subside into dismay as he learned that his beloved Miss Mitnick was to be married to another in the spring. The sight of Mr. Bosley keeping himself wrapped in coat and muffler well into the warm weather, hoping to hold spring at bay, was a nice one. And echoes of the melting-pot humor that had once seemed touching and relevant still stirred. When Mr. Parkhill, that dedicated teacher, ordered his pupils to prepare to "let Shakespeare's thoughts sink into your minds," the silent rustle of minds was delightful: twenty *tabulae rasae* sat up at the ready, welcoming an invasion that would make them all kings. When Mr. Parkhill had finished reading a passage from *Macbeth* and asked "Any questions?" twenty hands shot skyward like an instant army of lances. We laughed at the wholesale reflex because of *course* these near illiterates would have questions. And we laughed again because the questions weren't at all the ones we'd expected.

But in the meantime we had been puzzled, maybe a little bit

dismayed. One of those matronly housewives in the class had responded regularly with a loud "Oi!" No one, naturally enough (though it was not sidesplitting now), could pronounce a "w." There was an exercise in giving the opposites of words. For these ardent adult innocents, the opposite of "fresh" was "canned." The opposite of "new" was "secondhand." Mr. Bosley was so far from grasping the word "hobo" that he used it in the sentence "My hobo is hiking" (he meant "hobby," which must have seemed unlikely at any time, under any comic sun). At Ellis Island, gateway to the land of opportunity, the immigrants sang "maybe we don't belong" but "funny or not, we're here." An Irish cop on the corner, hustling classmates homeward, barked, "I was a foreigner once meself."

In the theater one's first reaction to this sort of thing was that the jokes were merely stale. After all, "Oi!" had never been anything more than a lazy bid for a quick laugh, and if "canned" as the opposite of "fresh" had once had an observant neighborhood-way-of-life flavor to it, the flavor had long since been lost in the chewing. In point of fact, librettist Benjamin Bernard Zavin *had* been careless enough to imagine that Abie's Irish Rose is a Rose is a Rose, and blooms freshly. We could have made the jokes when we were ten, going on Potash and Perlmutter.

But something else was wrong. The image of an American was now wrong. As things stood, Mr. Parkhill was the American of the piece, and the immigrants were the good folk who were trying to make themselves over in his likeness. They wished to pronounce "w" as he did, read as he did, hear as he did, think as he did. He, clean-cut and confident, was no doubt what we have come to call a Wasp. A good and earnest and likable Wasp. He was us, and they were they, waiting to become us.

That wasn't how our eyes or ears registered it any longer, though. Looking at the stage, we squinted and upset everything. The immigrants—above all the Jewish immigrants—seemed more American than he did. They were the faces and voices and inflections of thought that now seemed most familiar to us, literally second-nature. He was the oddball, the stranger, the fossil. We glanced at him, a bit startled, and said to ourselves, "Where did he go?" We remembered him: pale, poised, neatly dressed, briskly sure of himself. And we saw him as an outsider, an outlander, a reasonably noble breed in the act of vanishing. He was performing tonight as a molder of minds, but he was no longer in any sense the mold we had in mind. He had stopped being representative, and we hadn't noticed it until this minute. Not so emphatically, anyway.

Today a vast transition has reversed a picture out of the past. It's not just a matter of having been so exposed to Jewish entertainers and Jewish novelists that their tricks of rhythm have curled up in everyone's ears and come to feel at home there. That's happened, all right. Collecting Yiddish words and dropping them into Madison Avenue sentences has been fashionable for a long time now, so fashionable that it, too, is out of date. The Gentile who can't invert his sentence structure to make it sound pleasantly Jewish probably doesn't exist outside Kansas. (How is it in Kansas? I don't know.) Everybody today has a Jewish mother, whether she is Irish or what-not. And the Gentile, or for that matter the Jew, who now settles for a fast "All right already" or a sentence beginning with "So" in order to display his credentials as a sophisticate is all too plainly not a sophisticate. That's baby talk, affectation, even less than skin-deep.

Skin-deep isn't deep enough, isn't *true* enough. What has happened since World War II is that the American sensibility itself has become in part Jewish, perhaps nearly as much Jewish as it is anything else. And this is nothing so superficial as sympathetic identification (because so many Jews were killed) or a playful Gentile gesture of friendliness (because quirks of speech *can* be charming). It goes right to the bone, all the way in. The literate American mind has come in some measure to think Jewish, to respond Jewishly. It has been taught to, and it was ready to. After the entertainers and the novelists came the Jewish critics, politicians, theologians. Critics and politicians and theologians are by profession molders: they form ways of seeing. And America, at this particular moment in *her* history, desperately needed a new way of seeing. She had been moved, willy-nilly and by circumstances, into a world environment that called for an unfamiliar response: she had to learn how to deal effectively, courageously, and even humorously with irrational pressures that descended like lightning, with hostility, frustration, and despair. An experienced teacher was available.

Well, I should leave the how and why to trained sociologists, I suppose. But the degree of penetration, the spot that is touched when an American says "I," is now so marked that there is scarcely any "they" any more, any quaintness any more. The cast of mind is imbedded, firm, on the verge of self-recognition, increasingly flexible. The last sentence of Bernard Malamud's remarkable novel, *The Assistant*, has become prophetic. All of us, whoever we are or wherever we've come from, in some dim but ineradicable way now share the awareness of the young Italian who has wormed his way into a direct experience of Jewish days and nights. "After Passover he became a Jew."

And so, when we go to a perfectly ordinary musical for a perfectly ordinary evening's entertainment, we now go as someone other than we were when the words were first written down. The story rewrites itself in front of us, and we are thrown slightly off balance. The shoe is on the other foot, now. And whose shoe?

INSIDE MUSIC LOOKING OUT

Cabaret was a stunning musical with only one wild wrong note. The first thing you saw as you entered the theater was yourself. Designer Boris Aronson, whose scenery was so imaginative that even a gray-green fruit-store came up like a warm summer dawn, had sent converging strings of frosted lamps singing toward a vanishing point at upstage center. Occupying the vanishing point was a great geometric mirror, and in the mirror the gathering audience was reflected. We had come for the floor show, we were all at tables tonight, and anything we learned of life during the evening was going to be learned through the tipsy, tinkling, angular vision of sleek rouged-up clowns who inhabited a world that rained silver.

This marionette's-eye view of a time and place in our lives that had been brassy, wanton, carefree and doomed to crumble was brilliantly conceived. The place was Berlin, the time the late twenties when Americans still went there and Hitler could be shrugged off as a passing noise that needn't disturb dedicated dancers. Adapted by Joe Masteroff from the Christopher Isherwood-John van Druten materials that had first taken dramatic form as *I Am a Camera*, the story line was willing to embrace everything from Jew-baiting to abortion. But it had elected to wrap its arms around all that was troubling and all that was intolerable with a demonic grin, an insidious slink, and the painted-on charm that keeps revelers up until midnight making false faces at the hangman.

Master of Ceremonies Joel Grey burst from the darkness like a tracer bullet, singing us a welcome that had something of the old *Blue Angel* in it, something of Kurt Weill, and something of all the patent-leather nightclub tunes that ever had seduced us into feeling friendly toward sleek entertainers who twirled canes as they worked. Mr. Grey was cheerful, charming, soulless and conspiratorially wicked. In a pink vest, with sunburst eyes gleaming out of a cold-cream face, he was the silencer of bad dreams, the gleeful puppet of pretended joy, sin on a string.

No matter what was happening during the evening, he was available to make light of it, make sport of it, make macabre gaiety of it. Perhaps an amoral chanteuse with the mind of a lightning bug ("I guess I am a really strange and extraordinary person") was installing herself without warning in the rented apartment of an American writer, ready to share bed and bread but not for long. Perhaps the landlady was shyly and ruefully succumbing to a proposal of marriage from a Jewish grocer (she was rueful because she was old now, singing "When you're as old as I—is anyone as old as I?") and perhaps the Jewish grocer was beginning to feel the bite of things to come. Precisely as a brick was hurled through the suitor's shopwindow, Mr. Grey came bouncing from the portals to grab a gorilla in rose tulle. The two spun into a hesitation waltz with the prim and stately delicacy of partners well met. Let the world lose its mind, let the waltz go on.

Under choreographer Ronald Field's beautifully malicious management, Mr. Grey was superb, as were the dancers, the four girls who banged at instruments and called themselves the Kit Kat Klub Kittens (even the piano seemed to wear feathers), and the unending supply of tenors to give an Irish lilt ("Tomorrow Belongs to Me") to a contrapuntal pause in the tacky, rattling, bizarre and bankrupt goings-on. With the exception of an unlucky last song for landlady Lotte Lenya, the John Kander-Fred Ebb tunes snatched up the melodic desperation of an era and made new, sprightly, high-voltage energy of it, providing the men of the company with a table-to-table telephone song that came to seem rhythm in a state of shock, and offering Miss Lenya several enchantingly throaty plaints, notably a winning acceptance of the way things are called "So What?"

Miss Lenya had never been better, or if she had been, I don't believe it. Suitor Jack Gilford and non-writing writer Bert Convy were fine. Just one thing was missing: Sally Bowles. As the original narrative had had it, Sally Bowles was a fey, fetching, far-out lassie with a head full of driftwood and a heart she'd rather break than shackle. She was a temperament. She needed a temperament to play her. Instead, and unluckily, a pretty but essentially flavorless ingenue, Jill Haworth, had been cast in the role. Wrapped like a snowball in white fur and sporting that pancake tam that girls of the twenties used to wear whenever they were going to be photographed having snowball fights, Miss Haworth succeeded—at some angles—in looking astonishingly like Clara Bow. Her usefulness to the project, however, ended there; though the performer has certain skills she may be able to use in other ways, here she was trim and neutral, a profile rather than a person, not really worth more than her weight in mascara.

The latter part of the evening—the emotional part of the evening—suffered as a consequence. If you happened to remember a long-ago Katharine Hepburn film called *Morning Glory*, you realized that you were looking at it again, but without the glory.

Nevertheless *Cabaret* was able to ride over the gap because it had effectively opened the door—partway, at least—to a fresh notion of the bizarre, crackling, harsh and yet beguiling uses that can still be made of song and dance. Instead of putting the narrative first and the singers and dancers wherever a small corner could be found for them, it popped the clowns and the gartered girls directly into our faces, making them, in effect, a brightly glazed window—with a musical staff scrawled all over it—*through* which we could perceive the people and the emotional patterns of the plot. Instead of telling a

story into which musical numbers could be sandwiched when politeness permitted, *Cabaret* lunged forward to insist on music as medi-
ator between audience and characters, as lord and master of the
revels, as mocking conferencier without whose ministrations we
should have had no show at all. We were inside music looking out.
The show was a mask made of musical numbers, Peeping Tom
humming a tune.

In the end, I found myself wondering if the next logical step for
musical comedy to take isn't directly into picaresque territory. Supposing that we are going to go right on adapting novels and plays,
isn't it time to junk the routine novels and begin investigating what
have been called the "apocalyptic" ones?

Contemporary literature is up to its alert ears in the unreal real, in
the mocking, elongated, circuitous fantastications of Günter Grass,
Thomas Pynchon, Joseph Heller, Ralph Ellison, *et al*. The possible
virtue for the musical stage of these explosive, prismatic visions is not
simply that they are recent; it is that, in their structural openness and
in their free-association logic, in their irreverence and in their roving,
they invite rather than inhibit the stylized resources of choreog-
raphers, composers, designers and inventive directors. It's something
to think about, anyway, now that we have *Cabaret* to go on.

8

ALBEE, MILLER, WILLIAMS

TWO ALBEES

THERE ARE TWO Edward Albees, and they are both in *The Zoo Story*. In *The Zoo Story*, you will remember, a quiet man who is minding his own business, merely reading his newspaper on a park bench, is accosted by an unkempt, garrulous, desperately contemporary fellow who is determined to make contact at any cost. The neatnik on the bench is evasive; the beatnik circling him is fiercely direct. At play's end, the passive figure has killed the challenging one; the intruder has arranged things that way as a last resort. The relationship that could not be established by words is brought into being by a knife. It has taken death to do the trick, but the two have touched.

Edward Albee # 1 is the invader, the unsettler of other men's tidy little worlds, the unexpected noise on a summer day, the uninvited improviser. Not having been asked to speak, not having been offered any sort of subject for conversation, he bridles, invents, mocks, lashes out.

In this mood he can start from nowhere and in no time make a scene. *Virginia Woolf,* for instance, lunges forward for two long acts, emptying its lungs violently, without our having the least notion of the true nature of the quarrel. Its energy is boundless and gratuitous. The friends who drop in at midnight aren't friends and aren't wanted; in the living room two couples drink, shift uneasily, and relieve their embarrassment by confessional obscenities. They do not really have anything to say to one another, which leads them rapidly into saying the unsayable, the unforgivable, the unasked-for. Live people in a vacuum cannot stand the tension of their silent surroundings. Skin prickling, and driven by an internal need to fill the void, they are willing to blunder, quick to be blunt, committed to holocaust if holocaust alone will give them substance. We do not understand why Martha and George behave so savagely toward one another, certainly not before the last act and, strictly speaking, not even then. But the savagery nourishes our need to be engaged as it does theirs. It is a felt presence, like heat slowly filling a cold room and imperceptibly altering the disposition we make of our bodies. We were numb; we don't know why the heat was turned on; but we are anything but numb now.

So long as Mr. Albee is forcing to the surface something that seems not to have been preshaped, so long as he is prodding for response like the aggressor in the park, he is free with his tongue and adroit with his whip. Practically speaking, it would appear that his creative imagination snaps to attention whenever there *is* no ready-made scene to be played. He may be concealing his ultimate intention, and so forced to feint; perhaps sometimes he does not even have one. But if the situation is open or even empty, and if two people can be persuaded to walk out onto the stage, he instinctively knows what to do. He makes the two people scratch at one another to see what may peel off. Inside a mystery at least malice may be real, and with malice there is thrust and counterthrust, evasive action and headlong action, heads and shins cracking together. If no relationship exists, Mr. Albee will make one. His unleashed intuition runs beyond his intellect, and fury forms before our eyes.

But that is Edward Albee #1, the playwright writhing with great intensity toward a pattern that may never come; the writhing is the play, and as writhing it has authority. Edward Albee #2 is the passive reader on the bench, the man who doesn't want to be bothered looking into other people's lives, the creature of the cut-and-dried. In

The Zoo Story the indifferent man has everything accounted for—
nights and days, beliefs and rejections, what does and does not belong
to the Schedule. That is why he is indifferent. He has no need to
speak because his bed is made, his movements are planned, his course
is foreseen. The outline of his life has a certain prefabricated animation; but he is inert, having abdicated in favor of the outline.

The resemblance between this chap and Albee the Second asserts
itself in several different ways. It may turn up, as it does in *Tiny
Alice*, when a play is so schematically conceived, so rooted in a
philosophical predisposition, that the figures onstage have all they
can do to keep up with the marching propositions. It is as though
they had all read Mr. Albee's timetable—the New Thought, New
Haven, and Hartford—and agreed to appear on the right station
platforms at the appropriate times.

And the Other Albee turns up, most noticeably, in his adaptations.
Between original plays Mr. Albee likes to tinker with novels he admires, first Carson McCullers' *Ballad of the Sad Café* and then James
Purdy's *Malcolm*. But tinkering is the strongest word that can be
applied here; Mr. Albee does not feel obliged to question too deeply
the novelist's appointed rounds, he does not like to interfere with the
Schedule.

Malcolm is meant to record the impact of adult life upon an
innocent. The innocent, having lost his father long ago, is hopelessly
exposed. He cannot comprehend marriage between impotence and
whoredom; he cannot understand why men must surrender their
most cherished illusions; he cannot grasp the loss of friendship or the
fact that he is being "used"; he cannot survive the solaces of sex or
drink or irrational affection. "Everywhere I go the whole world is
flying apart!" he cries, and everywhere he goes he loses something of
himself. We last see him drained and dying, surrounded by the
sorrowing people who have helped make him their "contemporary."

During his journey of discovery, Malcolm has presumably played
out scenes with each of these people, suffering an injury here, a
shattering illumination there. But in fact he has played no scenes. As
Mr. Albee has fashioned the play, Malcolm drifts—literally, on a
treadmill—into one environment after another, observing relationships that are only standstill illustrations, and then drifts off again,

reportedly withering along the way. But he has not entered these environments to play a role. He never pokes a finger into the pudding to see what it is made of. Nor do the passing waxworks behave actively toward him, with the possible exception of a cabaret singer who is sexually aggressive and wishes to devour him nightly. His teachers, who are also his destroyers, put on small sideshows for him; but they are not even involved in their own adult cross-purposes, they are displaying rather than doing.

No connections are made: not with words, not with knives. In some way Mr. Albee is not challenged to discover scenes, not impelled to scrape or to badger or to probe. He has accepted another man's outline for the evening—rather as though Mr. Purdy had employed him and told him to be there from eight till closing—and, like a good bourgeois and unquestioning square, he has filed everything dutifully and minded his manners. The play is written by wristwatch, composed of cursory glances to make certain no chore has been neglected; one feels that, having done the required typing, Mr. Albee, primly satisfied, has retreated behind his newspaper on *The Zoo Story's* park bench.

Albee #2 is without urgency or initiative. His is the unrecognizable face, behind spectacles, that looks up at you from the receptionist's desk, welcomes you noncommittally, and then turns its attention to the necessary buzzers to be pressed. The playwright is preoccupied, confident in an abstracted way, virtually without identity. So long as he is chained to a prearranged routine, he is impersonal and not a little smug; it is only when the routine is shattered, and a blank page thrust before him, that his best energies are forced out of hiding.

It is perfectly possible that the passive Albee, pursuing schema rather than invention for too long a time, may kill off the active Albee, the restless, eruptive, run-on interloper—though of course that would make *The Zoo Story* much too prophetic and ironic. Albee #1 is the man to count on and to hope for. Starting from scratch he can scratch; and that, very possibly, is his mission.

LETTING IT COME TO YOU

This is an odd thing, but severely cerebral plays are always defended on the wrong grounds—on the grounds that they are not cerebral at all.

An instance of this sort of defense is the case Mr. Albee has made, or attempted to make, for *Tiny Alice*, though the position is by no means peculiar to him or to the play at hand. It was adopted when Tennessee Williams was having difficulties with *Camino Real*, and it has popped up, couched in virtually the same terms, whenever a play rooted in thought has not caught on with audiences.

The recommendation made to baffled audiences, whenever such plays are defended, is simple: don't think. "One must let the play happen to one," Mr. Albee has suggested to those who have expressed puzzlement. "One must let the mind loose to respond as it will, to receive impressions without immediately categorizing them, to sense rather than to know, to gather rather than immediately understand."

Mr. Albee acknowledges that his play has some sort of intellectual content, as indeed any play must. "The play is full of symbols and allusions, naturally," he goes on to say, "but they are to be taken as echoes in a cave, things overheard, not fully understood at first. If the play is approached this way, the experience of it will be quite simple." The author's specific directive is to "sit back . . . and take it in rather as you would a piece of music or a dream."

Now, this is a perfectly valid way of approaching the theater. In point of fact it is the commonest approach all of us make, certainly to plays of any complexity. Who can tangle with *Lear* while watching *Lear*? The only hope a man has of surviving *Lear* at all is to let himself float along on the accumulating wreckage. People have been making the same point about *Hamlet* for years. H. L. Bruckberger has recently made it again this way:

> I cannot *prove* to you that *Hamlet* is a great tragedy if you absolutely refuse to admit it. I cannot even demonstrate the dramatic credibility of *Hamlet*; it demonstrates itself on the

stage, just as movement is demonstrated in the act of walking. The credibility of a play is a fluid that comes across the footlights; if nothing comes across, it is because there is no fluid, no credibility. This dramatic credibility demonstrates itself in the degree to which the spectator finds, not that the spectacle is believable, but quite simply that he believes it.

Poetic truth is an existential business. What is accepted on the stage, on the spot, in the flesh and by one's own bones, can never be rationalized away, no matter how hostile clever critics may be. Nor can any degree of supple rationalization, of adroit explaining, breathe belief—after the fact—into a play that does not compel belief at first sight, directly upon acquaintance. The "let it happen to you" theory is entirely sound, and it is how we really deal with masterpieces all the way back to *Antigone* and *Oedipus*. First-rate plays are rarely reducible to tidy formulas. Even if they were, we should want to know them first and kill them with our exegetical exercises after.

By something of the same token, I cannot prove to you that Mr. Albee is either right or wrong about *Tiny Alice*. He says it is to be taken as a poetic, as an intuitively received, piece of work; I say that it strikes me, or feels to me, as though it had been manipulated into being by a series of thought processes which, in spite of some sleight-of-hand meant to conceal them, do not succeed in flowering into anything more than thought processes. But I am myself reporting to you a feeling rather than a mathematical certainty to which I can append Q.E.D. In fact I am reporting a kind of double negative: at *Tiny Alice* I felt no feeling. I was there and I heard no music, I was there and nothing dreamlike happened to me. Mr. Albee can say that I came to the experience too cerebrally, too much on the watch for detachable meanings; and he may be right. I can say that I went to it with a mind so "loose" as to be downright deplorable but that the play proper, providing no dream, forced me into trying to cope with it analytically; and I may be right. There is no resolving any such difference of opinion apart from the event as it took place in the auditorium: the audience either did or did not "sense rather than know," either was or was not satisfied in the sensing.

Here perhaps is a clue that can be worked with, though I don't mean to propose that *Tiny Alice* has been proved unpoetic simply because it closed after a short run. Once more the issue can be called ambiguous: perhaps the play was genuinely a piece of music but the audience was unattuned to this sort of music at this moment or put off it by tendentious reviewers; perhaps the play closed because it offered audiences very little that could actually be sensed. Take your pick, and hold your position.

But there is this to be suggested. Whenever a play provokes, as its very first response, a vast, clacking, agitated, argumentative public concern over its meanings, it has probably not exercised a very profound poetic command over that public. Thorough absorption in an experience tends to daze, to still, to dislocate slightly, to defer questioning until the quality of the experience has been savored fully and at long last expelled. *If* the sensing, the gathering, the submission, has in fact taken place, there is apt to be—very literally—a time of happiness, a time of nothing much more articulate than "I liked it," a time of affirmation on the part of the audience that will be broken only when heads are cleared of the dream and wish to understand what wonders may have produced it. Prodding now, alert minds may come upon oddities and difficulties either not first noticed or suppressed in the heat of the encounter; some alert minds will even regret that they were once taken in, while remembering that they *were* taken in. But the fact of the "taking in" goes uncontested, and there is a curious quiet associated with it.

Conversely, the play that *must* be explained, immediately, noisily, ardently or angrily, is probably a play that did not assert itself intuitively in the least. It prompted instant cerebration, throughout the town, because that is the kind of work it was: headwork asking for headwork, and getting it. I know, by this time, that the moment a playwright is heard saying "Let it come to you," he is a playwright trying to do a kind of work his play did not do. If it had done it, further urging would be superfluous. A buzz about meanings, and a request that the buzz cease, generally means—ironically—that the play is a play of meanings alone, without other life. I think we can recognize such a play by the anxiety it creates.

The standard defense in the face of such anxiety is both wrong and futile. It is wrong because it misrepresents the play: a playwright might do far better announcing his play as essentially schematic, a cerebral construct, in the hope of attracting just such audiences as may have a real taste for symbol-matching. It is futile because it cannot alter the nature of the experience on the stage, cannot transform into the gossamer of intuition what does not spin its own entirely natural, incontestable web.

And I make the point for one reason only. It doesn't cost a reviewer much to be wrong. A reviewer can be proved wrong ten years later and have nothing but his reputation, questionable to begin with, to lose. A playwright has his next play to lose. If, in the course of understandably defending his last play, he comes to misread his actual effect in the playhouse, he may come to make his next play in the false image. The one thing the theater cannot afford to lose is next plays.

THE GLASS HOUSE

In *Everything in the Garden*, Edward Albee carefully built an artifice and then killed it.

As Mr. Albee began his reworking of an earlier British comedy by Giles Cooper (black, black comedy), he was at infinite pains to assure us that we were not to take suburbia (not this suburbia) as quite real. True, there was Barry Nelson just outside the vast glass walls of his $40,000 home, mowing away at the lawn, and there was Barbara Bel Geddes tucked away on a sofa indoors, carefully counting the coupons that come with a certain inexpensive brand of cigarettes. Cozy and natural. Yet not exactly. There was already something about the room, and that emptyish landscape beyond, that seemed outsize, uninhabited, covered over with a uniform dry sunlight that Andrew Wyeth might have poured on it during an otherwise unoccupied hour. Even the lawn and the foliage seemed to have been given a remote coat of gloss, perhaps from the bucket Antonioni did not quite use up when he hand-painted the grass for *Blow-Up*.

Still, this was only a faint, faintly uneasy, sensation so far. If Mr. Nelson and Miss Bel Geddes talked a bit too much about money to be wholly plausible in our complicated world—indeed, they talked of nothing else, urgently and scrappily listing the power mowers and the greenhouses they wished they had—money is at least *one* of the subjects doll-headed suburbanites chatter about from time to time. We simply had been tripping the light domestic again, as in dozens and dozens and dozens of other plays.

Quickly Mr. Albee let us know that something less real was afoot, something tending to confirm our suspicion that there was a touch of outer space about that room. Robert Moore, a neighbor who might have pursued Miss Bel Geddes had he not admired liquor more, drifted in at the sliding windows. Mr. Nelson and Miss Bel Geddes did not hear him, though; they were on the instant transfixed, staring front glassily. For Mr. Moore was about to slip into that other outer space that exists at the footlights between the actors' world and our own, there to confide in us. "The months turn, people live and die, but I just wander around," he murmured, chuckling at us; he then went on to explain that he was very rich and that he might leave these pleasant folk his money when he died.

By the time he was finished with us, and had turned to join the action to which he did and did not belong, we understood that we had been nudged a little bit out of frame, placed three degrees south of simple belief. We were going to look at the events of the evening with his detachment now, and when Miss Bel Geddes, winning as could be, made a little joke about his going down to the basement and shooting himself promptly so that his money would come to them sooner, we didn't mistake it for an ordinary light-comedy pleasantry. We were planted on Olympus, at quite a cool distance, and we suspected that she might just possibly mean it. Mr. Albee wanted it that way.

He continued to want it that way as Beatrice Straight made her first appearance. Miss Straight, all lacquer and eyelashes held together by a smile like the crescent moon, was right out of Snow White, though her gold dust took the form of exceedingly green bank-notes. Graciously, and in private, she offered Miss Bel Geddes $100 an hour if she would go into prostitution, afternoons only. Mr. Nelson need not know, no one need know, many a greenhouse could be bought with the proceeds. Miss Straight did brush shoulders, swiftly and silkily, with others as she was arriving and leaving. Everyone whose shoulders were brushed by hers described her as a fairy godmother.

Now Mr. Albee had his game area laid out. This particular suburban household was, however subliminally and however precariously, poised in a never-never land in which fantastic things could happen quickly. We did notice that the essential happening was not all that fantastic: it was only a few years earlier that newspapers had excitedly informed us of the existence of a hurry-into-the-station-wagon ring of matronly whores. Yet the elevation into gold-dust artifice and out-of-frame comment had, or should have had, its clear advantages. Miss Bel Geddes could grasp Miss Straight's proposition with no more than one sharp twitch of her pretty head. She could accept it without going to the mat with her middle-class conscience; her thirst for greenbacks took care of *that*, thank you very much. When the money began to arrive in bundles big enough to suggest that Mme. de Pompadour was a novice, Miss Bel Geddes could lie to her husband with the sweet skill of an old pro. Mr. Nelson, asking the fewest possible questions, could clutch the newfound treasure to his heart, a liberated man. And all of the neighbors could be asked in for cocktails, so that all of the neighborhood wives could be revealed as colleagues in Miss Bel Geddes' chosen line of work. The vision thus conjured up might not be so brazenly heartless and cantankerously outrageous as the distorting mirror Ben Jonson would have made of it, but it was nosing in that direction. Space had been shaped to take a fast curve, ordinary belief was out of bounds, reflexes were smoothly styled. We were seated above the goings-on, looking down in bemused, if somewhat grisly, detachment.

Except that one thing went thunderingly wrong. Mr. Nelson began to behave like a human being. When he did discover what his wife was up to, the information went to his stomach, not to his brain. Suddenly nerves, flesh, pride and sickened affection took the place of the ready-made, impeccably oiled responses that had helped the play's polite puppets take their first seven-league steps. Wrenching his disbelief out of himself with a groan, unable to stop the spasms that turned his crumpled face into an exploding tic, he thrashed his way about the stage with the fury of an animal freshly blinded, sank at last into a humiliated defeat holding his soiled life in his hands.

Mr. Nelson, please note, did all of this quite brilliantly, just as Miss Bel Geddes shifted from a sunny calculation to quavering dismay without any sacrifice of personal grace. And, clearly, Mr. Albee had had in mind all along that we should begin at a level of light domestic cartooning and then descend into the abyss until we shared Mr. Nelson's revulsion with him.

We wouldn't and we didn't, even as we admired the performing. For the play had been precisely, judiciously built *not* to contain this sort of emotion. Genuineness had been banished, ordinary psychology outlawed, from the fairy-godmother outset. We had tried to suspend belief step by step, in order to let the author get on with his cold and impertinent argument. Now we were asked to feel, though the play had atrophied feeling in its eagerness to arrive at this point. It was like trying to stand on a landing from which we had ruthlessly removed all supports. Our stomachs turned, too, as we realized where we were. Our revulsion, however, was not with the black comic content, not with the behavior of the people, not with the reflection of a society that can condone prostitution of the self while taking a lofty attitude toward Negroes and "kikes." It was a revulsion with the play as play, with a form that was trying desperately to disgorge what it had not been created to swallow down.

Fundamentally, the distaste we felt for *Something in the Garden* was a distaste for Mr. Albee's misplaced seriousness. He had pretended to write a cauterizing comedy he never had been willing to write. The moralist in him was much too much for him; he was impatient with style and tone and the very detachment he seemed to insist upon; he could not wait to tear his little cartoons to shreds. Nor did he really wait until the moment of Mr. Nelson's awakening to let his private contempt show through; that was only the moment of most explosive disapproval. The fact that he detested what he was drawing seeped through all of the earlier portions of the conceit as well, preventing him from doing his lighter and more artificial work properly.

The beginning comedy was half-mast comedy, indifferently brushing in almost-*mots* on the order of "I can tell a lover from a friend," "How?," "Because in this country they're seldom the same." Mr. Moore's conferencier, perfectly well played, was a most curious conferencier: though he left the action to share secrets with us at the footlights, he had no secrets to share. He knew less about the principals than we did. Mr. Moore was an artifice with no real function except to *be* an artifice; perhaps that was why his language was so sticky.

When it was time to lay in the moral platitudes that constituted the true purpose of the play, they were baldly, literally laid in. "You're all killers and whores," Miss Bel Geddes was forced to say, heavily underscoring what we should, in a slyer play, have deduced for ourselves. The platitudes were not worth the seriousness, or the formal struggle, that had gone into them: love of money as the root of all evil, the news that we are all whores pretending to bourgeois virtue, and so forth. The taste of ashes on the tongue—yesterday's ashes at that—was constant.

We need waste no tears here paying last-minute tribute to Mr. Albee's talents. Wrong as the play was in its moment-by-moment and then in its final effect, we listened to every word that was spoken, commanded by the author's deliberateness, alarmed by its self-destructive drift. Mr. Albee's capacities were not at all in question. His pointlessly convoluted, stylistically perverse use of them was.

THE VIEW FROM THE MIRROR

After the Fall resembled a confessional which Arthur Miller entered as a penitent and from which he emerged as the priest. It was a tricky quick change, sometimes an almost imperceptible one; but it constituted a neither especially attractive nor especially persuasive performance.

I speak of Arthur Miller directly because the play seemed, quite simply and virtually all of the time, to be about its playwright, not at all about the shadowy alter ego he called Quentin. It seemed to be about Mr. Miller for two reasons, one of them less important than the other.

The less important reason was its patent use of the author's relationship with the late Marilyn Monroe. We were given no cause for doubt here, not in calling her Maggie or in describing her as a cabaret singer. In production, after one brief and appealing scene on a park bench, actress Barbara Loden swiftly acquired a feathery blond wig, a pair of pajama tops, and a moistness of eye and lip that led us without hesitation to the bridal gown, the broken contracts, and the suicidal dedication to sleeping pills by which we still chart in our nightmares one of the legendary careers of our times. About half of the three-hour evening was consumed with the hero's earnest, desperate, harsh and grating efforts to love this girl, to manage her, to chasten her, to save her. We did not attend to the scenes as though we were following characters in a play. We attended to them as though we had been given Mr. Miller's former address, and asked in.

The use of the materials, however personal, however intimate, need not have been fatal. Mr. Miller is a theatrical craftsman who has earned our respect. A craftsman can always be granted the freedom, indeed the right, to draw upon any sources meaningful to him. We shall not think him insensitive so long as he puts to this clay an imaginative hand, making something new, independent, complete and self-assertive of it.

It was here that the play failed most seriously, for there was no Quentin, no other man, no other life than Mr. Miller's. The nominal Quentin began by speaking to us as though we were on the other end of a telephone. He was exposing his mind to us in tiny bits and pieces, circuitously, sweepingly, handling the past like so many loose kites bobbing helplessly in midair. His father hissed disbelief as he was told of his wife's death; his mother pounded at a door with a child's sailboat in her hand, frantically; his first wife turned her back on him, in bed and in the living room, because he was cold and remote.

He struggled for the secret of his remoteness, his failures with at least three women. He seemed to find it in his promise, to all of them, of limitless love. But no man could ever have kept such a promise, he now knew. What lesser promise might he make that would be worthy of a man? He brooded, soliloquized, lectured, shouted, shrugged. In all of his search, however, there was nothing

concrete, nothing carved out of bone. The search was verbal, pontifi-
cal, rhetorical.

He had no sooner cried out, "We are killing one another with
abstraction!" than he went on to say, "This is a city full of people,
this is a city full of loves." But "people" and "loves" are themselves
abstractions. Vague, general nouns tumbled over one another. We
heard about "compromise" and "power" and forever about "truth"
("It is contemptible like all truth, covered like truth with slime!").
We heard, in a first-act sequence reliving the plight of former fellow
travelers reduced to telling on one another, that "They took our lust
for right and used it for Russian purposes!" Jason Robards, who first
played the role, seemed to be whirling a vast lasso of spinning words
above his head, aching to rope real emotion and to bring it slapping
down. He could not do it.

Because the playwright had not stood off a little distance, just
enough distance to imagine one other man, he ended up seeming to
discuss himself, to indulge himself, and in some measure, with
Jehovah's thunderbolt in his hand, to justify himself. Many of us
found this *mea culpa* disingenuous. Why, when the same charge
might as easily have been lodged against Eugene O'Neill in the
matter of A *Long Day's Journey into Night?*

I don't think the answer has much to do with the fact that
O'Neill waited until the members of his family were dead, and
indeed left instructions that all of us were to wait for the play until
he himself was dead, before displaying the drunkenness, the dope
addiction, and the lacerating domestic fury that had been the environment of his youth. Time is not of the essence.

A degree of detachment is. In dealing with such materials, and if
such materials are to be truly tamed and shaped, an author's eye must
move in two ways. It must first surrender its own claims, its egocen-
tric right to stand at the center of the universe taking the measure of
all things and passing judgment upon them. It must slip into a side
pocket, into a nearly neutral corner where the light is not so blinding
and where it may be able to see clearly, as O'Neill's did. The young
O'Neill is the least important, the least assertive, of the four major
figures in A *Long Day's Journey into Night,* a pale but observant
wraith looking, looking, looking—and trying not to judge.

Mr. Miller, instead, thrusts his hero into the center of things and makes him that center—sole reality, sole arbiter. We are given to understand that the fragmented and dispersed action we watch takes place inside the hero's head. To follow this conceit, we must imagine that head expanding until it has encompassed the stage and all the people on it, until it contains the whole visible universe. All that exists is bounded and defined by one man's self-centered reaction to it. The eye is "I," and the "truths" we see are wholly subjective. But we do not trust a wholly subjective truth.

Ideally, as an author's eye moves some distance away from the things it hopes to describe, it also finds itself free to move upward, downward, around, across. It begins to see in dimensions, to note weight and line and color, to build up an image out of sculptural properties—an image that will at last have the independence to live and move on its own. Having detached itself sufficiently to become in effect a third party, the eye is in a position to create.

Here we had only the view from the mirror.

THE OTHER ARTHUR MILLERS

"We invent ourselves" was the desperate summary Arthur Kennedy made of two possibly wrongheaded lives in Arthur Miller's *The Price*. We choose the roles we mean to play—the role may call for martyrdom or rebellion or whatever occurs to us at the moment of choice—and then wear the costume until it fits so snugly that it may, in the end, serve as a winding-sheet. And all the while it may not have represented us, really; it may even have killed what was most generous and best in us. A man may well wonder, as he looks down at the dusty policeman's uniform he wears or at the skilled surgeon's hands that now tremble a bit, what other uniform might have become him, what other work the tiring hands might have done. Thus the near conclusion of Mr. Miller's interesting inquiry.

It was interesting, in spite of its very evident thinnesses, for a special reason. Sometimes during his career as one of America's most admired playwrights—or at least as a playwright of whom much was expected and then demanded—Arthur Miller would seem to have been very busy inventing Arthur Miller, carefully and most consciously wrapping about himself the cloak of seer, prophet, founding father and dormitory prefect. We rather expected this Arthur Miller to pontificate; we may have wondered whether it was proper to applaud or to genuflect upon leaving the theater. With *The Price*, though, the master moralist had suddenly relaxed in two ways, and while I am in no position to say who the real Arthur Miller or the secret Arthur Miller or the total Arthur Miller may be, it was fascinating to catch a glimpse of two faces of the man we hadn't quite seen before. Fascinating, and attractive.

The first of the unfamiliar faces was an astonishingly droll one. Mr. Miller has never been much of a man for leavening his work with comedy, certainly not with comedy that is gentle and even forgiving toward an essential cynicism. Mr. Miller has never really liked cynics, compromisers, manipulators. But in the person of an ancient used-furniture dealer, going on ninety and carrying eggs, salt, and Hershey bars about with him for energy, he had literally opened an attic door to let guile in, guile with a scalawag charm to it.

The dealer shuffled in at the attic door, making his way through the dust on unsteady stork's legs that seemed to settle twice with every step, because two estranged brothers had come briefly together to dispose of the family belongings, remnants of the market crash of 1929. The building was to be torn down, and everything—the gaudy cracked harp in the corner, the Motorola radio, the gramophone with its Okeh Laughing Record still on the turntable, the chandeliers and fencing foils and tightly rolled rugs—had to be got rid of. The dealer was asked to name a price.

He was wonderfully patient about not getting to it, nibbling at the treasure trove he kept stored in his bulky overcoat pockets, admiring the family he so benevolently wished to serve, displaying such candor about his tactics that the tactics came to seem heaven-sent favors. When Kate Reid, wife to one of the brothers, pointedly announced that with every little delay she could hear the price going down, he clapped his hands for joy. "I like her, she's suspicious," he exclaimed, a seraph who had always surreptitiously admired devils. Suspicion was fine, it added zest to life, even though it was rather wasted on such an elderly fellow, a fellow who'd really retired and whose name—as he suggested—must have been got out of a very old telephone book. "I smoked all my life, I drinked all my life, and I loved every woman who would let me—so what do I need to steal from you?" was his philosophical answer to the urgencies of money-minded folk. Money was not for him. And the price went steadily down. The writing was softly sly, trickily inverted, and—this is what's important—affectionate. If Harold Gary was extraordinarily funny in the role, playing it as though he'd slept in it and had just turned out for a stroll, Mr. Miller himself displayed a becoming strain of wry kindliness.

The second and not altogether familiar face Mr. Miller offered us was one of uncertainty. His play had no real ending, and that was a dramatic defect in it. Two brothers badgered one another, all but knifed one another, all evening long; the fencing foils in the corner would have come in handy for the emotional work they meant to do. But when the work was done, and a hundred home-truths had been rooted out of them, they were no different. Whatever they had learned in the scorching match was powerless to alter the cut of the costumes they had so long ago adopted; they left as they had entered, blind enemies, and the effect upon us was dry and unresolved, rather as though we'd followed a good detective-story for nineteen chapters only to discover that someone had torn out the twentieth and last.

But his very inability to imagine a handy solution had a kind of retroactive effect upon Mr. Miller's management of the situation in mid-flight. It made the author rather more troubled and rather more human and it put him to the task of making each detective-story twist and turn—as two people dug for their identities—independently arresting, inch-by-inch vigorous. Occasionally there was too much vigor: certainly director Ulu Grosbard or the author himself ought to have suggested to contestants Pat Hingle and Arthur Kennedy that a roar becomes more exciting when it is interrupted by an undercut. Someone should have come in fast but low once in a while. Some of the surprises that were tossed in to keep two angry men regularly off balance were less than plausible, the Erle Stanley Gardner line "All right, I'll *tell* you what happened!" occurred too often for complete comfort, and the characters continued to have that sensitive cigar-store-Indian flavor that haunts Mr. Miller's work. Mr. Hingle was a boulder, Mr. Kennedy shivering steel; they were more nearly natural elements than observed people, and they spoke across a valley.

Nevertheless they made us listen; we wanted to dog them through each step in their bullheaded bout of self-discovery. We wanted to know why there was a cold reserve in Mr. Kennedy's eye when he was at his most gracious, why Mr. Hingle seemed ready to dissolve only to flare into fresh, implacable distrust. Mr. Kennedy was the son who had abandoned the family when the Depression wiped it out. He had gone on to become a successful doctor and had paid the price of his isolation: his wife and his health were gone. Mr. Hingle was the son who'd stayed, cared for a destroyed father, given up his own schooling and wound up profitlessly patrolling a beat: self-appointed martyrdom had come at a price, too. Now neither could be certain that he'd done what he did honorably. But neither could abandon a role adopted at such cost. Two men were in a bind, writhing to get free of it.

It was the bind itself that generated the energy of the play, not any promise of salvation. Which meant that Mr. Miller had come down from that mountaintop he has sometimes seemed to inhabit and got into the ring. If participation—with no conclusion foreseen—pushed him into melodrama, all right. If it forced him into patches of disbelief, so be it. Let's see how the footwork might go.

The sheer theatrical footwork went very well. And the necessity of slugging it out, without a clear moral planned beforehand, brought the playwright just a shade closer to us. We observed him feverishly at his work; we even caught him out at his work. But we knew he was involved in other men's troubles.

THE SOUND OF SELF-PARODY

During 1963 the town talked all season long about the fact that our most prominent and productive playwrights had, virtually to a man, come forward and failed. Instinctively, we tended to lump the lot together and say that the old guard was passing indeed, that a time of irrevocable change was upon us. This might or might not have been true. It was not really true, however, that all of the failures could be viewed in the same light, as though a single wave of the past had now broken upon the shore of eternity, breaking all of the old talents and all of the old molds in the process. Lillian Hellman, for instance, failed precisely because she was trying something new.

There was a possible link, though, between the failures of Tennessee Williams and William Inge, and it did have something to do with habit, with retread, with pressing on nerves that had been pressed too often before.

The unfavorable reaction to the excesses of Mr. Inge's *Natural Affection* was probably not going to cure Mr. Inge of his determination to present all men and woman as uniformly sick, any more than it was likely to cure the theater of its eagerness to see how graphically sickness can be illustrated.

True, the laboratory smear this time cracked in two before its author's eyes; audiences found themselves tempted to snicker at the sheer malodorousness of his specimens even as they continued to admire his technical craft. But while a playgoer might have come out of the theater whistling "They've gone about as far as they can go," he knew—in his heart—that they hadn't.

Someone was still going to write an entirely earnest play in which there were more open wounds per square foot of stage space than Mr. Inge had assembled for diagnosis. Admittedly, this would take work.

The next man up would have to carry us beyond (a) the mother who neglects her child while rolling around on the apartment-house bed with an insecure ex-bartender who won't marry her; (b) the son who develops an incestuous longing for his casual mother, molests a girl in the park, does a stretch on a work farm where he is whiplashed by sadistic guards, and ends his visit home by putting a carving knife through an appetizing blond stranger; (c) the woman across the hall who prowls the building's corridors in succulent pink pajamas waiting to leap at any man who will interrupt her obligations to her truly loathsome husband; (d) the loathsome husband who is either showing himself dirty movies or getting himself sodden drunk, and who spends Christmas Eve proving he is not a "faggot" by undressing himself, and attempting to undress his wife, in public. As I say, the dramatist who was really dedicated to "facing up" to the ugliness that stains this universe would have to assimilate these things, or their medical equivalents, and then go on from there. But one or another playwright would do it.

One would do it because shock value is thought to be commercial value, and in order to be more talked-about than the last man it is necessary to draw upon more and odder fears and fetishes. Another would do it because he honestly believes that this is the way the world is, because he knows the audience is peripherally aware of its own psychological unease and is willing to try to understand the contemporary condition by seeing it magnified or even distorted on the stage, and because certain of these very materials have, when held in a certain proportion, yielded up in the past substantial fragments of felt truth—as Tennessee Williams has so often demonstrated.

There is no precise point at which anyone can ever cry "Stop!" for the simple reason that no one can anticipate what the creative writer's intuitions will stumble upon and refine in the process of work. The rest of us can discover flaws, but only a playwright can discover a play; some very good plays have been discovered in very dark closets.

At the same time, the moment may very well have come for our playwrights to listen more carefully to themselves. If no one can properly tell them exactly what to do, they must become more exacting critics of their own doing, with their ears alert for the excess that makes the bubble burst. What they must learn to hear is the sound of self-parody.

The sound was to be heard, I think, in both Mr. Williams' *The Milk Train Doesn't Stop Here Anymore* and Mr. Inge's *Natural Affection*, though at slightly different levels of vibration.

Mr. Williams permitted himself the following scene, with caption. A dying harridan, Flora Goforth, was determined upon one last seduction. She wished to present her once-fabled body to a perpetual innocent who drank milk and wore lederhosen, and she had already tried to bribe him to her bed with food and cigarettes, though without success. As a final wile, fresh from a bath, she stepped into a warmly lighted room just offstage—leaving the door open so that the young man's view was excellent—and removed her bath towel, throwing it out to him as she began a verbal and visual inventory of the delights of her flesh.

The young man stood rooted to the spot, apprehensive, transfixed, the bath towel limp in his hands. Finally, he spoke.

"I came here hoping to be your *friend*, Mrs. Goforth," he said.

That, I submit, would take very little touching up to make a Peter Arno cartoon.

The self-parody in *Natural Affection* was not quite so assertive, partly because in this particular calendar year Mr. Inge was writing what he did write vigorously, whereas Mr. Williams was writing palely and more vulnerably.

But it was there, poised, ready to swoop down and destroy. When Kim Stanley's adolescent son came home from reform school for the holidays (you see, we were nearly in trouble already), Miss Stanley was fiercely determined that her unemployed lover should accept him as a house guest and help make his visit a festive one. It seemed that the year before when the boy was home he'd spent the entire time holed up with an ancient whore, who had paid him for his services.

"I'm going to show him a good time *this* Christmas," she insisted.

One hesitated to consider what she had in mind.

Other squeaky instances of borderline burlesque could be cited from both plays, but I'm not going to bother because this can become a form of baiting. What is wanted is not ridicule from the outside but a greater sensitivity at the source, within the playwright—not simply a sensitivity to pain or to peril, but a sensitivity that sets off an alarm bell whenever the sore spot is being scraped too hard or whenever the peril is becoming too much even for Pauline.

Why Mr. Williams and Mr. Inge should finally be caught out battering away at themes and devices that threaten to play jokes on themselves is not easy to say. Obviously, by this time each man may have worked his favorite theme over too often and too ruthlessly (Mr. Williams has shown us predators devouring an innocent at least four times, and *Natural Affection* was Mr. Inge's third flirtation with a fleshly romance between mother and son). These preoccupations may be now so drained of any vital juices they may have had that they can be forced into further action only by flaying. There is the further possibility that each man has concentrated so intensely on a single aspect of human suffering which seems important to him that he can now see no other aspect—not even of suffering. Bringing one thing into absolute focus can make it sharp and impressive. By isolating it altogether from the balance of the human landscape, it can also be made into a monster. Cruelty, carried far enough, can turn into Al Capp. A relaxation of the angle of vision, together with wider and freer observation, is probably the best way to ease eye-strain—and is no doubt called for in both cases.

FLOODWATERS

Like the characters in Tennessee Williams' *The Seven Descents of Myrtle* who were prepared to cling to the roof for dear life while floodwaters rose through the house, I was prepared to cling to the play. Whatever the rising winds may have been doing to three people trapped in a shaky relic of a homestead, the prevailing theatrical winds were right. Mr. Williams had stopped trying nervously to imitate the absurdist fantasies of the generation nipping at his heels and was neck-deep in materials he had mastered before: all the fears and frustrations and violent invasions of privacy that come of lust and pride in tandem. There was always the chance—it seemed a very good chance—that our finest playwright would for the ninth or tenth time declare himself.

And so, in the process of clinging, I began to play a little game of Blame. Things were subtly off, gestures tended to pull back before they could quite be completed, shadows roamed the downstairs kitchen and the rickety stairway restlessly without asserting themselves as more than shadows. Who's to blame here? I asked myself sharply, aware that the writing had some attractive overtones, the situation a sharp initial interest. I settled on director José Quintero first.

Why had Mr. Quintero been so careless as to permit a whole first faraway shouting match to be played unintelligibly? At curtain rise, a swarthy, hip-booted Chicken (Harry Guardino) was doing his chores under an overcast sky. Neighbors passed in a car offstage, paused to scream at him. All we really needed to know was that they were not truly friendly, that Chicken was in some sense a loner. But we scarcely got to know that much in the vocal screech over the wind; we were forced to deduce it for ourselves when the roar had subsided and Chicken had gone surly to his quarters, there to nuzzle a photographed nude with oversize breasts. (The floodwaters might or might not have been taken to stand for sexual energy, but that is a matter for later.) The evening had begun insecurely, its emphases and even its words unformed, and Mr. Quintero could easily have fixed that.

When Chicken's half-brother (by a "very different" mother) arrived in the person of Brian Bedford, bleached hair reaching to his shoulders, to display a silly goose of a girl he'd just taken for a bride, our curiosity came thoroughly awake. Mr. Bedford seemed fonder of the faded parlor than he did of his bride ("These drapes are velvet drapes, neglected lately"); he was quick to remember how to clean the pendants of a chandelier (his mother had taught him how); he was eager for his wife to misrepresent him to his brother as a "strong lover." We watched him, alert and puzzled. What had a bride to do with this evasive frond of a fellow, pursing his lips as though they could defend him from a world coming too close? More than that. Young, why did he seem to get about on an old man's bones?

Halfway through the first act he took a sudden tumble, crashing to the floor between kitchen and parlor, unable to rise by himself. If we were surprised, we were not surprised properly. There had been no rhythm to make us ready for the fall. We'd heard Mr. Bedford cough, we'd seen him walk like an ache, and we still hadn't come with him to the topple. In a flash, a single thought filled our heads. Kazan should have directed the play. He'd either have paved the way to the moment for us or hit us hard with its shock value. Quintero had left us between, disbelieving. And surely Mr. Quintero had *asked* designer Jo Mielziner for those cramped acting spaces: a parlor in which no one could move on impulse, an upstairs bedroom tiny and remote as a pop-up greeting card, a crucial staircase squeezed into place so treacherously that it seemed made of crumpled paper and plainly could not be negotiated with any sort of dramatic force. Yes, the fault was in the staging.

But still. Listening to the addlepated, slightly past-it bride chatter on about her onetime companions—all dead or deranged now—in a tawdry show-biz act, watching her ignore the accumulating truths about her new and virtually unknown husband (when Mr. Bedford asked not to be hated for having concealed the extent of his illness, she blandly replied, "When I love I don't hate"), we became aware that something other than the physical façade was out of sync.

In my own game of Blame, I turned my attention to Estelle Parsons, fussing about as the new bride. And in fact it was as easy to rebel against Miss Parsons' performance as it was to be half taken with it. The role was extremely well written. This girl—motherly, vulgar, vulnerable, pathetically confident of her own blowsy charms and yet frightened of using them—belonged, or nearly belonged, in the Williams canon of rattled women. You could overhear Blanche du Bois or Alma Winemuller any time you cared to strain enough; you could also overhear the differences, the little traits of cheapness and loyalty that distinguished her and insisted upon a personal identity card.

But the part wouldn't come whole, wouldn't rise out of the echoes to say "No, listen to *me!*", wouldn't detach itself from the green-and-white-striped wallpaper to stand and move as a cohesive shape formed of many shades. It was bleached. We saw the good things Miss Parsons was doing. This bride was at last told that though her husband owned the house and would like to leave it to her, he had weakly deeded it to his brother. She was to retrieve the deed, by any means; that was what he had married her for. As the actress decked herself out in the come-on finery of her vaudeville act, a preposterous failure in feathers, to stalk her prey in terror and on unsteady spiked heels, she indicated in severe outline all of the erratic responses that were meant to move us. Awkwardly parading herself like soiled merchandise, gasping and sputtering as asthma and fear contracted her courage, stammering into vacant bursts of silent laughter, crouching helplessly beside a trapdoor that might drop her into the waters below if the man standing over her decided that she should be dropped, Miss Parsons provided us with a complete and most accomplished catalogue of Attitudes to Admire. We did not forget how good she'd been in *Bonnie and Clyde*.

At the same time we were aware—and appalled—at what her voice was doing to us and to the part. Miss Parsons had elected to play the entire play at the shrill, colorless, fake nightclub pitch she used when she was screeching her way, deliberately tinny, into a half chorus of "Cuddle Up a Little Closer, Baby Mine." It was as though a complex woman, hurled into every sort of bizarre posture, were being funneled to us through the nasal single-note of Adelaide in *Guys and Dolls*. Coloration vanished, crisis piled on crisis without any shift of sound, identity itself became blurred under the constant calliope pressure. What would this girl have been like, how rich might she have seemed, if ever she'd changed key? We were forced to filter a graphic performance through an earache.

In the end, though, the dodges wouldn't wash. Mr. Quintero might have helped more, Miss Parsons might have tried less hard. But the play was not filling its own outlines, wasn't coming up like the flood that was so constantly threatened. There was a reluctance about it, a caution about possibly saying too much too soon, that rather resembled Mr. Guardino's reluctance to enter the action. For most of the play, Mr. Guardino simply prowled the lower back room of the house, uninsistent, hiding out, sneering when approached but without the moral force to initiate any one confrontation.

I suspect that this hesitation was more Mr. Williams' than the character's, and it might very well have come from an apprehension about stirring memories. Aware that a faint Blanche du Bois halo hovered about the girl in the case, Mr. Williams might have drawn his hand back from prodding his potentially explosive Chicken too urgently. He might have turned out to be Stanley Kowalski. In any case, the author avoided him, let him stew on his own terms without telling us what those terms were, postponed and postponed him until it was too late for him to affect the vital movement of the play. The play went all one-sided as a result: everything that happened happened tentatively from upstairs. The passive characters were forced to carry the action—and carry it to a man not wholly present.

And it was difficult for Mr. Williams' girl to assume so heavy a burden because she was not herself moving from one clear pole to another. The play ended with the assertion of Chicken as life-force; only a sexual partner could save Miss Parsons from the flood. She had to join it to endure it, leaving her impotent "husband" behind. But if this was to seem a kind of advance or even change, and if Miss Parsons' terror in approaching it was to be emotionally justified, the girl had to begin at some other point on the fever chart. She had to be frigid, or sick of sex, or in some way desperately committed to neutrality. She wasn't. It wasn't clear what she was, or where she stood, in relation to the last-minute scurry toward sexual safety and a possible future. If anything, she seemed to be promiscuous from the outset; various perfectly good jokes were made about her just happening to be standing "on a street in Memphis, for no particular reason." Thus there was no troubling transition to be got through: you felt that Mr. Guardino could have wrapped up the play whenever he wanted to simply by snatching the girl's wrist. One end of the play's lifeline was unanchored.

The Seven Descents of Myrtle, then, was unfinished, not so much ill-conceived as unrealized. With some luck and some openness and some urgency, it is possible that it could someday be finished. Mr. Williams has rewritten plays before, including—as in the case of *Summer and Smoke*—some that scarcely needed the careful after-thought. There were things to be salvaged here: an environment, a provocative symbolic structure, a girl of idiot but actual quality, effective contrasts, whole blocks of language that were teasing in the familiar Williams way. I'd still hate to see them lost, flood or no flood.

In any case Mr. Williams should be accepted as a permanent house guest: a status for which our theater makes no provision. Mr. Williams had now come a cropper thrice running, and, as though the hostile reception given his earlier *Slapstick Tragedy* wasn't good enough for him, he had been more or less embalmed by the Broadway morticians. We tend to conjugate careers: a man moves from "is slipping" to "has slipped," and there is no reversing the orderly progression of things. The morning after becomes all mourning after, with no sense that the interment may be premature or the failure of energy temporary.

We all know perfectly well that the creative impulse is an erratic one, given to inexplicable disappearances for very long lost weekends and then turning up again, without apology for having been away, in remarkably fit condition. Oscar Hammerstein once took an ad to proclaim his ten years of disaster; the very fact that he could pay for the ad indicated that disaster was now done with. The capacity to do confident work comes and goes, and we will all do well not to get our tenses wrong.

But a playwright of stature should be protected during his off hours, weeks, and years, made to feel at home and not exiled to Macedonia. Above all, he needs the hum and throb of his own creative powers about him, present not as dim memories but as live evidence. Consider how happily inconsequential occasional failure must have been—apart from a brief gnawing at fingernails—for Shakespeare or for any of his most productive contemporaries. (Mr. Williams is our most productive contemporary, as well as our American best.) A playwright attached to a permanent acting company which has kept his more profitable plays in repertory is in a singularly indestructible position. He can afford to write *Timon of Athens* any old time, and afford to forget about it, because *Hamlet* and *Lear* will go back on the boards to fill up the vacant space. He is literally a continuing playwright, pride of the pack, still at his best because his best is still on view. Minor accidents are of no importance; his self-assurance surrounds him. That is probably one reason why you can get a *Tempest* at the tag end of such a career.

I don't mean these remarks as added mourning, as a lament for lost practices as well as for Mr. Williams' mishaps. I wouldn't bring the matter up if we hadn't had quite recent testimony to the feasibility of what may seem a daydream. Less than a year before *Slapstick Tragedy* Mr. Williams' *The Glass Menagerie* was revived as an independent production on Broadway. It managed to keep itself there for five or six months. *The Rose Tattoo* was later done separately, successfully. Considering that *The Glass Menagerie* and *The Rose Tattoo* are only two out of eight or ten revivable plays the author has given us, it is almost conceivable that a Tennessee Williams company might be formed and not founder too soon for want of material. It might also spur the creation of new material, and so prove self-generating.

Well, I'm not seriously advocating that we build one house for one man. That might put rather a strain on any author, and wear out the audience as well. But what is really to prevent someone from banding together a handful of playwrights, each with a backlog of reputable and hopefully still viable work, so that what exists as past glory might be turned to present comfort? More than comfort. The confidence that comes of being current.

We feel a good many obligations these days, obligations to brand-new work, obligations to very old work that hasn't been done properly in years. But we might make room, somehow, for one more; we might accept the obligation to keep in-between work alive. For only in that way, I think, can we make it in-between work and not the end of something. We may then see that *Summer and Smoke* or *Suddenly Last Summer* comes in between *The Glass Menagerie* and who knows what? It would be good if we could stop thinking in terms of inevitable periods and have at least one playhouse devoted to commas.

9

FREE ADVICE

CUTTING

JUST A WORD to playwrights. Don't cut the first twenty minutes.

The figure is hypothetical, but I have been thrashing about trying to explain to myself a phenomenon that constantly plagues Broadway. The curtain goes up on a play. Various characters enter, and we run through our programs to establish their identities. The characters exchange a few hasty remarks, and suddenly—much to our surprise—they are screaming at one another or bolting out of doors. Comedy or straight play, we are swiftly in the thick of things. There is noise, motion, and, in the play's brain, a slight trace of dizziness.

The play has plunged into its middle without quite having begun. I don't mean to say that everything thereafter is pace, punch, and passion, right down to the homestretch. Very often such a play, for all the clamor that is going on, seems as slow and as sluggish as the months of midwinter. In fact, nothing really slows a play down so much as not having had a slow beginning: if you've missed the introductions and never really discovered who all those people in the room are, a party can be dreadfully monotonous.

But the flaw, often fatal, is lately a very common one, and there are pressures which bring it into being, pressures which ought to be resisted and which we may as well discuss as part of our own resistance movement. On one recent evening, after I had filed my review and while I was driving home in the gloom, my wife turned to me and asked a question. "Will you kindly tell me," she demanded in a tone that hinted I might have written the play, "what that play was *supposed* to be about?"

It was a good question, because the play was an ordinary one, cast in a perfectly familiar domestic vein, and certainly everyone in the theater had followed—all too clearly—the comings and goings, the caterwaulings and the reunions, that had taken up nine-tenths of its acting time. But behind all of the activity there ought to have been a *why*, and she'd missed it. Everything was intelligible except the first little push on the lever meant to set the machinery in motion: the play hadn't had a starting point.

If I was able to answer the question, it's not because I am any brighter than the ushers (though I sometimes wonder about that as people who have crawled past me crawl back again in order to crawl into some other row) but because I have been training myself, pen at the ready, to jot down the very first, and generally the only, three or four lines near a play's opening that have something to do with the cause of it all. If a character stretches out with a tall Scotch and says he's happy, I make a note of that. If a friendly psychiatrist drops by and mentions in passing that our character is *too* happy, I put that down, too. Chances are that these two seemingly innocuous remarks, never to be amplified or so much as repeated in the long course of the evening, constitute the entire driving force of what is to follow, and if I'm not quick about it I won't be able to answer my wife's questions, let alone write a review. As it happens, on this particular occasion these two lines *did* constitute the whole plot, or at least the prime cause of it, and if confusion reigned later it was because playwright and actors had treated the lines as though they were embarrassing family skeletons which ought to be clapped into closets as quickly as possible.

I said that there were pressures operating on the playwright to reduce his exposition, his formal introductions, his establishment of plot points, to a minimum, and there are. As a rule, when a playwright first writes a play he writes out his preparatory stages at length. After all, he himself is just getting to know the people, their habits, their hopes, and so he lets himself go on paper until he feels he has settled down with them, snug as a near neighbor, after which he has a degree of acquaintance to build on. Probably, in most cases, he overwrites the opening scenes—a bit. But once the play is put into rehearsal, or opened before an out-of-town or a preview audience, these initial scenes suddenly seem three years long and obviously the product of an encyclopedist.

There are two fundamental reasons why they now seem so long, so wordy, so lazy. Everyone connected with the production by this time knows the plot. It's the oldest, most obvious, most dismissable factor in the proceedings, grasped in its entirety many months ago before a single actor was hired or a single stage ashtray purchased. As the song says, it's like breathing out and breathing in, and people who have been around for a while quite forget that they are breathing at all. Now they can no longer bear to listen to the simple basics learned by dawn's early light, cannot endure the laborious repetition of what they have come to take for granted. And so, if the show is overlong and needs cutting, their eyes fasten greedily upon what most bores *them*. Snip, snip, snip, go the scissors—and out of the play come most of the vital statistics. The first stretch to be tackled out of town or at previews is, inevitably, that opening twenty-minute stretch, which usually arrives on Broadway as one fast Scotch, downed in not more than one hundred and twenty seconds.

In the meantime, of course, what has been forgotten is the audience, which hasn't the faintest notion of who these characters are (or were) or what they had in mind when they were so loquacious on paper way back in a writer's room. Backstage, in Boston, a notice should always be posted: THE AUDIENCE DOESN'T KNOW THE PLOT.

The other reason for ravaging the first twenty minutes—this is especially true of comedy but applies to soberer ventures as well—is that no response can be felt welling up in the auditorium. The audience is silent, in effect uninvolved; silence is always held to be ominous, and until some clear sign of emotional involvement can be detected all authors, directors, and producers pace the parterre in panic. This part of the play isn't getting over, isn't "sending" them. Naturally everyone chafes at the bit to get on to the good scenes, the big scenes, the scenes that crackle and pop. If only the deadwood can be got out from under, the show's collaborators tell themselves, we'll start fast, hit hard, and get to the marvelous drunk scene half an hour earlier. And off to the races they go, leaving a litter of small life-studies behind them.

The curious thing is that they never do achieve runaway force any earlier, after all. It still takes the audience twenty minutes to warm up, to dig in, even to hear properly—which means that some of the good moments the producers were hurrying toward are now no longer good moments but effortful ones. And the damage in lost information, in theatrical map-making, can be severe. Nervous writers and directors should take what comfort they can from some sage's hallowed remark that "any audience will give you the first act," meaning that the customers never really wash out a show unless it's still bad after the intermission. Heeding this advice, our craftsmen can set about their laying-in of fundamental pieces with patience and fortitude and scissorly restraint. Momentum will sooner or later be necessary; but to begin with it's nice to know the score, even the players.

COUNTING

Logic, that ancient nuisance, is generally conceded to be rather more important in the theater than it is in life. In life we allow for all sorts of coincidences, because we keep bumping into them daily. We're always running into the very people who told us they were going to be out of town this week; and people who have been sitting together, profoundly silent, for hours on end *do* open their mouths simultaneously to say exactly the same thing. In life we know that the scales are rigged by an insane demon who has the drop on us, and we put up with the preposterous simply because we have to. But when we go to the theater we demand that the demon not be given a seat beside us, or even permitted in the building. What happens upon the stage is supposed to follow a course which, unlike true love, runs smooth. A nice little cause begets a nice little effect, and all their descendants resemble them. When the play is over, it has been plausible in a mathematical, rather than a listen-to-what-happened-to-me-yesterday, sense. In short, we have been looking at a fantasy, which is what strict logic is.

But yes and no. Put coincidence into a play and everybody in the bleachers will yell "Foul!" Put too much logic into a play and the whole thing may crumble before your astonished eyes. The theater is like the weather: fair, if it doesn't happen to rain. The theater is inexcusable: it insists upon absolute coherence until it gets it, whereupon it looks sheepish and ashamed of itself. The theater stands staunch and incorrigible on a spot exactly midway between logic and lunacy, and woe betide the man who cannot intuit its quicksand temper.

For instance, I spent months one season trying to figure out the precise instability that had overtaken a bit of stage business used in a quick failure. The play presented us with a passionate middle-aged woman who couldn't, just couldn't, keep her hands off a very young lad. In the circumstances she did what women always do, on the stage, these nights: she shot her fist forward and tore open his shirt. We are here in the realm of the logical but unlifelike. That is to say, if a woman is mad for a chap and the chap has a shirt on, it is certainly logical for her to want to shred away that shirt; even I see that. On the other hand, no one has ever torn *my* shirt off—not since I was five years old, anyway, and that was done by a mean fat kid down the block, who was not even a girl—and I cannot, as a result, be persuaded that the situation is lifelike. Of course, it is always possible that I am not the type who has to fight them off and that other men everywhere are having to deal with this problem all the time. But I know a man who works in a laundry and he tells me that my shirts come in looking just about like your average shirt—not unduly mauled—and so I dismiss this possibility with some relief. I am insecure enough as it is, and don't need further shaking from playwrights whose women are all mad things.

But the shirt itself isn't the essence of the matter. In the particular scene to which I am referring, the woman ripped the fellow's shirt straight down the front so that all the buttons came off. *All* the buttons. That's what I can't believe. I believe a good woman could get three, maybe four, buttons at a single swipe, depending on her reach and physical fitness. I believe that one other button might suffer strain, so that it would be left dangling there by those two threads that generally linger for a day or so before giving up. But I believe, and I cannot be talked out of this, that at least one button would remain defiantly in place, and that it would either have to be unbuttoned or subjected to a second decent rip.

My experience is that some buttons are vulnerable to the least little tug and that some buttons can't be dislodged without the help of one's mother, one's wife, or one's surgeon, and when I go to the theater I want to see a balance struck. I want to see the mess of life duplicated, with all of its gritty resistances, to a reasonable degree. Logic, okay. But let's respect the scientifically observed behavior of buttons, too.

The thing is, once you let dramatic logic get the upper hand it goes crazy with power. It never knows when to quit. For instance, you may think that in the play in question the playwright, riding rough-shod over nature in his anxiety to make things speedy and keep things neat, was content with that clean sweep of six buttons. He wasn't. A short while later it became necessary for the principals to find those severed buttons. The young man was putting his shirt back on preparatory to leaving the apartment and facing the world again, but it was perfectly clear that unless someone sewed him up he was going to face not only the world but a probable bronchitis. He and his sure-fisted friend therefore dropped to their knees and began searching about on the floor to see what buttons they could retrieve. Listen carefully, now. In no time at all, they found *all six*.

You see the problem here, the insoluble clash between logic and life. Logically speaking, they had to find those buttons pretty quick. The audience wasn't going to wait all night while a woman and her lover crawled around on the carpet getting the palms of their hands dirty. Drama calls for a certain expedition, a certain—what shall we say?—getting on with it. Audiences tend to leave the theater around eleven o'clock. But who do you know that *ever* found all the buttons they were looking for? And right off the bat, too?

Chances are that you can always find one button by stepping on it, though of course in that case it will break. You can reasonably expect to find another by the dodge of pretending not to look for it: I have discovered that if you just sit in a chair, avert your eyes, and hum to yourself for a little while, the button—challenged and frustrated— will voluntarily force itself upon your attention. You could probably get a third by removing the furniture to the sides of the room and shaking out the carpet. But beyond that—nothing. Buttons, as I have known them, are not friendless, subservient little creatures pining away for the touch of a remembered hand; they do not stay where they are in hopes of a pickup, or cluster together like so many volunteers eager to serve. They are proud, ambitious, and resolutely far-ranging, and I say that if six get away only three come back. You could live the rest of your life in that room and find all sorts of treasure: nickels in the sofa cushions, matches wedged between the floorboards, hairpins in the ashtrays; but you would never again see anything you could plausibly sew to a shirt. And that is why, as I watched the actress calmly gather the six and just as calmly affix them to the shirt, giving no hint whatsoever that she was involved with the miraculous, I began to disbelieve *her*, too. Disbelief is a disease; it creeps from the inanimate to the animate, corrupting everything in its path. Let one thing be *too* unlifelike and dramatic necessity will get you nowhere. Here logic had gone just three buttons too far.

BELIEVING

There's nothing else for it. If a playwright is going to write seriously, and be taken seriously, he's going to have to make us believe in good people.

That's a large order these days, when we've all become accustomed to the notion that we're wicked through and through, but I see no way out. Evil has plainly and simply become a fun thing.

Take Norman Mailer's dramatization of his own novel, *The Deer Park*, as a not unrepresentative example. Mr. Mailer is a moralist and concerned with unmasking evil wherever he finds it, which is everywhere. He finds it in bitch-goddess mothers, in bisexual sons, in ladies of the evening in the evening and in the morning. He finds it in patriotic aviators and in movie producers, in pimps and in pretty young call-girls who are really and truly looking for love. I'm sure he'd have found it in the backstage electricians if they hadn't had a union to defend them from such canards, and I imagine he's still taking a long look at the ushers. What *does* go on when those little flashlights go out?

There was no one in *The Deer Park* who had not been daubed with the mark of Cain, and everyone in *The Deer Park* had been sullied not once but twice or thrice. The characters seemed willing to bait and betray one another, bedding down betweentimes, seven nights in the week and then to play Wednesday and Saturday matinees besides. They were, make no mistake about it, corrupt.

And how did we respond to them? We waited eagerly for the next laugh. We didn't recoil in horror from Rip Torn's carefully slimy, sleepily smirking cynic: we watched him almost idly offer his current mistress the sleeping pills that would shut her up permanently; we listened to him proclaim his virility while snuggling up to a male who had his own interests to get on with, and—Mrs. Grundy forgive us—we smiled. The murkier the stage got, the deeper the mire, the more we were amused. Indeed, we waited for the next outrage with the confident expectation that it would be even more outrageous than we could possibly have imagined; and we waited with a glint in our eye because whatever is outrageous enough always has the taste of a joke about it.

Mr. Mailer is of course not blind to the fact that unmitigated evil invariably creates in the viewer a happy impulse to hilarity. He played directly into this truth, "used it," as actors say. Wherever he could, he caricatured, turning grossness of mind and greediness of appetite into dancing cartoon-shapes, veritable Mr. Magoos of malice. His greatest success came, surprisingly, with that cliché among clichés, the Louis B. Mayer–type movie mogul.

Will Lee performed the antics, which included dive-bombing blond starlets who didn't want to marry homosexuals and blowing kisses across the flat of his hand at creatures so loathsome that even he kept his sanitary distance, and if Mr. Lee was superbly over-wrought (even his thinning hair seemed excitable) the role had been cunningly imagined to begin with. The cliché breathed under Mr. Mailer's heart massage. When this tycoon modestly dismissed a compliment on his own acting ability with the firm statement "I can't act, I'm too sincere," we knew that we were in the presence of a grotesque with a real genealogy, a goblin who believed in himself. Inevitably, during the play's eighty-odd scenes, we waited for him to come back. We knew that he would always put us in a good humor because he was so totally (and therefore so sincerely) a fraud.

Mr. Mailer exploited the undercurrent of comedy that exists—and is bound to crop up—in all visions of massive corruption in certain other, less satisfactory ways. A curly-headed young star spoke with callous indifference of a girl who had killed herself out of unrequited passion for him, then broke into a toothpaste-ad grin as flashbulbs went off about him. This sort of irony was stock; but it did remind us that the author was once again trying to beat a tittering audience to the punch. He wanted to paint the grin on evil before his audience did it for him.

Before pursuing the point, I should mention that the evening was not dull (except for the last fifteen minutes), that a decent tension was sustained even when the play was merely circling its cesspool (the author has an interesting knack for breaking scenes into two and three pieces without letting the pieces fall from his hands), and that the overall atmosphere was genially freakish rather than repellent.

But that does bring us back to the point. Mysteriously, the moralist's passion for rubbing our noses in it, for showing us how thoroughly defiled with pitch all those who dare to touch pitch come to be, for parading degeneracy in full bloom and painting all clouds bruise-purple, invariably provokes in an audience a demonic grin, a compulsion to giggle.

This seems always to have been the case. In medieval drama, it was the Devil who turned into the first Fool. He was much too damned to be treated seriously. Think of a play in which *all* of the characters are wicked and you'll find yourself thinking of some comedy by Ben Jonson. It is difficult *not* to think of Nero or Caligula as a joke. Sobriety just can't survive too much depravity. The foul pestilences around Hamlet eventually become too foul for earnest philosophy; Hamlet takes refuge, then, in exasperated wit.

Not even the theatrical innocence of the nineteenth century could be sustained for too long: eventually everyone saw what was funny about villains as deep-dyed as the notorious Jem Dalton, whose mustache was so black, whose exit lines were so sneaky, whose soul was so unredeemable. *Ten Nights in a Barroom* was probably pretty stark for its time; its time didn't last long because laughter caught up with it so quickly.

Who's Afraid of Virginia Woolf? is ninety-percent funny (on purpose, but also unavoidably). There is something in human psychology that responds to uniform venality with a twinkle. Whether the twinkle is believing or disbelieving I can't say (probably slightly disbelieving; usually this kind of cackle comes from having spotted a disproportion of some sort). In any case, the man who wants to mount a vision of unrelieved chicanery, of utterly conscienceless behavior, had better *be* a comic playwright or the audience will rather quickly turn him into one.

Serious drama, on the other hand, seems to derive from a concern for goodness, from an effort to paint or at least to very desperately pursue virtue. Oedipus is a good man. All things considered, it would be hard to think of a better one. Antigone is nearly perfect. Hamlet is a splendid fellow who wants honesty, chastity, loyalty, and friendship to rule the world. Othello is a figure of such stern integrity that it takes Iago an excruciatingly long time to make him do so much as one wrong deed. The hero of *A Man for All Seasons* is careful to do nothing wrong. Willy Loman only wants to be liked.

All of these "good" men must tangle with evil, of course. They are meant to inhabit our planet, where evil is. But the successful *seriousness* of each play grows from the effort to sustain virtue, to achieve justice, to find rectitude. We become sober in proportion to the persuasiveness with which the struggle toward virtue is recorded. Whether the struggle is successful or unsuccessful doesn't matter too much. No one smiles at Oedipus for all the mess that he makes. We don't listen to *Death of a Salesman* anticipating the next pleasantly outrageous joke. A play escapes comedy when enough of its principals behave well, or at least mean to. And when the playwright can make their goodness convincing.

Mr. Mailer, by the way, could not manage this last effect, and it was as he turned to a film director who had done his best to behave decently over the years that *The Deer Park* became pompous and more than a bit foolish. Good deeds and high ideals were here recorded in language that was both inflated and empty. Mr. Mailer's knack is for the nastiness that, in its everlasting insistence, diminishes man enough to make us snicker at him—and that keeps us, in the end, from being able to take what we are seeing seriously.

Generally, we don't think of vice and virtue in these reversed roles. We think of vice as our most serious concern and hastily conclude that the play most deeply immersed in it will therefore be most serious. If we think of virtue at all, we think of it as something so unlikely and so fabricated that honest men must snigger at it. But it works the other way around, I'm afraid. Whores and wastrels, wasps and wantons, almost always wind up amusing us. It is those intensely earnest, lamentably square, doggedly determined clamorers after virtue who make us think, and worry about them, and frown.

NAMING

A simple truth that our dramatists are going to have to relearn is this: a statement of fact opens the world wider than a vast, indefinite summary does.

In trying to make plays mean more, playwrights so often make them mean less. No playwright today wants to limit his statement to an isolated instance. He doesn't want to say that the action takes place on 12th Street, at 2 o'clock, in April. He doesn't want to say that his heroine came from Chicago and that she came, during winter weather that frosted the steam on the windows, on the Pennsylvania Railroad. He doesn't want to say that anyone ate a tuna-fish sandwich for lunch and then went shopping at Klein's, where garden hoses were on special sale that day.

He is fearful of producing nothing more than a diary; the day of the sociologist's nitpicking for trivia, or of the psychologist's absorption with case histories crammed with unique and unpredictable detail, is pretty much done. The new playwright shuns narrowness, particularly the narrowness of seeing his characters as individuals or their acts as independent gestures. He is after life at large, life as it is lived by the generality, life as someone viewing it from the perspective of another planet—broadly, impersonally, grasped whole from a great distance—might see it. He wants *all* of it, not a piece; and to get All he must suppress the particularity of parts.

So he tells us that the play takes place "in one room," perhaps, but he is careful not to say more. If we ask "one room of what?" as

we glance about the bare concrete walls, we are refused an answer by
the deliberate design. The place is not a place—not a house, not a
hotel, not a museum, not a prison—so that it can be everyplace. No
matter where we may choose to go, in our meaningless shiftings of
foot and gear, we are always here, at this standstill, in this permanent
and "universalized" human environment.

"The time is now, as it could be," the program informs us, crossing
our eyes so that vision shall be indistinct. "As it could be" means, of
course, that it is not really "now." If it *were* now, no hypothetical
subjunctive would be necessary or possible. Each half of the sentence
deletes the other. Actual time, like actual place, has been deleted in
the process.

"There's not a house on the street with a number on it," muses the
principal character of another such play as he stares into undivided
space. The cancellation of numbers, of separations, of identities, is
conscious and very careful. Whatever is concrete, localized, or recognizable must be erased from the face of the earth.

Why? In theory, so that we shall be able to see the face of the
earth—see it in its totality, however bland, however blind, as we see
the face of the moon. Playwrights want us to know the ultimate
story, all at once, without comforting distraction along the way.
Names, places, dates, familiar things are all comforting distractions:
we become caught up in them, because they are so tangible and so
immediate, and lose sight of truths larger than they are. If we wish to
face larger truths we must surrender all of the smaller ones.

Well, there are justifications that can fairly be offered for the
method, or at least for the impulse that prompts it. The small play of
individual psychology, especially of aberrant individual psychology,
has indeed been drained dry by this time. Some sense of universality
is desirable: the world is bigger than any one man's case history and
we are all looking around to see what things we share, even what
dangerous things, what destructive instincts, we share. But the universalized method, as it is now most often practiced, does not work.

There are no more vacuous plays, on Broadway or off, than those
which promise us this sort of expanded vision. We look at rooms that
have become universes and we see neither rooms nor universes. We
listen to characters who have no names—sometimes they are given

generic labels such as Father or Grandfather, or, in coyer pieces, Fa and Grandfa—and we agree that they deserve no names: they are, collectively, no one. We study behavior which is significant only in having no immediate significance, or even interest. If a character falls asleep within two or three minutes of the beginning of a play and never awakens thereafter, we may understand that he represents an area of Silence, a disappeared chord, in our lives; but we cannot pretend that he has been a person worth meeting for the evening. If a character spends a great deal of time trying to flush a toilet that will not flush, we may very well realize that the toilet is meant to stand for something bigger than it is, perhaps bigger than the man is; secretly we expect him to be swallowed down the bowl, completing the symbolism. But the action proper—as prolonged as it is imper-sonal—could be of genuine interest only to a plumber. The pursuit does not engage us, particularly since in nowhere it doesn't matter whether a toilet flushes or not.

The reaching playwright has overreached himself, shot his arm past everyone else's elbow without so much as grazing it, bumping it, touching it. He has so divested himself of the actualities of our days that he is impotent to haunt our nights. What's Hecuba to us if she did not live in Troy, if she did not have a husband and sons, if she is not now awaiting the mailed fist of a named conqueror? Inside the generalization there is no kernel of fact—the kind of fact we are—to keep us company. Because we are in no way related to the disem-bodied figures onstage—we don't drink their coffee, they don't ride our buses—we cannot share their vast destinies, either. The moon view fails. We need a snapshot in our wallets before we can get to know all mankind.

The principle isn't new, of course, but it obviously needs hammer-ing home again. The best way to intimate universals is through practical particulars; the best way to know all men is to know one man intimately. One fully realized actuality will buzz and nearly burst with great big hints, whereas a broad hint that is only a broad hint—with nary a fact to feed on—will come to ground with a *whoosh*.

I was much struck, while reading Thomas Pynchon's novel, "V," by the power a handful of tangibles have to move in two directions at once—to draw one precise face and to suggest, through the lines of that face, a thousand others. Let me quote you a passage from what is actually an experimental novel dedicated to striking, through selected specifics, broad overtones:

> That night Profane shaved, bathed, donned suede jacket, levis and big cowboy hat and went a-roving down Kingsway, looking for amusement. He found it in the form of one Brenda Wigglesworth, an American WASP who attended Beaver College and owned, she said, 72 pair of Bermuda shorts, half of which she had brought over to Europe back around June at the beginning of a Grand Tour which had then held high promise. High she had remained all the way across the Atlantic; high as the boat deck and mostly on sloe gin fizzes. The various life-boats of this underelict passage east were shared by a purser (summer job) from the academic flatlands of Jersey who gave her an orange and black toy tiger, a pregnancy scare (hers only) and a promise to meet her in Amsterdam, somewhere behind the Five Flies. He'd not come: she came to herself—or at least to the inviolable Puritan she'd show up as come marriage and the Good Life, someday soon now—in a bar's parking lot near a canal, filled with a hundred black bicycles: her junkyard, her own locust season. Skeletons, carapaces, no matter: her inside too was her outside and on she went, streak-blond, far-from-frail Brenda, along the Rhine, up and down the soft slopes of the wine districts, into the Tyrol and out into Tuscany, all in a rented Morris whose fuel pump clicked random and loud in times of stress; as did her camera, as did her heart.

This girl, Brenda, appears late in the novel and has very few more lines devoted to her. But no more are needed, here or ever. The girl is as tangible as a toy tiger and the black bicycles, concrete and complete in a paragraph. But so are the thousand girls not named Brenda who constitute one dizzying time-of-our-life mass, girls of the junkyard, clicking their cameras. The vision is double, evocative both ways.

Getting back to the theater, we can always take another look at Tennessee Williams' *The Glass Menagerie* for further evidence. The play is made up of what are described as memories and what are certainly gestures as graphic as facts: a mother cannot pass her son without dabbing her finger at her tongue and using the moisture to flatten down the boy's cowlick. The detail is homely, prickly, exasperating, sorrowing. The alley in St. Louis is real and really in St. Louis. But the play, so anchored in reality, has infinite room to breathe. If it inhales Mr. Williams' fact, it exhales everyone else's. A mother's maddening gesture is translated infinitely across the auditorium, becomes other gestures of other mothers and then something more than that, becomes the harrowing of love as all men know it. *The Glass Menagerie* touches everyone by touching home base first, says more than it seems to by saying some things exactly.

CHEATING

I'd spent an entire evening looking at television, for reasons we will not go into now, and as I watched show after show flip mechanically by, including some movies which had been sold down the golden river, I found myself constantly and severely oppressed. Scarcely ten minutes passed without direct and deliberate violation of the image I was looking at, almost as though some evil genie were determined to challenge the validity of each succeeding frame by imposing an alien frame upon it, and in the end I had the sensation that (a) I was seeing double, and (b) double is nothing.

Let me explain. A dance team, lovingly introduced, had begun to stomp out a rhythm, with an encompassing swirl of cloaks, and I had begun to attend to the patterns with as much interest as I could bring to anything so overpraised to begin with. Then, sixteen or eighteen beats into the act, a swift flow of words, blocked out in capital letters, suddenly invaded the screen, moving with resolute importance from right to left across the dancers' feet. We were getting a news bulletin about an important event of the day, and we were getting it—miracle of miracles—*without* its interrupting the program. Thanks to the electronic trickiness which has meant so much to our culture, the dance could go on, the news could be assimilated, and all without wasting so much as one second of our valuable time.

But of course the dance *was* interrupted. As soon as the printed words began their authoritative march, our eyes leaped to them. Nothing so alerts the world nowadays as a news bulletin appearing in an out-of-the-way place. And by the time the message had been grasped—it turned out to be inconclusive, and might well have waited till midnight—the beat of the feet had been blurred, the build of the patterns had been cracked, the dance was dead. Whether or not it was a good dance, whether or not we missed anything, I can't now say. We had been effectively prevented from seeing the dance as it was intended to be seen.

Even so, that is not what distressed me. I'm missing dances on television all the time without worrying too much about the loss. What was most violently wrong with this ingenious use of the medium was that it called attention to the characterlessness of the medium. It told us that we were not watching a dance at all, we were watching a television show—a mechanical, prearranged, readily manipulated *thing*. Indeed, the medium was busy expressing contempt for itself. It did not regard its having captured a dance on video tape as anything of value, as anything in the least worth preserving; it regarded it as a stretch of neutral material extending a certain length of time which could be used to occupy a vacuum tube so long as nothing else was occupying it. Nor did it attach any particular importance to the news bulletin, either. If it had, it would have given it separate time. As things stood, it simply threw two different things into the tube at the same moment—feeling proud of itself, no doubt—because it did not consider either of the items worth the undivided attention of the viewer. The medium, freely violating its promise of either entertainment or information, wound up acknowledging that —in its own estimate—it had no particular identity at any particular time. It could cancel itself out because there was nothing it believed in as inviolate.

I will not go into the dozen or so minor defiances of eye by ear that kept reminding us all how impersonal and how indifferent to any sort of significance the strung-together programming was, though I would like to record my own frequent descent into near madness whenever I tried to read the rolling credits that followed most programs. I read credits because I am interested in identifying actors I haven't seen before, and sometimes because I want to know the name of the director. But the practice has grown up—we are in the presence of contempt again—of superimposing on the credits a sound track extolling the virtues of some other program to be seen later the same evening or perhaps next Tuesday night. I find it virtually impossible to fix new names in my head while announcers are simultaneously tossing dozens of other, irrelevant names at me, and I have finally decided that if television doesn't care who those actors and directors are, neither do I.

The business of habitually dismissing what is being seen as of no particular consequence, however, has consequences. The habit is catching, and it goes some way toward explaining, I think, the willingness of actors of some distinction to appear in commercials. On the evening in question, at least two performers for whom I have considerable admiration appeared briefly as pitchmen for one or another product. "Why not?" I suppose they say to themselves. "Especially since the money is good and everybody knows it's only a commercial, anyway." In effect, they are trusting the audience not to believe them. But there is a very good *why not* for such people. They violate their own images, deny their professions. Invariably they identify themselves ("I am So-and-so") in the course of the commercial. But they are plainly, appallingly not themselves, not as we have known them, not as we have admired them. In each case the personality we have learned to like dissolves, queasily, and a hollow, somewhat self-despising substitute, neither actor onstage nor true man at home, takes over. Suddenly actors, too, become *things*—not people but objects that can be bought, used, manipulated. We are less likely to be entranced by them next time we see them on stage or film.

Film itself has over the years damaged itself by corrupting the matter seen and heard. "Process shots" violate the form—unstable backgrounds that do not match the players in front of them—because they warn us that we are not seeing what the camera says we are seeing. The camera lies about itself. Dubbing comes to the same thing: little slips in the lip synchronization make it swiftly clear to us that we cannot believe what we hear. Once again there are unlooked-for consequences, as I was reminded during my evening of viewing. If, for instance, a director makes a film he knows is going to be

dubbed, he naturally sets about his task in a certain way: he composes as many of his shots as possible to conceal lip movement, so
that it will not prove troublesome later. He may now drive you up
the wall with endless "reaction" shots, so that you are always looking
at the person listening rather than the person speaking. This ultimately produces a certain Martian effect, or at least suggests that all
communication is by walkie-talkie. Or the director may decide, as
so many directors have done, to solve the problem by shooting over
the actors' shoulders, so that we catch the muscles of one cheek
twitching but never do see any performer's mouth. The effect in this
case is to make every filmgoer his own Peeping Tom. One film I
watched for a while presented me with such a forest of shoulders that
I thought I'd never see a human face again.

Well, out of all these careful denials of what was actually going on
I thought I saw a blessing for the theater. In the theater, once the
curtain was up, the actors couldn't be cut, spliced, angled, or trod
over by block letters; they were on their own and what they seemed
to be doing they had to *be* doing. The theater was not subject to a
contradiction of its own terms.

Then, alas, I came upon that now celebrated nude male figure in
Marat/Sade, and I knew I was wrong. What other forms can do—
cheat themselves by claiming actuality while canceling it out—the
theater can do, too. In *Marat/Sade* the actor playing Marat rose from
his tub, his back to us, and moved forlornly upstage. The image was
meant to be shocking, not in the clumsy sense of being sexually
shocking—to speak for myself, I had come two hours earlier from the
steam room of a health club and was probably not going to be
stunned in any case—but in the sense of exposing man, as a species,
for the pitiful, helpless, essentially naked thing he is.

The moment had a purpose. But to achieve that purpose and to
subject us to shock it had to persuade us that we were indeed looking
at poor, shivering, ravaged, unadorned man, at vulnerability bare.
Unfortunately, perfectly visible between Marat's skinny buttocks was
a narrow clamp of some sort, obviously designed to support, and to
defend against visual mishap, the actor's genitalia. On the instant we
were not looking at naked humanity; we were looking at a protected
actor and wishing him safe-conduct. It was a wonder we could hear

the next ten minutes of dialogue for speculating on precisely *what* sort of device the property man might have rigged up. What was intended as dramatic shock became mild amusement. By pretending to offer what it could not securely offer, the image confounded itself, calling direct attention to the mechanics that made it a half lie. Not so much as a half lie could be afforded here, because the image was meant to be uncompromising. The theater had, after all, found a way of compromising itself.

FEELING

I have sometimes thought that when the twentieth century is finally consigned to a paragraph in the history books, or when it is finally represented by a single piece of statuary in a very long corridor in the Museum of Time, the image it will leave us as a legacy will be that of a perfectly decent-looking man, rather youngish, with his face screwed up in a small spasm of bewilderment and self-doubt, cracking his knuckles and staring outward vacantly because he is really staring inward, repeatedly asking himself, "Why can't I feel anything?"

In short, he will look rather as Hal Holbrook did in Robert Anderson's *I Never Sang for My Father*. Mr. Holbrook began the evening by coming toward us—it was necessary for him to confide in someone and we, perhaps, were history—to speak in a low-keyed, candid, honestly reflective but faintly fussed way about an emotional relationship he could not bring into being. For as long as he could remember he had wished to love his father. No, that is not the right way to put it. He had wished to *feel* love for his father. The old man was near death now. The feeling wouldn't come.

As Mr. Holbrook turned away from us to pursue the object of his frustrated ambition, to circle the eighty-year-old tyrant who was all too happy to have his son sit beside him silently before an endlessly glimmering television set but who could not face that son and embrace him without hedging, the focus of the evening shifted firmly to

Alan Webb, crusty, filled with false heartiness, demanding, commanding, and sealed off on his own mountaintop. Mr. Anderson had written the part, and Mr. Webb played it, with a kind of spiky reserve, never cheating, never sentimentalizing, always stopping just short of making an intensely *present* man likable. He was there, in all of his contrary colors; we were not expected to hug him.

The detail, in its fustian and in its frosty detachment, was beautifully worked out. Mr. Webb, frail but fond of Schrafft's and the Rotary Club, was eternally, expansively ready to buy his grown son a drink. He had never noticed, however, exactly how grown that son was—he was a widower on the verge of a second marriage—and so invariably ordered the lad a Dubonnet, inducting him slowly into the mysteries of manhood. There was talk of death all about them, there was even a funeral; at the cemetery the old man could not place one of the headstones, that of the son's dead wife. He remembered, of course, with an automatic "of course" when he was reminded. The patriarch was self-made: he would repeat, at the drop of nothing at all, the whole sterling saga of his rise; he would even write it out all over again in answering a simple note of condolence on the death of his own wife. At his own wife's funeral, he never spoke of his wife; his attention was centered on himself and on the mother he had buried so long ago ("She was a little bit of a thing").

He was affable. Accept his invitation to dinner at a restaurant in town and you would hear jokes. The jokes were the same jokes, clapped out with fresh confidence. If the family couldn't laugh this time, Father had a ready retreat. "Just trying to get a rise," he said, face beaming and flushed with triumph. He was seriously obtuse and pleasantly obtuse. After wife Lillian Gish had died, he wouldn't have a housekeeper on the premises. Not *alone* with him, he confided in all goatish innocence. He was tough. The son would by God live with him, freshly remarried or no. And when he was tucked in for the night, he was a wrinkled scarecrow in pajamas. No surprise that Lillian Gish had died before he did, though. He'd been calling attention to her failing powers—not quite gloating over them, mind you—for years. He'd been barking, "Can't you turn that thing up?" at her and her hearing aid all along, unaware that she could hear him when she chose.

He was a prickly bastion, a fortress flying a deceptive flag of friend-liness, fending off in his contrary variety all efforts at penetration—astringent in the writing, superbly armored in the playing. You believed in the firmness with which Mr. Webb put his arms halfway about Mr. Holbrook's shoulders, and also in the decisive withdrawal that said halfway was quite enough. You believed, too, in Mr. Hol-brook's interior desperation as he turned to mother Lillian Gish and sister Teresa Wright for help. Miss Wright's advice was to cut off and cut out, as she had done earlier when Dad had resisted her marrying a Jew. Miss Gish would have freed him of his unfinished search as well, though in a subtler and less possible way. She would have had him leave them both before they became "burdens." But her very generosity was an unwitting trap. She could not realize that her unwillingess to become a burden became the greatest burden of all. The actress held to a very fine, cautiously controlled line as she balanced, ever so gently, her practical love for a martinet and her practical love for a son she could not really help. For she stood midway in the relationship; she too was something between, her love of both a barrier between them both.

Barriers to feeling, then, were the meat of the play. They were also the method of the play: we were not to be let in where Mr. Holbrook was left out. But this whole matter of feeling and not feeling had certain curious effects upon the way the play worked in the theater and, apparently, the way it made audiences respond. For one thing, the evening was inevitably a sustained standstill. Mr. Holbrook did not wish to do anything. He only wished to feel something. That meant that we were simply to stay with him while he tried, futilely, to stir a kind of response in himself that the object of his aborted affection was drawn not to invite. We could not move; we could only examine impregnable aspects of character. We were going to repeat without advancing, end in stalemate. This difficulty, on the whole, was very nicely taken care of by Mr. Anderson's ability to sustain on the stage prodding confrontations between two people, by the strict discipline of the performing, and by the private-eye intensity with which director Alan Schneider kept narrowly after his quarry, never letting his emotional have-nots out of sight or off the hook.

Yet there was a further difficulty. What, and how much, were we to feel? We were not to feel for Mr. Webb what Mr. Holbrook could not feel; that would have made an ass of Mr. Holbrook, or at the very least kept us from understanding him. I found myself fascinated by Mr. Webb, and even developing a grudging respect for his cock-of-the-walk energies; but I didn't exactly like him, nor was I meant to. (Such a double play is undoubtedly possible, but it would require an ampler vision, a kind of poetic umbrella, that Mr. Anderson's spare speech and tethered characterization did not aim at.) Were we to feel for Mr. Holbrook's absence of feeling, then? Tricky.

Still, it was probably this last invitation that seemed to split the theater down the middle on opening night. Around me I could see various members of the audience dabbing at their eyes; I could also see a great many who weren't, as I wasn't. No doubt those of us who sat interested but unmoved felt thoroughly guilty about it.

And this may be the nub of the whole matter. In the twentieth century we are inclined to feel guilty unless we can respond, with every pore open and every nerve quivering, to each and every opportunity for love. Because those opportunities are infinite we are certain to wind up frustrated, accusing ourselves of heartlessness, nagging at our psyches because emotion won't always come. It is not even love we are after. Love just might consist of knowing and then doing, understanding and acting generously toward what is understood. What we demand of ourselves is the *sensation* of loving, a ready tingle of the flesh, a tickle at the stomach, a warm and gratifying glow that stirs in the bowels and suffuses the whole body until the body is persuaded that it is totally involved, totally sensitive, all athrob with participation. Mr. Holbrook demanded this of himself in the play: he could not bear it that he felt so little sitting beside his father, watching a western. Conceivably Mr. Anderson has demanded it of himself at one time or another and so wished to write about it. I suspect that those who did cry in the theater had brought some of their tears with them, rightly or wrongly, out of past failures to feel all that they held themselves responsible for feeling, out of past guilts. I don't know.

I did sense that there was something excessive, something uncommonsensical, in the play as in the posture, an urgent need for a sensation that was out of proportion to the evidence offered. We

were given Mr. Webb, on a platter, to look at. In all honesty, was
there any need for Mr. Holbrook to feel anything more, or do anything more, than he had done? Some part of his suffering was
gratuitous, self-generating, as some part of the play was overinsistent,
asking more in the way of emotional return than its figures were
shaped to justify. This son's concern was altogether genuine; but it
was, after all, more for himself than for his father. "Why can't I feel
anything?" is the standard phrase we began with, and perhaps it
should be inflected to call attention to that *I*.

When we feel less than we feel we ought to feel (you see how
complex the matter is), are we being hardhearted or are we only
harassing ourselves? Above all, what are we focusing on, the figure in
need of care or the interior reassurance of caring? It's a puzzle, and a
universal pressure. The pressure may in the end create contemporary
man's most recognizable stance: a faint cringing in fear of not having
felt absolutely everything.

RESTORING

The theater has won a small and belated but I think decisive victory.
Ever since the night of Lincoln's assassination in April of 1865,
Ford's Theater in Washington had lingered like an untreated sore in
the American consciousness. The building was there, all too intensely
there for what had happened in it. It could be used, if anyone could
think how it should be used. An attempt was made to reopen it in
the very year of the President's death—as soon as the convicted conspirators were hanged, in fact. Two hundred people bought tickets
for an announced performance of *The Octoroon*. They were met at
the doors by a possibly dangerous crowd, by a troop of soldiers, and
by an order from the Secretary of War closing the building. Someone
had threatened to burn the place down if an actor dared set foot on
the stage.

Once it had been abandoned as a playhouse and later reduced to a
shell, the battle of morbidities continued. There was constant agita-

tion to restore it; after all, Mathew Brady had photographed it so thoroughly that even its ceiling designs could be flawlessly copied. But weren't the restorers' motives morbid? Why would anyone want to go into such a reconstruction except to feel that titillating little shiver of regret and distaste that the prying like to get in the presence of remembered catastrophes?

There is always something particularly garish about catastrophe in a theater, an obvious mismatching of intended gaiety and actual disaster, blood on the clown's face. The sentimentalists who wanted the playhouse back again were suspect: necrophilia in the wings, as it were. And of course those who so bitterly opposed the notion of brightly lighting what they preferred to think of as a tomb were plainly morbid, too. A place was damned by a deed; it could scarcely be passed without making a sign to ward off evil. With superstition on the one hand and a kind of corrupt nostalgia on the other, what good could possibly come of the battle or the bother? I am told that even now the government department that has so lovingly put every last bit of lace curtain in place—are you surprised to hear that the playhouse has lace curtains in its boxes?—is faintly uneasy about permitting continuing performance. What *do* people think and feel as they come ostensibly to be entertained?

I can tell you what I felt, and it surprised me. Although the President's box, with its flags draped out of symmetry just as they were when Booth's spur caught in one of them, asserts itself plainly and prominently at the right side of the auditorium, I spent no time at all thinking a man had been killed there. The only thing that entered my head was how much he had liked to come there.

The house makes the difference. It's an enveloping house, a rippling house, an easy embrace that makes a casual but unmistakable gesture of community. This is where to come not simply to see a play but to see neighbors. The stage is a graceful scallop, curving so far forward that it passes and absorbs the four boxes on either side, moves into the area where the audience is. The two balconies undulate in response to the apron, overhanging and echoing its outgoing impulse; they begin not at the rear or even halfway through the house but at the very point where stage and boxes leave off, seeming to link arms with the platform on which actors walk. To sit in the balconies is to hover over the stage, peering directly down into players' faces looking up. It is as though we had all gathered at first- and second-story windows to lean out and over a busy event in the courtyard. Heads don't quite converge, but you feel that they might.

The walls and ceiling are white, or a very lively near-white, infrequently broken by exceedingly simple line-decorations. This is, at first glance, astonishing. White walls, or even light walls, are thought taboo in our own playhouses, for most definite reasons. They pick up too much reflected glow from the stage, pulling our eyes away from what is going on under the proscenium, diffusing our attention as they attract needless notice to themselves. While a show is going on, who wants to be conscious of the auditorium proper?

As soon as you settle into the proportions of this playhouse, though, you see why the walls can afford to insist upon themselves. We aren't looking at the stage through a tunnel of darkness. We're in it, nearly on it, joined in the same friendly space. The actors' walls are our walls, more or less; we're more nearly in the ballroom of a mansion than in a corridor with a distant door, and it is proper that we should share the same gas lamps. Proper even that lace curtains should be draped here and there. Lace curtains are used in homes, and we have not gone all that far from home tonight. This is a meeting, not a magic-lantern show.

I should say at this point that the National Repertory Company, which opened the theater with a new staging of Stephen Vincent Benét's *John Brown's Body*, was by no means taking full advantage of the most striking characteristics of the theater. Contemporary acting and staging habits are not that easily broken, particularly by a company not overly imaginative to begin with. Director Jack Sydow was still in love with the vast deeps under and inside the proscenium; for the most part he huddled his actors there as though backstage were home base, letting them advance only occasionally—one or two at a time—to explore the resources of the courtyard we'd really come to. (Hadn't he noticed how the players' voices suddenly acquired timbre as they got past the curtain line, or how responsively audiences sat up on the cane-bottomed chairs when they felt they were at last being approached?)

This is a house, and a forestage, built for "asides," for full-throated confidences. It is the sort of place in which one actor can converse with one side of the auditorium, another with the opposite side, while all of us together hear and relish the crosshatched intimacies of both. At no time did Mr. Sydow attempt to explore the possibility, though the fragmented and impressionistic parallels of the Benét poem readily lent themselves to—even seemed to call out for—such felicitous simultaneity. Neither did the director ever escort one of his actresses to the wavelike lap of the apron and encourage her to follow its inviting swell, brushing eyes with us the long and supple way across.

Not until the second half of the entertainment did he use the one real virtue of combining backstage with forestage: that of propelling an actor out of the dark and distant reaches on a strong trajectory that seemed to cannonball him in our direction. (And when he did, the actor hesitated just shy of us, wary of our presence instead of welcoming it.) The Brady photographs, by the way, show that the scenic walls and doors for *Our American Cousin* were stationed flat at the curtain line, shutting off the area that was being most used in this production and making no bones about the fact that ideally the play is to be played where the audience is. It was immediately urgent that a play be mounted in this manner, not because there is any virtue in being piously antiquarian about nineteenth-century practices but because now that we have the building we should discover what it was built for. We have the decor; let us also have the experience.

Ford's is a fine laboratory, not just for research but for intimating change—for making our awareness of change real. We have no other house (nor do we need one; this will do) capable of suggesting to us the subtle social differences between an experience of theater at one earlier point in our history and our customary experience of theater today. We're much interested in altering our own overfamiliar and rather tired experience; if we weren't we wouldn't be spending so much time on arenas, on thrust stages, on pattern-cracking happenings. And though snuggling inside a sensation earlier than our own certainly isn't going to tell us what to do the day after tomorrow, it can help alert us to the fact that there are no theatrical absolutes and that some theatrical relatives may be cozier, or more direct, or even more binding than others. The strongest sensation I had on coming away from Ford's was that if Lincoln had lived he'd have been back next week.

The sense of his pleasure is stronger, much stronger, than the sense of his death. That is why I've called the reconstruction a victory for the theater: in effect, the stage's purpose has won out over Booth's. The house smiles. It is gregarious. It has a character and reflects a character. Going into it is almost like meeting a person. More like meeting one than losing one.

10
REPERTORY
IN LABOR

WHY *THIS* GRASS?

S<small>UGGESTED</small> <small>PRAYER</small> for actors, directors, and producers with serious artistic ambitions, to be recited daily or weekly as opportunity permits or fervor dictates:

"Oh, Lord, give me successes that are not simply successes but contain just enough quality to let me feel I haven't wasted my life. Give me long enough runs to pay my bills and then, when I am rich, get me into repertory. Let me make wise decisions with regard to my career, but when I cannot be wise let me be undeservedly lucky. Let me be praised, let me be paid, let me be proud. Give me the strength never to announce my plans beforehand, give me the grace to get through interviews safely, give me the fortitude to survive my collaborators. Humbly, I ask all this, and Sardi's, too. But, dear Lord, there is one thing I do not want. Whatever else you give me out of your unbounded generosity, never, never, never give me a building."

Buildings are the curse of the creative man. One has but to hear that a philanthropist has allocated seven or ten or twenty million dollars for the erection of a new edifice generously designed to house an acting company to begin shuddering. The pattern is all laid out in advance. First there will be lunches in boardrooms, cocktails for the press, and promises to the community that the American theater is about to have a permanent, stable, comfortably padded home.

An architect will be named and he will consult with absolutely everybody, trying to decide whether the dressing rooms shall be a quarter mile or a half mile from the stage, whether the auditorium shall be ski-sloped or shoebox-shaped, whether the stage machinery shall come up through the basement or down through the roof. With a confident smile, the architect will announce that he has satisfied everybody by compromising everything, and construction will begin.

During all the time of planning, and during all the time of construction (which can, mercifully, be a very long time), euphoria reigns undiminished. As the girders are slipped into place, between work stoppages, more and more happy facts become available to the public: this new building has overlooked nothing, it can accommodate eighty actors decently, store as many as eighteen productions for repertory, admit 1,200 or 2,000 paying customers each night.

It is only as the building begins to look dangerously near-finished that other, unseemly questions crop up: what actors, what plays, what customers? Board members now dig their gold pencils into the tables at which they sit, gouging out unsightly and utterly unilluminating little holes; some have even been known to raise their voices. "Something's got to open this place!" is the first scream of order. What's worse, it's got to be cultural. *The Merry Widow* can always be sneaked in during the summertime, but winter is colder and more high-minded; people wearing furs want class. But who's got the culture? Ellis Rabb? Roger Stevens? Herbert Blau? That fellow who used to be in Seattle? And where the hell *is* Tyrone Guthrie, anyhow?

The future is in the fire now, turning to ash. Mr. Guthrie isn't available to be *everybody's* building superintendent; Mr. Stevens has a building of his own in Washington to worry about (and don't take bets he's not worrying); Mr. Rabb's A.P.A. seems to be getting along on its own at the non-twenty-million-dollar Lyceum, and everyone else has a black mark against him (he's been successful on Broadway, he's never been on Broadway, he's been fired from three municipal theaters, he's been in one municipal theater for eleven years and must be extraordinarily unadventurous). The debate rages on while the marble façade gets its final polish.

Eventually, of course, a managing director is invited to enter the building, on tiptoe, with the board at his back. He is already in trouble. He is in trouble simply because the building, as the mountain climber said, is there. Here are mountains of money, masses of stone, acres of architecture, seascapes of carpeting, pyramids of promises all to be lived up to. The director enters a void big enough to frighten the most hardened existentialist. "Here," he is told as he is handed the keys, "fill it."

And he knows that he must fill it with actors who are not only bigger than Burbage but bigger than Rockefeller, with productions that do justice to Ben Jonson and Jean-Paul Sartre equally, with audiences in furs and audiences in pea jackets who mustn't cancel their subscriptions in fury after the first wispy season. Who wouldn't quail? Who wouldn't quiver? Who wouldn't fail? (It's often been suggested that the A.P.A. take over Lincoln Center's Vivian Beaumont Theater; the suggestion has always made me faintly apprehensive, because I've never wished to see an effectively functioning group take a building, as well as a production schedule, on its back.)

Good acting companies are not brought into being by monuments. They are created by being free to work where it doesn't matter much if they fail. In New York such a company would be most likely to emerge from a loft or a Café La Mama. More probably—because New York, with its many professional distractions, generally doesn't permit actors to stay together long enough to play together—the next good acting companies we get will come from the sub-road, from catch-as-catch-can university campus performances, from summer stock used as a kind of survival kit, from wandering the byways—in however gypsylike a fashion—until harmony and cohesiveness come along as the results of a kind of companionable endurance-test.

"Why this grass?" Rosemary Harris is said to have asked as she dug her toe into a lawn somewhere in Michigan or points south, wondering what she was doing circling the world's tacky outposts. *This* grass because it was free grass, unimportant grass, trial-and-error grass that *could* be scuffed. You can't dig your toe into the planted grass confined in small cement squares at the foot of some intimidating, gobble-you-up edifice.

If the A.P.A., of which Miss Harris has been a member, is getting along nicely in New York just now, it is because it made its mistakes —or a lot of the early necessary ones—while vagabonding, feeling impoverished, no doubt, but suffering no undue penalty for failure. William Ball's American Conservatory Theater, adrift on the road before it settled in San Francisco, came to a simmer in something of the same way. (Why does no one want to remember that Molière tried Paris as a callow youth, failed dismally, was arrested for debt, and then went to the countryside, where he made do in any old circumstances for fourteen years until he was ready to invade Paris again? The fourteen years made Molière out of him. The Comédie Française was built later, as a monument to work completed.)

Well, we have some of the buildings now and must perforce deal with them. What *are* the immediate problems that actors, playwrights, directors and producers have had to face as they walked in the doors, lemminglike? We might look at them separately.

ACTORS IN REPERTORY

Playing in repertory can do one of three things to an actor. It can make him surprisingly flexible, it can teach him to make the most of his equipment by permitting him to specialize in a line of stock-company parts, and it can unnerve him altogether.

We have lately been in a position to observe all three eventualities. At the same time that the original Lincoln Center company was taking its first hesitant steps in Washington Square, other repertory companies—varying considerably in age and weight—were flooding the city: Israel sent us the Habima, France sent us the Barrault-Renaud troupe again, and of course the American hinterland passed on to New York the traveling players of the A.P.A.

Flexibility is the proud possession of the Barrault company, which is able one night to dive headlong into the antic mannerisms of Molière, Beaumarchais, or Feydeau, the next night to attend with impassioned seriousness to the formalities of Racine, and then to declare a holiday by singing and dancing Offenbach. What such players cannot sing, they can orchestrate with their bodies; and because their speaking voices are so highly trained, singing itself becomes easier. By this time the Parisians are able to respond on cue to many different cues.

But all repertory has a built-in tilt. It leans, like that tower in Pisa, toward soft ground and the inviting laws of gravity. It yearns to become a stock company, for reasons that are not wholly despicable.

Once a performer has been brilliant, say, as a crotchety father, the temptation to use him again as a crotchety father is quite irresistible, especially if you badly need a good crotchety father. The pressure toward typecasting is quite as severe in repertory as elsewhere, perhaps more so. And the actor who begins to specialize in crotchety fathers gets better at it; after a while it's a shame to waste him, and the management begins to pick plays in which crotchety fathers appear. We can be quite certain that once Shakespeare saw an actor play Falstaff well, he did not particularly want to cast a good Iago in the part. There is even some suspicion that Shakespeare wrote Falstaff less well in *The Merry Wives of Windsor* because the company had in the meantime lost the player who first brightened the role. All *commedia dell'arte* companies were repertory companies, acting out scenarios so variable that the plot for tonight had to be pasted up backstage; but in the end every member of such a company played a single role his whole life long.

The good side, the plausible and profitable side, of this inevitable tendency is handsomely illustrated whenever Pierre Bertin is docked by tugboats in a Barrault production. (I never have the feeling that M. Bertin enters a scene under his own power; some vast section of the stage gives way and a tide rises to fill it.) M. Bertin almost invariably plays obtuse elderly gentlemen. He has so perfected a slow and astonished roll of his eyeballs that you feel a constant alarm: if those eyeballs should ever come to ultimate rest in either corner of his eyes, his head would go out of balance and fall off. He is florid, but slow to inflame: he must be pumped full of air, as though by a bellows, before his bleat can be heard. He is always funny, but he is composed about it. He knows his effect from a thousand and one nights, and is certainly not thinking of going into any other line of work. Who would change him?

During Lincoln Center's initial season in Washington Square, the situation was a great deal different. One enormous surprise jumped out of the box: David Wayne, wearing coats of many colors. Mr. Wayne has always been an engaging performer, but one would have supposed him as much a disarming personality as anything. But of the actors then assembled it was Mr. Wayne who was richest in diverse tones. In *Marco Millions* he was able to raise his voice, and raise a righteous Oriental row, with ease and amplitude. In S. N. Behrman's *But for Whom Charlie* he hurried onto the stage as though he had been waiting in the lobby for the beginning of the second feature, and when he settled cross-legged in an armchair, studying a cigarette as though he expected it to speak to him, we saw at once that he'd turned himself into a sharp-witted, dreadfully honest, self-acknowledged failure we had never met before. It is hard to say where Mr. Wayne might have met him; in some secret rendezvous, no doubt, where flexible actors are born. But neither the author nor the repertory principle was at all well served by the balance of the acting. Here we come upon the third of our possibilities: players who, good as they may have been at one or another time in their careers, simply flounder when they are asked to become virtuosos, to do unfamiliar things.

Ralph Meeker had never before played a well-heeled, superficially cultivated, sleekly charming deceiver, and he wasn't playing one now. He was gasping at the role, blue in the face. One expected Salome Jens to manage the sultry invitations of a much-married temptress, confident of her own charms, with poise and flair; the poise and flair were nearly there, but it was suddenly and unexpectedly clear that Miss Jens lacked lightness, as it was suddenly and desperately clear that the attractive Zohra Lampert—appearing as the Princess in *Marco Millions*—could not hope to do repertory work until she had made a responsive instrument of her voice.

Mr. Behrman's play, whatever its merits, was seriously damaged by having fallen into the hands of earnest players who could do some things skillfully, but not many. Playing in repertory over a period of time does not necessarily ripen all actors in all directions; it can merely baffle and discourage them.

There are actors whose temperaments are outgoing, observant, quick to snatch at a fragment of life and inflate it freshly, actors who take delight in revealing different strands of themselves or strands that are different from themselves. Repertory wakes them up and uses them. There are actors who tend to examine infinitely the possible nuances of a single kind of role until they become, in effect, archetypes. When they have become superb at what they do, reportory can make room for them.

But there are other actors who are not at all to be despised and yet are relatively useless when variety is the main thing wanted. Variety is not an absolute goal for every actor; it is only good for an actor when the actor is good at it. Players who have been born blessed with a strong stamp of personality, or who have been lucky enough to fall once into the kind of role that might employ them forever, or who have limitations that simply cannot be overcome and need not be publicly displayed, would do well to ask themselves, "What's in it for me?"

Sometimes there is nothing in it for author or audiences, either, and all may profit by being candid about the matter. There is a long-run commercial theater at hand which functions on another basis and pays well for typecast quality work.

PLAYS IN REPERTORY

Generally we speak of repertory as though its principal function were to serve the needs of actors. But as we plunge headlong into the practice of maintaining stable acting companies and a rotating library of plays we might well pause, briefly at least, to ask ourselves how repertory may be expected to serve plays. The issue hasn't been given much thought. We suppose that generally better acting may show off the plays a bit better and that a certain number of rarely produced plays from the theatrical past will be given the rehearing they are denied in the commercial theater; and that's about it, which may be enough.

It isn't enough. If we are really going to take advantage of the permanence of house and householders which repertory affords, we are going to have to conceive the play—and the particular production it is first given—as something more than an overnight guest with a temporary claim to the closet. We're going to have to think of it as a child of the family, capable not only of growth but of radical shifts in temperament.

Let's be plainer. When Lincoln Center downtown took on S. N. Behrman's *But for Whom Charlie*, the play—a new one—was at best mildly received. Audiences didn't come running. After what amounted to little more than a long weekend in the life of a repertory company, the play was dropped from the working library—as indeed all plays which have worn out their welcomes will always be dropped from repertory schedules.

But we've skipped a step, or rather repertory has. In its short life, *But for Whom Charlie* profited exactly nothing from having been given to a repertory company. Indeed, as a good many people noted at the time, Mr. Behrman might have been much better off in the hands of a commercial, one-shot management. Such a management would have been able to give the play its exclusive attention rather than one-third of a very busy mind; more importantly, it would have been free to typecast the play from a thousand and one applicants instead of doling out the parts among a ready-or-not group of twenty. These things, however, are simply success-or-failure calculations. Something else, and something subtler, was at stake.

What *should* Mr. Behrman have gained from letting his play be done by a group with a permanent address? Not thirty or forty or even four hundred performances. The number of performances can never be guaranteed; if no one shows up on a snowy night, even repertory can read the silence at the box office. But the play should have been guaranteed three or four *productions*, or as many productions as were needed to prove the piece good or bad. So far as I know, it got exactly one production, the one that was displayed on opening night.

The play was palpably miscast in several of its principal roles. Now, if repertory is to have any meaning at all for a playwright it must mean that what is first miscast can be instantly recast. In the twinkling of an eye, or—to be more realistic about it—in two or three nights, another member of the company who has been in the building all along can be popped into one leading role, to be joined another night or two later by a fresh face in the role opposite.

In theory, repertory is a talent pool which can be tapped on short notice. Ideally, repertory is always double-cast, or triple-cast, with players ready to swap costumes as readily as Rosemary Harris and Nancy Marchand did in *Man and Superman* for the A.P.A. And because a full-time director is bound to the theater, living in and doing his washing there, restaging should be swiftly possible as well. The commercial theater doesn't really allow for the play's being done over after its Broadway opening: the director is off to Hollywood, the actors can't be replaced without scandal, there are no prior successes to be thrown into the breach while the fledgling is being taught to fly. But all of these things *can* be done where the job is steady, in repertory. And because they can, they should be. The possibility becomes an obligation.

The matter is important simply because we are paying no attention to it. I don't know that anyone considered, or even thought of, tossing Mr. Behrman's unlucky play into the Lincoln Center air until all of its parts came floating down into different hands. Instead of an up-for-grabs treatment, and a quick look around the premises to see who might alter its balances this way or that, it was given the commercial headshake and a quick heave-ho. The Broadway habit of regarding a play as finished—in both senses of the word—on its opening night proved too strong a habit for any repertory principle to override. Yet repertory will have no identity for us until it claims all its rights.

Whether or not Mr. Behrman's play might finally have been salvaged is beside the point, though it seems clear that Emlyn Williams' version of Ibsen's *The Master Builder* in London received an enormous boost from the replacement of one fine actor, Michael Redgrave, by another fine actor, Laurence Olivier. The British National Theater, working as a repertory unit, is flexible enough, one might say impertinent enough, to do just that.

The point, in the case of the Behrman play, is that nothing was done to it to justify a playwright's handing it over to a particular kind of company in a particular kind of house, and the point may prove to be a critical one in future if repertory is to be given any brand-new plays. Those players who are now trading off roles are generally doing it in classics, where the plays themselves are felt to be secure and the trading-off is principally beneficial to the players.

I think one of the things repertory must look forward to is assuming its obligation to the new and insecure play, marshaling its own various advantages in such a way as to escort the baby not over the threshold alone but past adolescence and into something like maturity. That, after all, is what Shakespeare's repertory company did; it is clear from the wide variations in the texts we have that the playwright kept right on tinkering, and no doubt shuffling his actor-friends around, until he had got the thing nearly right. Even Ben Jonson's *Sejanus* was kept on the boards, and probably worked over, for as long as audiences would tolerate it, though of course Jonson didn't think that long enough. But then *Sejanus* is an exceptional bore.

Presumably repertory companies are going to want a partial diet of new plays, if only to keep them from looking too much like museums. To get the new plays, and to keep playwrights in a generous frame of mind, they are probably going to have to cease thinking of themselves exclusively as actors' training schools and begin thinking of themselves as quick-witted rescuers of plays that have temporarily gone wrong. The two goals are most compatible, but one of them isn't being mentioned in so much as a whisper, not yet.

True, when this sort of activity does begin, reviewers are going to have to go back to shows five or six times. It serves them right.

DIRECTORS IN REPERTORY

It was easy enough to throw up one's hands in dismay over Elia Kazan's production of *The Changeling*, but where was that going to get anyone? It had been fashionable to express dismay over the Lincoln Center Repertory Theater from the beginning, and while the dismay was justified, it gradually became something more or less than genuine. There was some glee in it.

Not satisfied with pointing out the defects of the first season's three productions—and the defects were real, real as real could be—a goodly number of critical voices had elected to saddle the venture not only with its own sins but with all the sins of the American theater, and particularly the commercial American theater, for twenty years past. Because it had not sufficiently broken with the Broadway system the new organization had been treated as though it had invented the Broadway system, and perhaps murdered William Desmond Taylor as well. Scorn was not enough for it; it had to be put on the sacrificial pyre as expiation for everybody's crimes. Directors Kazan and Robert Whitehead could only have been baffled by the inherited blood-guilt heaped on their heads.

And now, with his production of *The Changeling,* Mr. Kazan had put himself helplessly into the hands of his detractors. The production was an utter failure. It was more than that. It was foolish. The choice of play was foolish. *The Changeling* is one of those potboiling shockers with which the Jacobean audience contented itself once the great fire of Shakespeare was dead. Here and there it has a degree of the old fever, principally in the grim determination of its villain to possess a woman who loathes him and in the woman's realization, once she has been possessed, that her sensuality precisely matches his.

But as serious drama it is calculated claptrap; any absurd motivation, or no motivation, will serve to make a path to the two or three explosions of lust at its center. In something of the way that we have sick comedy, it is sick tragedy, though its sickness is more nearly lowbrow leering than sophisticated. To cast such a play with a company of actors taking its first tentative steps into the cold ocean of the classic repertory was to ask for the disaster we promptly got; only a superb company of actors, trained to the teeth, could have hoped to mask the play's inadequacies and make the most of its verse violence.

Having handed this razor blade to babies, Mr. Kazan himself behaved in altogether uncharacteristic fashion, obviously because he felt out of place in a world of metrical passion. If the play had been a contemporary one, he would have known exactly what to do with it. He would have searched for an inner source of the heroine's virginal bloodthirstiness, her willingness to do murder though never to lose her maidenhead. And he would have found it, whether the text supplied a motivation or not. He would have imagined a heat for his players, and got heat from them. He has ideas about contemporary men and women upon which he can draw to fill in a dramatist's lacunae. The flesh, at least, would have leapt.

Here his natural instincts were put entirely to one side, as though they had no proper place in earlier drama, as though earlier drama were an artifice wholly divorced from the real. The heroine became a preposterous mannequin, whipping a beggarwoman with her rosary beads while speaking like a mechanical doll. The hero was out of A Child's Garden of Verses, or perhaps Puss in Boots. The comedians felt it necessary to make literal illustration of everything: if a clown spoke of his knee he slapped it smartly, as though otherwise we mightn't know where it was. No one—with the exception of villain Barry Primus—led any sort of natural life beneath the flowering ruff at his neck. Classics, the production seemed to say, are contrivances.

Thus Mr. Kazan, having put his instincts into cold storage, contrived and contrived. He brought on bands of archers to shout "Holla!" or some such thing to no purpose other than to make a picture; he arranged walking ballets in which ghosts and lunatics did nothing but did it spectacularly; he dropped a dummy from a tower window almost as though he wanted us to *know* that the dummy was not a human body, and he stripped a woman naked so that we could see the pink cheesecloth that covered her. Even when he approached the kind of earthy sensuality he has always done well, he artificialized it. Mr. Primus, as the maddened villain De Flores, whipped off his great gray cloak and threw it over heroine Barbara Loden, who was lying outstretched on the floor. He then crawled under the cloak himself and there followed a few moments of unidentifiable movement in which, presumably, De Flores deflowered his victim, though it would be quite impossible to say how. A smirking sexuality was one of the evening's few constants; but none of it was lifelike.

The play was performed not on an open stage or an apron stage or a thrust stage but on a broken stage. The acting area was chopped into three basic segments connected by tiny footbridges; getting from one to the other meant one man at a time, and that man was well advised to watch his step. All spaces were cramped, fussy, over-decorated with Gothic gimcracks; seen together they did not make a unit, not even under the embrace of an overhead crucifix. We were in a prop shop, or in an armory, or in a waxworks.

Play, company, staging and stage were made of wax in a way that was not to have been expected. But we are nearer the heart of the matter now. What was to have been expected?

It was to have been expected that the initial efforts of a company to don costume, speak verse, and move about in an environment three hundred years distant from its own should be experimental, groping, unfinished, preparatory. A company must begin somewhere. We were to walk patiently with these players as they inched forward, taking our satisfaction in the knowledge that they were on their way, willingly suffering someone else's growing pains.

Yet that wasn't the problem at all, for we *would* willingly have suffered a company's growing pains if there had been any indication that the company was growing. Here the situation was quite different. A child was being taught to walk by someone who didn't honestly see the sense in walking.

Mr. Kazan was not guiding twenty or thirty apprentices toward the bright beacon of poetry or of period style for the simple reason that he himself has no apparent affinity for poetry or for period style. The very fact that he abandoned what he knew and substituted imitation carnival-time snake-dancing for it was substantial evidence of the fact. No one needs to be told that Mr. Kazan is a brilliant director in the best contemporary mode. But it was necessary to notice that he was uncomfortable, insecure, imaginatively unresponsive in his present circumstances, and these circumstances would seem to include the kind of stage on which he was working. The director did not seem challenged and involved at Lincoln Center downtown; he seemed wistful and alienated, an outsider trying hard to make gestures fundamentally false to him.

He was vigorous in his public defenses of this particular repertory-company operation because he was sternly determined, I think, to teach himself how to manage styles he had not dared before. One could only admire a man bent on extending his reach, above all a phenomenally successful man who had very little to gain and a great deal to lose in the daring.

But we were left with the realities of the situation. A company that needed to be taught was being guided by a man who needed to be taught, or at least by a man who was far from having mastered the specialized materials he and his pupils were working on. Captain and crew were equally at sea, and it was getting dark. Exploration is an attractive word, and there is something comfortably democratic in the notion of master and men finding their bearings together, shy one compass. But it is also a good way to get lost.

Lincoln Center's Repertory Theater could not allow the sky to get very much darker before setting a clear course; the institution was far too necessary to us all for that. Unless it was ready to reach out and collar directors—from anywhere—who knew precisely what to do with materials unfamiliar to the American actor, it was not going to teach the American actor much about doing them. It was going to produce more *Changelings*, more avoidable embarrassment, more confusion in the ranks and bafflement at the top. One calls for a plumber when a pipe leaks and an electrician when a wall fixture spits sparks; the jack-of-all-trades is a vanishing breed. If Michael Cacoyannis is known to be a fine director of Greek tragedy, then Michael Cacoyannis becomes the man to introduce youngsters to Greek choral patterns. You can add your own experts. But you must heed them.

I didn't—and don't—subscribe to the proposition that the original management of the company had been commercially cautious or aesthetically snow-blind or in any way less than honorable in its intentions for the group. On the face of things, the Messrs. Whitehead and Kazan were risk takers, though they may not have taken the risks you or I might have wished them to take.

What was needed at this point was less risk. What was needed—during a training period, during a mountain-climbing expedition—was directors who had been there, and had liked being there.

DOUBLE DISASTER

When Lincoln Center was still dreaming of its new Vivian Beaumont Theater and of the repertory company that was to be installed in it, Robert Whitehead, then artistic director of the slowly forming project, made a radical proposal. It was his contention that any new repertory company would require at the very least a two-year period of making thumping mistakes before it could begin to consider itself even halfway ready, and that it would be best not to initiate this period of trial and probable error with a splashy formal opening at a glittering uptown house.

He therefore suggested that while actors were taking their baby steps, while directors were experimenting with an unfamiliar stage, and while one and all were engaged in the tricky business of trying to determine precisely what plays belonged in a playhouse representing repertory in general and the American theater in particular, the work might well be done on a side street, so to speak, where the atmosphere itself would attest to the unfinished business at hand. Against considerable opposition, Mr. Whitehead succeeded in erecting a temporary structure in Washington Square and proceeded to fill it with productions which, if they failed, would not irretrievably tarnish the ultimate hope. Literally, deliberately, he put up a house to make mistakes in.

He made them, as did the colleagues he chose to work with. Beyond doubt, he made more than he had hoped he'd make. In two seasons of attending the downtown playhouse I never saw a production that struck me as firmly right. For most people, a feeling of disappointment, if not of outright dismay, hovered cloudlike over the venture.

But there were two things to be said about the then state of affairs. One: the whole purpose of the proceedings was to risk dismay now in order to prevent despair later. Mr. Whitehead had been candid about that; the playhouse itself stood where it did to accommodate the likelihood of disaster—and then to look beyond it. The other thing to be said is that the temporary project freely invited attack—that is what it was there for—and that every outcry, from critic or paying customer, could be taken as part of the shaping process. Testing was being done in public and the public was playing a valuable if unfamiliar role in helping to fashion the kind of municipal stage, and the kind of theatrical consciousness, that might eventually speak for it. It was at least saying what it *wouldn't* have; and that was something for producer and staff to be learning.

The learning process was plainly under way. Mr. Whitehead had originally estimated that it would require two years for some sort of clarity, and some sort of maturity, to assert itself. By the middle of the second season changes were in progress. It had become all too apparent that the original acting company was not robust enough for the demands repertory made on it. As a result, some players were leaving and a much more flexible policy of inviting outsiders in for particular productions—and possible tenure—was being tried. Elia Kazan, having found the stage and the system incompatible with his talents, had resigned his official position and the door was being opened to other directors, one of them a young man whose earlier work had been done off Broadway. The original emphasis on contemporary American, and more or less commercial, plays was similarly giving way before public pressure. Molière was about to go on the boards.

In the transition under way, fresh mistakes would unquestionably be made. But they would be fresh mistakes, profiting from earlier *don'ts*, and it was possible to begin to think of the venture as partially self-educated. It would not, in any case, have had to repeat its earlier fumbles.

At this point the powers that rule the Lincoln Center complex as a whole panicked, though the theater was in fact going through just the painful growing process that had been envisioned for it and though the growth rate was approximately, if less than blissfully, what had been prophesied. Mr. Whitehead's departure was effectively arranged, and the Vivian Beaumont Theater uptown, now ready for occupancy, was offered, without an experimental period, to Herbert Blau and Jules Irving of the San Francisco Workshop. The Messrs. Blau and Irving patched together a company partly composed of San Francisco regulars and partly of Lincoln Center's downtown holdovers and went to work on Georg Buechner's *Danton's Death*, which thereupon formally and ambitiously opened the Beaumont. With *Danton's Death* we were farther behind than Mr. Whitehead had been two years before.

The playhouse was ready, the people inside it were not. Buechner's infrequently performed though sometimes academically admired play is a turgid assembly of fragments, a kind of philosophical *pot-au-feu*, in which the power struggles of the French Revolution are seen piecemeal by lightning light. Bleak, jagged flashes crisscross the historical countryside, picking out Danton toying with the fleshpots,

Robespierre sucking softly on his puritanical teeth, the common people quarreling mindlessly among themselves, dozens of conspirators going their own ways in the near dark. Uncohesive, assuming familiarity with the political intricacies of the time, the work selects its images at random, a technique which has here and there been described as anticipating German expressionism but which, in this performance, more nearly resembled inept Shakespeare compounded by early Goethe and relayed to us all by a man with soap bubbles in his mouth.

The soap bubbles were often Mr. Blau's; he had adapted the text to make it windy at all times and brutally out of key at some. The line "Honesty will be out of breath before it can run the breach between us and these decent people" was almost instantly followed by the promise to give someone "a kick in the ass," and if I had to choose between the quasi-literary vacuousness of the former and the anachronistic, thoroughly artificial toughness of the latter, I must say I'd have chosen the latter. But neither attack possessed any actual dramatic energy. The poeticisms were merely inexplicit, loose gatherings of verbal fuzz. The effort to shock the play forward with inappropriate colloquialisms was startling only in its naïveté. And when the two strains were drawn together, as in "Madness is a whore, she fornicates with the whole world," we had surely overleaped thought and arrived at parody of thought.

As director, Mr. Blau commanded neither the meaning of his play nor the full presence of his actors. He kept the enterprise moving, but only as a waterwheel is kept moving. Great tribunals rode toward us bearing justices who would shout; a curved segment of the stage floor floated the recently dead away; panels opened in the proscenium wall to admit the defiant or the jailed; when the stage machinery was not in transit, hordes of costumed supernumeraries were, milling about in undesigned mob patterns until the dimming of lights cued them to rush, roaring unintelligibly, away, But no two pieces of illustration joined together to illuminate a point. Even when an obvious contrast seemed called for—Danton stalking off in challenge, Danton returning immediately on his knees—the significance of the paired images was blurred: Danton seemed simply to have come back onstage too soon, or seemed a fool for ever having left it. There were endless trailing threads to be looked at as they vanished into space; but there were nowhere any ties.

The players were uniformly without pasts or private lives. They appeared, briefly as a rule, to speak certain lines, vociferously as a rule, and then to depart with a flourish that was also a kind of collapse: it was as though they had, in those few moments, emptied the full contents of their heads and were now going to the wings to be inflated again. The sense of person was always absent; these were walking wigs, parroted imprecations, painted leers. Gesture was arbitrary, automatic: I was glad I had not begun to count the number of times one or another housecapped harridan flung her palm forward and up, curled clawlike, only to fling it back down as accompaniment to a curse, or the number of times a jaw tightened fiercely to indicate, cartoon-style, a malice that was not felt.

The blunted nature of everything we were going to see was hinted at, ominously, with the stately rise of the vast gray front curtain. We were momentarily distracted by the deep perspective of spiderweb that designer Jo Mielziner had drawn, in black and white, from proscenium arch to back wall. Our eyes responded quickly to the harsh suction of the converging lines and we blinked in anticipation, though we were later to discover that the production design was altogether eclectic and this first tease was without stylistic significance. But our momentary interest was at once foolishly dissipated: Mr. Blau now staged a dumb show in which a young man in frock coat darted up a ramp, ran this way and that, met various threatening symbols of the power he could not evade (the symbols were female, for no very pertinent reason), and then submitted to being disemboweled by what I took to be France carrying a cutlass. The staging was as ragged and unpointed as it might have been in a graduation exercise; and the meaning was either as simple-minded as I have made it, or obscure. In any case, *Gorboduc* was what came to mind.

But all of this is to say no more than what we have already said: that Lincoln Center uptown had arranged to have opening night and amateur night at the same time. The fumbling had begun again, late. What passed on the stage for passion was noisy hysteria; what offered itself as dramatic color was the garish surface posturing of penny dreadfuls. The glowing new playhouse was pleasing to enter, and the massive machinery that rolled forums forward and back was impressive. But, as we tried to attend to the play, we became uncomfortably aware of the predicament we were in. What we were looking at, alas, was a million-dollar dreadful. The money had been spent, and we were once again in kindergarten.

The stage itself remained a question mark. It was conceivable that the pool of playing space which comes of combining the area under the proscenium arch with a fair-sized circular lip in the auditorium proper might yet be used with such vigorous imagination that we should learn to see the advantages of combining an old-fashioned, picture-frame house with new-fashioned apron-stage projection. Any new piece of architecture must always have secrets to yield; we could afford to wait a time for the unveiling of those that might be hidden here.

One thing should be emphasized, though. *Danton's Death* was not being performed on a thrust stage. The term "thrust stage" has come into use fairly recently, and it is too often applied to any activity in the playhouse which escapes, however minutely, the confines of the old proscenium. Actually, there are two simple enough tests for determining thrust-stage effect. Supposing that we are not in any case to employ the old full circle of the Greeks, and supposing that most productions are to be acted in what amounts to a visual rectangle, the issue is: where is the rectangle? Does it extend across the curtain line, from right to left, as it always has in the proscenium theater? Or has it been wrenched entirely sideways, so that it extends full length into the auditorium and invites the actors to do all of their work there? At the Beaumont not only were the actors doing nearly all of their work near, or at, or inside the curtain line; we ourselves were looking at the rectangle of action precisely as we would have in a proscenium house. Our angle of vision was not altered in the least.

The other simple test has to do with the far arms of the semicircular auditorium. How far do they go as they wrap themselves around the central acting area? Do they go so far that someone sitting at the extreme side wall could not see under the proscenium arch if there were one?

When they do go so far, the action is forced—literally thrust—forward into the auditorium in order to be able to satisfy all of the spectators. At the Beaumont the wraparound stops short of this, which means that we are once more invited to attend primarily to our old stamping ground, the curtained stage.

There is no law that says a new stage must be a thrust stage. Hopefully, we shall have hundreds of new stages, all of them different, before drama's work is done. But there is a virtue in keeping definitions, as well as experiences, clear in our heads, so that we shall not begin to imagine that we are having, at *Danton's Death*, say, the same kind of projected experience we might have at Stratford, Ontario, or in Minneapolis. As the Beaumont stage is gradually brought to a color by directors determined to understand it, we may want a word for whatever fresh happening overtakes us, and then we shall have to coin one. On the occasion of its baptism, the identity of the physical stage was as blurred as the real temperaments of the actors were.

Ground had been lost. The downtown house, the old house, had opened as insecure professional theater. The uptown house, the dream house, had opened as insecure college theater.

WRESTLING WITH BRECHT

Everyone said they were meant for each other, and the marriage turned out to be a mistake.

Thus the meeting of the ardently pro-Brecht new management at Lincoln Center and *The Caucasian Chalk Circle*, long reported as the most readily manageable and indeed the most charming of Bertolt Brecht's plays. There were many reasons for looking forward to this final production of the first season in the Vivian Beaumont. The season had, until now, been a series of stumbles; surely the Irving-Blau directorship would at last feel at home with a play that so precisely reflected its image of the rebellious, stylistically radical theater it hoped to bring into being here.

And nearly every last man of us was waiting to see Brecht whole. Brecht has for many years been advertised as one of the truly influ-

ential movers and shakers of the contemporary theatrical consciousness—advertised, but not effectively/ represented in New York. Aside
from a few suggestive performances of early and not altogether
definitive plays, notably *In the Jungle of Cities* at the Living
Theater and an independent off-Broadway mounting of *When a
Man's a Man*, every attempt to come to grips with the later Brechtian
blockbusters had broken the backs of the eager wrestlers engaged. It
remained possible, of course, to know Brecht in theory, to track down
each word he'd published in explanation of his iconoclastic techniques, and to arrive at tentative agreement or disagreement with
certain of his premises in the silence of the library. But where theater
is concerned, the library does not have the last word; performance is
crucial. Now, at last, we should be seeing a production done by such
sympathetic hands, hands shaped to the bent of the Brechtian tools,
that the issue would be proved out, or at least handsomely illumi-
nated.

No such luck. The very worst, far and away the most frustrating,
aspect of the Blau-Irving *Caucasian Chalk Circle* was its ineptitude
in projecting what is unconventional about the play. We don't go to
The Caucasian Chalk Circle looking for conventional pleasures,
familiar excitements. Brecht made a distinction between the theater
of action and the theater of narrative: this is the theater of narrative,
in which a middleman stands between us and the story constantly
reminding us that we are objective observers, not emotionally involved participants. The technique is called "epic," and it permits the
narrator to range freely over the history of an issue, in this instance
the issue of whether things belong to people by natural right or by
demonstrated aptitude for dealing with them; time may move forward or back, events can stretch out laterally until the social, political, and even psychological implications of all conceivable side-issues
have been investigated, comment from singers or from principal
actors can intrude upon the development at any time. Brecht intended no "development" in the ordinary sense. He asked not for
"suspense in awaiting the outcome" but for "suspense at the process"
itself. We are not to wonder anxiously whether the foster-mother
who has reared a child will win permanent right to the child at the
climax; we are to take our satisfaction from knowing that each con-

tributing factor to the problem has been exhaustively and independently examined: the price of milk, the draft status of a potential husband, the differences in class that make some women greedy and some long-suffering, the venality of ironclad soldiers while they are disinterestedly making arrests, the manner in which judges are elected and in which they may quite irrelevantly behave. Rejecting the notion that "one scene exists for another" in an orderly, unfolding process of growth, Brecht issued a command: "each scene for itself."

Now, all of this places an extraordinary burden upon the individual scene as it passes: it must function at such a high level of intellectual intensity that it occupies us wholly, without any fretting about what has preceded or what will follow it during a more than three-hour span. The intensity *is* intellectual: Brecht wished to wave to one side the kind of play in which the spectator is allowed to have feelings or is "drawn into something." The spectator is not expected to share the life presented on stage. Instead, he is "confronted with something."

During the first silent moment of director Irving's *Caucasian Chalk Circle* there was an abrupt sense in the playhouse that just such a confrontation might be realized. A handful of peasants, bearded, shawled, and booted, appeared with little warning before a vast metal-and-burlap curtain that seemed a damaged but defiant shield. The peasants simply stared at us. Their heads were up, their eyes were cold and penetrating, their bodies were braced to issue even physical challenge. Our attention was arrested immediately. A righteous anger, or a steely arrogance, was about to be thrust under our noses, we felt. The posture was bold, and it promised us nothing but the right to listen. We were to be engaged in a new way: no catering to us, just challenge.

Almost as quickly as it had come the sense of an assured and demanding manner vanished. In a moment the principal storyteller, Brock Peters, had left the curved platform to roam through the lower reaches of the auditorium, apparently to confront latecomers who were struggling toward their seats and to impress upon them their formal, dispassionate relationship toward actors in makeup. We were all one in this discussion, boots or no boots, and no nonsense about stage illusion, please. The remaining peasants waited patiently before the curtain while their spokesman and describer strode from aisle to aisle across the Beaumont's red carpeting.

But the gesture deflated on the instant the first brazen image we had been given. Confrontation was not carried into the auditorium; it was diminished and made foolish. Mr. Peters in no sense dominated the latecomers; embarrassed though they were, they dominated him. There were more of them, they were in the right place and dressed properly for it, and they alone were busy doing something. He was the impotent interloper, unable to alter what was going on. Suddenly all impact was dissipated and we were breathing dead air.

I dwell upon this first incident precisely because it was not an isolated one. It was simply our first illustration of the stylistic insecurity, the inability to grasp what would exert command in a novel situation, that Mr. Irving displayed throughout the evening. Pressed to make each moment arrest attention on its own, the director did not dig for what might be argumentatively stimulating in the moment. He brushed past the argument, letting the players slur their speeches as though language counted for no more than sentiment in the Brechtian vision, and reached for anything in the way of scenery or odd stage business that lay ready to hand. Years ago I saw an Eddie Cantor film in which the comedian was riding the rear end of a fire truck, swaying wildly on a loosened ladder. "Do something!" he screamed. The man driving the truck did something and the ladder soared high in the air, carrying Mr. Cantor with it. "Do something *else!*" Mr. Cantor screamed. The memory popped into my head as I watched the epic fable unfold, for Mr. Irving was doing Brecht as though doing Brecht consisted not in seeking one defined effect but in simply doing something *else*.

Else was all over the place. In a sequence devoted to displaying the heartless indifference of an aristocratic mother toward her infant, the mother chose to sit where there was no stool while a servant frantically slid beneath her to hold her up. Meaning? Possibly that the rich tend to sit on the poor. If that was the moment's intended metaphor, it was a laboriously obvious one. But the fact of the matter is that any such meaning was superfluous in the sequence, as intrusive as it was clumsy. We were looking at a sight gag from some ineffectual revue sketch, at a use of the stage which failed to respect the intent of the passage or the texture of the play. Nothing like it was ever employed again; desperation tactics were being resorted to on a catch-as-catch-can basis in exchange for a very few titters.

Elizabeth Huddle played the kitchen maid who rescues an abandoned baby and rears it as her own. Hurrying across the ravaged countryside with her hastily bundled burden, she came to a time when it was necessary for her to sing "The Song of the Rotted Bridge." A narrator clad in goatskin and caracul-wool cap, and accompanied by a twanging of carefully unsweetened instruments, told us so.

The girl stood poised above the bridge—a fearful ladder of disintegrating slats—swaying as she clutched a slender lifeline thousands of feet high over a gorge. The naïveté of the situation was deliberate; the cliff-hanging was calculated to remind us of ancient theatrical trickery at the same time that it detached us from its foolish suspense. Two things were set at odds here: the familiar picture with its overtones of mere thrill, and the fact that the girl froze on the precipice to detain us with formal song. The theater turned inside out: we were to see it through the other side of the mirror, understanding it instead of submitting to it.

But the meeting was botched both ways. There was no sharp stylistic cutoff to frame our vision in a crisp, crystalline, fiercely angular new way. The universe did not, for the moment, go into deep shock. And when the song had been blurred through, the old, shaky, next-to-absurd realism of watching a heroine navigate a presumably threatening gorge was done with the clumsy and undesigned earnestness of an Eliza surviving the ice once again.

We were given neither formal nor illusory satisfaction, much less the clear contest between the two that might have brilliantly silhouetted both. Again, the kitchen maid's brother, who had temporarily given her shelter, looked toward the skies to say that when the snow melted she must go. Without pause, he announced that the snow on the roof was at last melting. Here something odd and attractive should have happened in and to the playhouse. Time should have doubled back on itself as our senses dissolved, and perhaps delighted, in our awareness of what it means to be in a *theater*, where such things really can happen. At the Beaumont nothing at all happened. The actor simply spoke the second line perfunctorily, and we simply wondered whether we had heard the first or the second line wrong. Mr. Irving was never ready to give Brecht, or the all-important Brechtian *scene*, its special definition. He seemed merely in a hurry to call the richly costumed extras back on stage, as though visual color could do what the human intelligence, contending with ironies and issuing fiats through fierce concentration, could not.

I do not think Eric Bentley's translation was of very much help to him. All of us are in debt to Mr. Bentley's scholarship in the field. But when lines for actors are laid out on the same meticulous file-cards that are native to scholarship, they are apt to sound flat in the playhouse. Subject, predicate, object, together with all phrases and clauses between, come in something like military order, minding their linguistic manners. But here, as in most of Mr. Bentley's translations, there was a constant feeling of having lost the theatrical force of the line. Writing for actors is not the same thing as providing responsible trots, and I am not in the least thinking of such awkward thrusts at humor as "Lady, you are running straight into the arms of the armed forces" or "I find it most unusual—from the taste angle, I mean." Spoken rhythms must perforce find their emphases at points where written rhythms would not. These points are nearly always elided in Mr. Bentley's work, so that we come to the end of a speech feeling we have navigated a tunnel in which there were no variations of shape or course. The thought is completed in the writing, but it is not forcibly projected on the stage. Mr. Bentley's ear would not seem to be attuned to the auditorium.

Overall, the bad luck we were faced with in this rarely evocative, generally tedious production of a play considered close to foolproof forced us to ask certain unpleasant questions. If we were to look at the credentials of the principals involved and conclude that what was now on view at Lincoln Center was representative Brecht, we could only exclaim, in genuine dismay, "Oh, is that all there is to the man?" On such a showing, Brecht could be written off as, for the most part, a bore.

Or, as an alternative, we could simply say that a management team devoted to Brecht had utterly failed to show us Brecht, had in effect built a Berlin wall of its own. But this meant that Messrs. Blau and Irving were themselves without any powerful or very practical theatrical sensibilities, that they were less than professionally equipped. Certainly the acting company they employed during their first season had consistently seemed well below New York professional standards. But it was the managers who had both selected and directed the members of the company, and it was the managers who had to assume responsibility for the players' flabby and unpromising state.

It doesn't really matter that a fledgling repertory company should produce a certain number of failures. It matters very much when there is no promise of better things in sight, no evidence of movement, of growing awareness, of talent nearing the turning point. As things stood, there were no shoots ready to burst—or even showing springlike signs of life—at the Beaumont. The playhouse threatened to become a wayside stop, a detour, a dim and dismissable cul-de-sac on the New York scene, disappointing above all in its failure to make the unconventional speak clearly for itself or to make its own announced rebelliousness invigorating.

Subsequent seasons have improved matters very little. A few good actors—Philip Bosco and Aline McMahon in particular—have been added to the company but have rarely seemed at their best with the company. Other good actors have occasionally been jobbed in, vanishing after single performances. Repertory has not happened: no production has ever been strong enough to be returned regularly once its six or eight weeks were done. The choice of plays has been increasingly "safe," revivals of *Saint Joan, Tiger at the Gates,* and *Cyrano de Bergerac* among them. With the departure of Mr. Blau, Mr. Irving seems to be wooing the matinee audience, the subscriber who routinely goes to what in high school he came to regard as "culture."

Meantime, the A.P.A., which is the best repertory company we possess, has continued to extend its reach beyond the pleasant pastiches which established it on Broadway—revivals of *You Can't Take It with You* and *The Show-Off*—to include such contemporary dramatists as de Ghelderode and Ionesco while continuing to do excellent work with the likes of Pirandello and Molière. And in San Francisco director William Ball continues to mount as many as sixteen productions in a season as well as to shuttle some forty actors through daily classroom sessions in which a new stress is place on the techniques required for stylization, period pieces, and verse. The job *can* be done, backbreaking and underfinanced though it may be. It is perhaps best done when it is at first underfinanced, even unhoused, relying upon knowledge and inspiration to call it to our gratified attention.

11

IN THE NAME OF LAUGHTER

DANCING TILL DOOMSDAY

IN A WAY, comedy is the greatest hypocrite of them all, for it is essentially a dark form dedicated to looking into locked closets and underneath the bed while pretending to be lighthearted about everything it finds there. That is its dirtiest and most delightful trick; it points to a blemish and does nip-ups over having discovered something so utterly unimportant and so utterly delicious. It is, you see, kidding. Its habit is to make merry over what really ought to be reported to the police.

But it does, oh it does, need elevation. Nip-ups must go *up*, must forever stay airborne, must loftily insist that the murderous matter is of no consequence at all. That is what is so pleasantly outrageous about comedy: it is always dancing over danger as though it hadn't the faintest notion the danger was there. Comedy is blithe because it is blind, but it must always be both at once. Unless the fundamental lie, the affectation of a false and foolish indifference to the abyss which gapes beneath capering feet, is steadily maintained there is never going to be much laughter. Ignorance needs altitude if it isn't quickly to become painful.

I turn to these thoughts because comedy in our time is increasingly being drawn down into the abyss over which it has a sworn duty to skip. Instead of ignoring the pitfalls, and so making us laugh, it is peering directly into them. The excuse that is most often given for such morbid behavior is that the times are dark, which is so. In an age living next door to holocaust, what is comedy to do but come out with the truth, face up to the facts? So runs the argument.

It is an argument bound, in the nature of things, to produce rather poor results. For instance, you may have heard about a certain sketch in *The Committee*, an improvisational revue brought to New York from San Francisco. You may have heard about this certain sketch because nobody—so far as I know—liked it. The jest in question had to do with an electrocution. A humane warden, a humane chaplain, and a humane governor stand by to give comfort to a condemned man; when the switch is thrown and the power fails to kill its victim, the three humanitarians turn upon him and stomp him to death. Joke.

But it isn't. It may constitute a fair enough comment upon certain actual practices we engage in today; it may indicate to us discrepancies between our virtuous chatter and our vicious habits; it may be thoroughly up-to-date in its attitude toward capital punishment—but none of these things makes it comedy. Comedy isn't fact, it is forgetfulness of fact. Nor does the twist at the end of the sketch make it comedy. Comedy doesn't consist of simple reversal or simple surprise. A nice boy carrying a hatbox may turn out to be carrying a severed head in the hatbox, but the surprising discovery does not announce comedy; it announces macabre melodrama. The only twist that truly guarantees comedy is the twist that makes sport of something which is not in the least sporting. There is indeed such a thing as gallows humor; but it always achieves its standing as humor by politely or even airily pretending that there is no trapdoor, that the occasion is an attractively social one, that business may go on as usual.

What is happening to so much of our latter-day, or doomsday, comedy is that it is resolutely putting a single face on things, whereas comedy invariably requires two. The mask of comedy is double: it is ugly, and it is smiling. What makes us laugh, really, is the inappropriateness of the smile on such a countenance. We see warts and moles and a whisky nose, we see a kind of ugliness: that is one face. We also see a cheeriness, an almost mindless effervescence, which makes it perfectly clear that ugliness couldn't care less: that is the other face. The two together tell the truth and shrug it off, look in the mirror and imagine beauty, put on a battered hat and tilt it modishly. Comedy comes of the complexity, the denial, the mismatch.

In the case of the sketch we've been mentioning there is no complexity: there is only a perfectly straightforward, progressively logical statement in which one ugliness is twisted into an uglier. The face of comedy has been flattened out, pounded down, rolled into evenness like so much dough. A commitment to the truth has been kept, all right; but it has not been kept by that comic indirection which elaborately points right when it is left you are meant to notice.

This one sketch would be a mere mishap and not worth extended attention if it weren't symptomatic of much of the humor that has grown up—in nightclubs, in revues, in some avant-garde plays—as a result of our deepening nervousness over the facts we must live with. The comedian, the comic playwright, feels that he must take the bull or the bomb by the horns—and so, no doubt, he must. Having got hold of the horns, however, he fancies himself funny merely because he has been bold, merely because he has been candid, merely because he has mentioned the unmentionable, merely because he has proved himself "in the know." But the work of comedy is not done so easily. Comedy wants another step.

It wants a step off into thin air so light, so insouciant, so impervious to its own untenable position, that we double up in glee at the preposterously confident behavior before us. That this very step can be taken with aplomb, and without ducking issues, was made clear to us by the gentlemen of *Beyond the Fringe*, gentlemen who arranged for nuclear warfare and even the end of the world without ceasing for a moment to behave like gentlemen. Demented gentlemen, to be sure; but of course that is what we look for when we feel the urge to laugh. Not the least of Jonathan Miller's secrets is the helium he must take intravenously; it becomes easy to be funny about disaster in the cellar if you report it while soaring like a stork across the rooftops.

Nor would I wish these remarks to be taken as a sideswipe at "sick" jokes. There are good "sick" jokes and bad ones. A bad one occurs, figuratively speaking, when a fellow who has been telling you about the endless stomach operations he has had to undergo interrupts himself for a moment to vomit. Vomiting is funny in some circumstances; in these it is merely logical. A good "sick" joke occurs when the same fellow, describing the same endless operations, unbuttons his shirt to show you the zipper. The illness is by no means over; but it is going to be dealt with more efficiently from now on.

Surely these are elementary things to be saying. But again and again there is fresh cause for saying them. A sketch in which a man begins by speaking pacifically on the subject of Vietnam and then is shown a series of increasingly inflammatory photographs ends with the man becoming violently inflamed. What else should we expect, and where, dear clown, is the mismatch that makes for entertaining mockery?

Back to first principles. When, in *Modern Times*, Chaplin roller-skates on the edge of a cavernous drop he doesn't know is there, he roller-skates dashingly, elegantly, suavely, fastidiously, making his arabesques with the finesse of a ballerina. The grace is as essential as the precipitous drop. The trouble with much contemporary comedy is not in our times: the times can be reported accurately enough. It is in the peculiar behavior of some of our would-be entertainers, who imagine that the roller-skating sequence would be improved by having DANGER signs erected everywhere and then having the skater go over the edge anyway. There is a simple one, two, three about this kind of comedy, and one, two, three is out.

LAUGH SIZE

A laugh is such a little thing, it's a wonder it's so hard to get one.

Perhaps the best rule is to let it be little. Don't bug it, don't bruise it, don't blow it to the size of a nervously overexcited balloon, don't insist that it graduate *summa cum laude*. Just give it the easy chair, tell it it's summertime, and see if a sudden snicker doesn't bubble straight up from the first sun-warmed sigh.

That's the way they decided to go about things in *You're a Good Man Charlie Brown*, anyway, and the results should have been studied by all uptown managers, by miked nightclub comedians who make you want to put the napkins in your ears, and by the obviously deaf manufacturers of television laugh-tracks. *You're a Good Man Charlie Brown* was a sort of musical paper-chain made out of the meanderings of the comic strip *Peanuts;* it opened in an attractive off-Broadway bandbox approximately the size of Snoopy's doghouse; it was inhabited by exactly six youngsters who walked—did not run—to the nearest piece of brightly painted playground equipment to discuss Beethoven and lost ball-games; and it moved on cat's feet all the way, even when the feet belonged to a dog.

Snoopy was a dog—no offense intended—and he was never in much of a hurry to leave his perch on the doghouse roof, where he rather imagined he resembled a trophy commemorating some distinguished event. Once in a while, though, something came over him, something primeval and mysteriously passionate. Hadn't he once upon a time been a member of a hardier jungle breed, cousin to the lion or the leopard or some such predatory type? Shouldn't he roar, and assert his lineage? People might respect him more, and bring him dinner faster.

The thought coaxed him down from his king-size siesta, though tentatively. He would, perhaps, emit a ferocious roar. He cleared his throat, as singers and public speakers are wont to do. Then he let us have it. "It" was, shall we say, on the inadequate side, the sound of a lad whose voice is changing but heaven knows into what, the insulting scrape of worn chalk on a weary blackboard. "How humiliating," he said, returning thoughtfully to his place of rest, and sorely in need of it.

That's all. A little itch, a little effort, a dreadful surprise, and two resigned words that squarely, dogfully, faced the facts. And we were with the show, won for the evening, because we hadn't been worked over, we'd been gently jostled into a rueful appreciation of how blighted some lives are. As actor Bill Hinnant, whose head somehow seemed to hang lower than his tongue did, slunk into his Snoopy-droop to contemplate the additional fact that he'd always been a dog and always would be a dog, we came to feel as keenly as he did the eternal pea beneath his mattress. "There's so little hope of advancement," he murmured.

Lucy, a bit of a witch on the surface but a vixen underneath, might seem—on the face of things—to be a pushier comic sort. Charles M.

Schulz often draws her with a mouth wide enough to accommodate the Lincoln Tunnel traffic at six in the evening. As Reva Rose played her, however, she was a creature of tidy effects. She was, to be sure, all queen, and would grow up to rule. But the simplicity, the sheer grace, of her thoughtful condescension as she lightly lifted a hand to let her abject subjects know that they might now rise in her presence, was modesty personified. Miss Rose commanded, but she did not command us to laugh; she hinted that it might be appropriate if we did, provided we cared to. Why fuss about a thing like that? Weren't we friends?

At her most ferocious, she was genteelly controlled. Let's say that her crabbiness quotient was running high at a certain moment and that she was about to intimidate one or another member of the world's unluckiest baseball team. Did she bleat, or pounce, or blast her way through? Never. Slowly, and really rather sweetly, she raised an open palm aloft, so that her five ladylike fingers were plainly in view, and—with the tender concern of a schoolma'am who hopes no further accidents will happen—explained how swooping claws function.

"These five fingers," she said very earnestly, "individually are nothing, but when I channel them together they constitute a fighting force." You sensed that they did. In fact, you saw that they did. They'd turned into talons even while Mistress Patience was speaking. But there was no need for them now. The polite, precise instruction in the realities of power politics had already made its effect, and no one—not Linus, not Schroeder, not Charlie Brown with the "failure face"—was about to say another word against Lucy. Conquest is easy if you're calm and level-headed and very plain about your purposes. Count ten before you strike and everyone will be out of the area by nine. The result is a ten-strike.

IN THE CLOWN'S SHOES

In speaking of the rich and stubborn humor of Dustin Hoffman's performance in the British comedy *Eh?* at Circle in the Square, a

number of reviewers noted a certain resemblance between Mr. Hoffman's mask and mannerisms and those of the late Buster Keaton.
Watching the entertainment a week or so after it had opened, I was
much more struck by the differences. They are exactly as wide as the
gulf that has opened between the kind of comedy you and I grew up
on and the kind of comedy that insists upon having its say today.

There was a limited sense in which Mr. Hoffman had adopted a
Keatonesque personality—a Tower of Pisa body that leaned forward
as though its shoes had been nailed to the floor, a habit of walking in
strict rhythm with the man just ahead, a stare where an expression
should have been—just as some of the situations in Henry Livings'
freehand play brought back memories of the silent film comedian's
reluctant but relentless battle with the mindless universe of matter.
Here was a saphead gazing at a monstrous machine again, wondering
which of its movable parts would make it purr and which would
make it turn on him with the fury of Moloch unleashed. Rouben Ter-
Arutunian had designed a satanic tangle of ladders, valves, and
wildly splayed boiler-plating that looked in general like a disemboweled armadillo, and it was a machine that a man of the 1920's or
a man of the 1960's would think twice about daring to flirt with.

But those differences. They begin in the nervous system of the
clown himself. Buster Keaton knew that the world was insane. But he
did not think he was. If his bent-forward posture indicated anything,
it indicated that he was ready, on no notice at all, to dive, dodge, and
deal with the enemy on the enemy's terms, adapting himself instantly
to the prevailing winds. Mr. Hoffman's posture suggested that his
arms were going to fall off.

Indeed, this night watchman in a completely automated dye-factory
distrusted *himself* at least as much as he did the factory's buzzing
control-board. He could not cover so much as three feet of ground
without recovering at least half of it in the same broken stride. His
feet seemed to retract like a robin's just when he needed the lope of a
leopard. He was *out* of sync with the world and the weather, not an
alert and responsive grace-note in its rushing, lunatic harmony. "I'm
mostly apprehensive about everything," he said, adding that he
probably needed treatment, though not necessarily the shock therapy
he got. (Shock therapy was provided in the dye works by a woman
from Personnel who was able to emit piercing sounds that seemed

anti-mating calls, capable of shattering glass and the human ganglia at one and the same time.) Mr. Hoffman's very eyelids seemed ashamed, and when he got married he immediately put on a false nose to defend himself from the new man he wasn't. Unlike Keaton, he smiled. The smile was tolerant and forgiving, because he had given up. When it was time to go to sleep, he marched directly to a bunk bed and, still standing, dropped his head onto the top tier like a broken-necked puppet. He was something to put away for the night, and perhaps for eternity. Eternity was close at hand anyway, for he was blowing up the boiler room as the comedy sighed to its end.

Beyond the differences in temperament, there is a difference here in narrative tension—a rejection of narrative tension, in fact. It works this way. When the twentieth century was younger, comedians came to implausible crises through an initially strict logic. With Keaton, say, there was always a sequence of reasons for the city streets' turning mad. The clown might pass a barred prison window and pause to peer in. He might peer in at just the moment a criminal was being photographed. The criminal might trick things so that the clown in the window was photographed, not he. The criminal might then escape. It now naturally followed, as the night the day, that the police—industriously trying to recapture the criminal—would plaster the town with enormous WANTED photographs of the clown.

The clown would thereafter find himself in a universe where he was pointed at by total strangers, where women fainted in his presence, where he was vigorously chased without reason. An irrational hostility engulfed him; he was battered back and forth along alleyways as inexplicably as an innocent out of Kafka; he found himself hiding on freshly sculptured statues of horses that—being so freshly sculptured—slowly sank in surreal horror beneath him. But all of this was irrational only to *him*. We knew the why of it, and felt comfortably sane ourselves.

The most experimental new comedy denies us our security. For logic, as we view it in the Age of McLuhan, is one of those sequential little artifices we have rigged for ourselves in an effort to make "sense" of our lives, putting A before B and B before C and pretending that D will always obediently follow after. But of course, as someone has begun to notice, D doesn't. Not always. Ever?

The current philosophical climate has made us aware that, even if matters *can* be sorted out in retrospect and given a natty cause-and-effect progression in time, experience doesn't come to us in that way. Life happens all at once, in an irrational explosion of doorbells and bad moods and good luck and stale bread (there is no *reason* I should feel rotten today, why is the fall weather so beautiful and who killed the cat?). It is a bombardment, not a law brief, and I respond to it while I am under bombardment, not after some logician has got through tidying it up for me. Each of us is *in* it, in it up to his neck, while it is still in a highly irrational state. That is what we know, or feel, now.

Thus *Eh?* disdained the business of making A, B, and C lead to an intelligibly preposterous O. It insisted that O was there from the beginning, behaving bewilderingly enough to jostle A right off the platform, perhaps never to be seen again. The dye works needed a night watchman because there was no work for a night watchman to do. (Is that so far afield, or haven't you been following employment proposals lately?) Furthermore, the night watchman didn't want to do it; he was very proud of his rights as a human being. Human rights are human rights, except that no one knows what a human being is. "Will somebody invent me a man?" the owner of the machinery cried. "What am I, if there's nobody here?" the employee wondered. When he was absent for a moment, no one could remember what he looked like. He was there only when he was there. There—here—is nowness, simultaneity, and total confusion.

What has happened is simply this: we have all slipped into the clown's shoes; we live and see as he does. There are no privileged positions in the bleachers.

SCHISGAL (SOB!)

I like Murray Schisgal because he is one step ahead of the avant-garde. The avant-garde, which is supposed to be ahead of everybody, has spent some years now scraping its aching feet against the dusty,

inhospitable earth while standing in exactly the same place. Pick up a
foot, put it down, move not at all but complain of the pain. The
place where the avant-garde has been standing is known as the Brink.
On the brink of despair, on the brink of the void, on the brink of a
park bench, the defeated have been observed waiting for Godot,
waiting for love, waiting for a word that would make communication
possible, waiting for someone or something to put them out of their
misery. Occasionally they have tried to hang themselves from inadequate trees; sometimes they have succeeded in getting themselves
disemboweled; mostly they have survived to disintegrate in the failing
light, patient candidates for the trash heap.

There has always been some aptness in the image: modern man
does feel estranged and abandoned and all that. But there has often
been something else in the image, especially as it began to repeat its
nausea *ad nauseam*: there has been self-love, self-dramatization,
romantic self-pity in it. See how drained I am, how devastated, the
squirming near-cadaver says, proud of his position as The Man Who
Has Been Most Badly Treated. The lower lip trembles but the eyes
look up: where is that spotlight that will display me as victim? Come
closer, spotlight; I have a very good speech ready about the abuse the
silent universe has heaped upon me. The universe may be silent, but
I will not be. Hear my moan. Isn't it something, really something,
how I am ravaged?

I like Murray Schisgal because he hasn't stopped at this point,
content to assume that we have come to the end of the line beyond
which no bus runs and only ragweed grows. Mr. Schisgal doesn't
necessarily deny that things are tough all over; he just sees how
preposterous it is that we should take such *pleasure* in painting the
clouds black.

If the avant-garde, up to now, has successfully exploded the bright
balloons of cheap optimism, Mr. Schisgal is ready to put a pin to the
soapy bubbles of cheap pessimism. Whatever social and philosophical
stalemates we may have come to, wit at least need not be halted in its
tracks. Wit may still venture forward. It may go right on to notice
that the woe which has become so fashionable *is* fashionable; as such
it is subject to some nose-thumbing. Wit may notice how thoroughly
professionalized our postures of despair have become, how prepack-

aged our sorrows are, how slickly and sweetly the lozenges of lament roll about on our active tongues. Wit may look at the man who is trying to hang himself and say, "Come off it."

That is one of the things Mr. Schisgal does in *Luv*. *Luv* was an extraordinarily funny evening in the theater, beautifully performed and maliciously directed, and I shouldn't be making it sound like *The Critique of Pure Reason*, even if it was quite plainly a criticism of fraudulent, opulent heartache. There was a park bench in it, validating its avant-garde standing, upon which impassioned characters compared their unhappy childhoods, growing ever more furious at the thought that anyone, anywhere, might have been more maltreated, at nine, than they. There was a lamppost in it, from which baggy-trousered Alan Arkin tried to hang himself after he had several times failed to leap from a bridge. Naturally he did not succeed; if he had he'd have had nothing to complain about. All three of the play's characters sooner or later packed knives. So did their author.

Mr. Schisgal's knife—a very sunny one, glinting brightly as it slashed—was out for people who wear black on black while lovingly congratulating themselves upon the profundity of their losses. In the second act Anne Jackson turned up very smartly in black dress, black stockings, black boots, black raincoat. She couldn't have been happier. Tragedies filled her life. She had been married twice, first to Eli Wallach and currently to Mr. Arkin, which meant that her capacity for suffering had been enormously enriched. "Now that I've lived with you," she confided in the deep, rolling tones of the old Roxy organ to Mr. Arkin, "I find you utterly obnoxious as a person." She didn't say this unpleasantly; she said it *sincerely*. Nor did Mr. Arkin resent it. He listened, deeply sympathetic, then nodded. "All right," he said, "that's a beginning." He understood the ground rules of contemporary life, the shared horror upon which all secure relationships must be founded. With luck, matters might get a good bit worse.

"I didn't ask for universal education, Harry. Why am I educated?" Miss Jackson cried in honest, succulent dismay. That was another of her tragedies. She knew so very, very much. And what she didn't know she could easily make up, for she had read a great many books, including some with hard covers. She finally intuited, among other things, that Mr. Arkin was really in love with Mr. Wallach. Latent, of course. The spectacle of Mr. Arkin digesting this information, weighing its possibilities with a wary roll of his eyes, was very, very funny, in an underground sort of way. It is difficult, you see, for any modern man to reject any suggestion that is sufficiently distressing. A fellow could be thought square, or could lose caste, if he denied out of hand a guilt that hadn't yet occurred to him.

As it happened, Mr. Arkin decided that this was one burden he did not care to take on. But it was about the only one. Knowledge has made nebbishes of us all, and we had better learn how to comport ourselves as the angst closes in. Miss Jackson did know how to comport herself. With an attitude on tap for every soul-searing occasion, she was now Phèdre fingering a cigarette, now Tallulah Bankhead caressing a growl, now any new-wave film heroine abandoning herself to existentialist necessity and the nearest male.

Because all human emotions are subject to ready analysis and readier revision—downwards, usually—there is some question whether any emotion dare be felt at all. Thus Miss Jackson delivered Mr. Arkin a most serious blow. She announced that their new marriage was a failure. Mr. Arkin did not panic. After a moment of apparent paralysis, he simply crossed his legs comfortably and thought about what he had heard. The question was: "Hmm. How shall I react *now*?"

Men do not live by bread or love alone, they live by affectation. Director Mike Nichols knew precisely how to display—in half a hundred zany visual images—the splendidly heartless disparity which has come to exist between the choked-up speeches we make and the frequently noticeable fact that we don't mean a word of them. Mr. Arkin dearly wished to soothe his despairing friend Mr. Wallach, who was stretched out beating his fists against the floor of a bridge; he sat on Mr. Wallach while consoling him. Mr. Arkin was elated to hear that Miss Jackson loved him. He stamped violently on her foot and walked away. "Do you *still* love me?" he wanted to know, sneakily, a moment later.

Due to the fact that our fashionable postures have become somewhat detached from any actual processes going on in our minds, passion—particularly anguish—can be applied to absolutely anything. "It was a cinnamon doughnut!" Mr. Wallach screamed at one point, though we had no reason to believe that he had anything against cinnamon doughnuts. He simply needed one more injustice to charge against this miserably inconsiderate world.

I like Murray Schisgal because he has not only made his vision— that of Everyman wrapped in a cloak of borrowed pain—coherent; he has made it hilarious to begin with. Occasionally he settles for a merely constructed joke ("Do you know I'm more in love now than the day I married? But my wife won't give me a divorce") as occasionally, though very rarely, Mike Nichols stooped to the easy humor of producing chamber pots. Ninety-nine percent of the time author, actors, and director were occupied drawing brilliantly buoyant cartoons which did not have to struggle to Say Anything because they so perfectly contained—within their comedy—the "Come off it!" that lately needs to be said. An exaggerated drape of Miss Jackson's leg, or a Promethean lift of Mr. Wallach's chin, was enough to do the trick. The spurious does not have to be explained when it is standing there, palpitating steadily, delighting us in the very overripeness of its stance.

A JIGGER AND A HALF

Whenever a playwright manages to be hilariously funny all night long—and Neil Simon managed to be hilariously funny all night long in *Plaza Suite*—he is in immediate danger of being condescended to. He will be tolerated, of course; somehow or other what is unmistakably entertaining is always tolerated. But he will be given a pat on the head that also suggests he should be sent from the room. He is, after all, only a genial, cunning gagman, perhaps a master of the one-liner who ought to be working for Bob Hope. The proof? The jokes are the proof. They keep coming so fast. No man who can turn a laugh so readily, so unfailingly, so *compulsively* really, could possibly be mistaken for a serious craftsman. He is a professional funnyman, and though we may be quietly grateful that he is steering large numbers of people in the direction of a theater, professional funny-men properly belong on television. The message to the audience comes down loud and clear: laugh when you will, applaud if you must, but never, never admire.

I admired *Plaza Suite* very much, and not for the most obvious reason. The obvious reason for tipping one's hat to it is that this sort of apparently idle, always amiable, cork-popping improvisation is exceedingly difficult to bring off; if it weren't, we'd have hordes of such "trifles" instead of one good one every two years. Mr. Simon, unlike most of the hopefuls who save up quips until they've got a hundred and twenty pages of them ready to be typed, knows precisely what he is doing. But there's a better reason for saluting him than that. What he is doing is precisely *right*—for him and for the form he works in.

To explain this I'll have to touch on those jokes. *Plaza Suite* did indeed have one-liners, lots of them. The evening was composed of three separate playlets set in the same hotel room. A couple married twenty-four years, or twenty-three if the husband happened to be right about it, stopped overnight to celebrate whichever anniversary it was. A Hollywood producer, short a wife at the moment, invited an old high-school sweetheart from Tenafly, New Jersey, to share vodka and its consequences with him. A father and mother took over the quarters in order to get their daughter married in the ballroom below, though the daughter quickly locked herself in the bathroom and wouldn't come out. Each visit was self-contained; Maureen Stapleton and George C. Scott, however, keep reregistering under different names and different wigs.

When the twenty-four-years-married Miss Stapleton glowingly re-counted the blessings heaven and a husband had showered on her, and included in these unbelievable miracles "a maid who doesn't drink," that was a one-liner. Something else could have been substituted and still delivered the laugh. When Mr. Scott told the dazzled matron from Tenafly that he had invited her up because he'd seen her picture in a newspaper "winning the mother-and-daughter potato race," that was a gag. The words were funny, whether the race had been or not. When Mr. Scott all but demolished himself trying to put his well-dressed shoulder through that bathroom door and

Miss Stapleton combated his rage with her own by shouting "Don't wave your broken arm at me!" that was still a jokey joke. A slight trace of madness had crept in here, the kind of madness that once might have made a Thurber cartoon, but you could see how the quick humor had been arrived at.

Perhaps it was just as easy to spot the setup when the enchanting Miss Stapleton got an enormous laugh by murmuring to herself, "I must be out of my mind coming to the Plaza in the middle of the week." Or was it? Was the line at all funny unless one knew something—a pathetic little something—of the habits of middle-class suburbanites who seek heaven only on weekends, and only in hotels? If there was a trace of pathos there, wasn't it entirely on the level? We won't push it. We won't push Miss Stapleton's regret as she stood beside billowing window-curtains and looked in vain for the lost Savoy Plaza, either, or her half-pleased, half-disgusted realization that she knew only one other couple married as long as they'd been and they were the most boring people in the world. These were put-together lines, all right. But one of the things that had been put together was a modest experience of the way things actually are.

In short, a shadow of substance had become the base for the joke. The joke wouldn't work as wordplay alone. To get on with it, what about a line like "I'll let you know" or "Would I fit in with your crowd?" or "I don't know where Humphrey Bogart lived"? These were all solid, lobby-shaking laughs, I assure you, but I'd never suggest you try them out at parties. The fun had been carefully calculated; to have it, though, we found it necessary to slip past the simple business of knowing how inconsiderate life at fifty can be—in Tenafly or Tuckahoe. We had to know what it was like for these particular, just-a-little-bit-real people: how dumb their dreams were, what they'd missed that still teased them, where they'd put the scrapbook and what was in it. Nothing profound, mind you: only enough to make certain that a straight line would turn turtle in the isn't-it-too-bad circumstances. Let's just say that Bob Hope would never have gotten yocks with the excerpts.

Well, natural enough. Even the most commercial of light comedies must have some homey streak of recognition in it, something that went on in the kitchen before the invitation to drinks came. But we're not quite done. There was a most striking moment in the first playlet when Mr. Scott simply had to tell us what was eating him. He'd been a success in the Navy, a success in business, he'd got the wife and the home and the children he wanted, his figure was trim at fifty. And he wasn't happy. Miss Stapleton, funny-bewildered and mercilessly blunt, kept at him to find out what was wrong. "I don't know," he said at first, setting his teeth. She pressed the attack, floundering but stubborn. He seemed to dig himself into the stage floor, feet apart. Then, eyes fixed intensely on nothing, he answered her. "I want to do it all over again," he said, hopelessly.

That, I submit, is an honest line. The situation was familiar and we had arrived at it in casual amusement; but the insight was real and serious and freshly stated. You jumped a bit on hearing it. I should add that Mr. Simon followed it up by giving Miss Stapleton a wise-crack not half wise enough for the woman we'd been listening to, and the echo of vaudeville promptly stirred. But for a moment, at least, we had touched something that ran like a gentle undertow beneath quite a bit of the nonsense.

Was the trace of seriousness spurious? Was it a sham gesture toward mild weight forced into the rattle-on fun to keep it from rattling too transparently, a vein borrowed from more responsible playwrights and only shallowly explored by way of cooking up a plot? Not at all. We come to the point I have been edging up on. This was exactly the degree of substance proper to light domestic comedy. No less, no more.

One of the crazy mistakes we make in the contemporary theater is that of supposing that if something is serious at all it must be thoroughly, thumpingly serious—and must promptly be put into a bigger, deeper, soberer play. That is how we get our overinflated dramas in which almost nothing happens, certainly nothing ample enough to account for all of the soul-scratching, conscience-prodding, emotion-begging writhing that goes on. The play becomes over-wrought because it is making too much of a small truth. There *are* small truths, and they are comic truths; they are truths of a size that can be accommodated in—and almost cheerfully covered over by—a quip. We quip them into statement, and then into silence, every day of our lives. Feeling fifty, and having energy that can never be properly used again, is one of them. Being bowled over by celebrities, especially if we have come within inches of brushing lives with them, is another. They are legion; they are not tragic (they are too ordinary for that and we are all helpless in their damnable hands); they are shrug-off truths, silly imprisonments and hopeless reflexes that can be dealt with only by pretending to laugh. By actually laughing, finally, more or less as George Scott laughed—with desperate exuberance. The highest home of such truths is the epigram, which is, of all things, a one-liner. But there are some so commonplace that a wisecrack will take care of them, and thank God for that. If all men are trapped, some have the sense to see that they are trapped in a circus ring.

Mr. Simon seems to me a man of sense, using just the jigger and a half of substance that will make a decent drink, observing what he observes and cradling it in a joke that is about the right fit for it. His work is not only smooth and sunny, it is nicely proportioned—which is more than can be said for that of many of his perspiring fellows. He has no identity problem.

CANCELLATION STAMP

What is there about the British state of mind just now that insists upon the complete rejection of feeling?

This curious phenomenon, which crops up most often with the label of "comedy" attached to it, is stubbornly, coolly, in a way expertly illustrated by Frank Marcus' *The Killing of Sister George*. The play, however, is no loner. Its dryness of tongue is anticipated in Joe Orton's *Entertaining Mr. Sloane*, and there is scarcely any need to mention the vast terrain that has lately been opened up in the name of black comedy, sick comedy, or, more conventionally, dark comedy.

A kind of jungle law governs this country in which no heart beats. The playwright generally begins, as Mr. Marcus does, with what would normally be regarded as a simple satirical thrust at some contemporary fad, foible, or commonplace foolishness. Addiction to radio soap opera is the point of departure in *The Killing of Sister George*. Sister George is a jolly, generous, ever-so-wise country nurse who scoots about on her motorbike hailing Ginger, the local pub-keeper, as she passes by, singing hymns at the top of her lungs as she turns down crooked lanes where the ailing await her ministrations. All of this for the benefit of credulous London housewives who turn on their sets at 11:15 in the morning to soak up, sentimentally, the quite synthetic cheeriness and benevolence that is missing from their own lives. The mythical Sister George is truer than truth to them.

Easy enough to satirize, and Mr. Marcus doesn't mind availing himself of some of the easier satirical ploys. When it is time, for instance, to write Sister George out of the script—she is to be "killed," still singing, by an unfortunate encounter with a ten-ton truck—something close to a day of national mourning is in order. Bereaved listeners send flowers—sticky crosses formed of roses. An executive of the BBC stalks onto the stage in black, bearing lilies. Not only housewives believe in the spurious; the very people who perpetrate so much commercial fraud pay it lip service, too.

In Mr. Marcus' fable, some of this mooning over the demise of what never existed at all is funny in a familiar way. The lady in black with her lilies is broad enough to have come out of *Once in a Lifetime* or any other thumb-to-nose sassing of the entertainment industries. But Mr. Marcus also holds a checkrein he wants to pull up sharply before we laugh too much. The evening is only part parody; it could—if anyone wished it to—engage us in pathos.

For the actress who plays Sister George believes in Sister George herself, up to a point. She can recite, over her gin bottle, whole reams of ersatz philosophizing battered out for her by some hack, and she can do it in a warm, motherly voice that trembles on the edge of actual conviction. Being written out of the script is literally a death sentence for her; the person she was, or imagined herself to be, will cease to live in this room or be recognized on the streets. As an actress, she is offered a sop: she can take over the role of Claribel the Cow in a new children's program, if she wishes. Her furious "I can't play a cow!" really means that Sister George can't play a cow; an actress who hadn't turned into a myth could, of course, do it. And when, at evening's end, she sits alone in her award-cluttered flat, forlorn and increasingly sodden, to look bitterly into the unspeakable heavens and moo three times in self-mockery and ultimate distress, we might very well be touched by the breaking of a woman who has let illusion rule the roost.

But, but, but. We must *not* be moved. Although pathos inside parody might prove a neat enough discovery for one evening's outing, the pathos itself must be scratched, carefully defaced, before it creeps close enough to tease us into a fondness for the play's people. Sister George is a monster. The thirty-four-year-old "child" she lives with on Lesbian terms is an opportunistic ingrate with a nasal whine where her brain should be. Sister George may splatter a fresh scone all over her slavey and companion just to keep her in line; but that is the least of it. When Sister George barks, Childie must drop to the floor, kiss the hem of her garment, chew the stub of her cigar, go to the still-steaming tub and drink Sister George's bathwater. When Childie misbehaves, Sister George threatens to tear the heads off her pet dolls. Sister George is savagely jealous and certain that Childie is seeing men on the sly; the iron pills the girl takes are probably contraceptives, the old harridan insists. And the younger woman must be tormented with half jokes, jokes that seem to despise themselves while they are being made. Childie is reminded that a man who had seen her stripped remarked that she could use sunglasses for a bra. "You're my flatmate in more senses than one," her sarcastic lord and mistress concludes.

Now, there are other emotions that might invade us as this brawling, clinging, distrustful and yet desperately needed relationship is disclosed. We might feel revulsion, for one thing; that is an emotion. Or we might as readily feel pity. But here the play resolutely coils back on itself, rushing malicious humor into the breach. What is revolting must be ridiculed; what might have aroused pity must be squashed under the bootheel of caricature. Is the situation ugly? Laugh. Are the principals miserable? Laugh harder.

All of the potential emotional facets of the play—humor, pathos, revulsion, pity—are carefully, constantly brought together so that they will cancel one another out. No response can begin to stir without being undercut by its opposite. The image that is left is deliberately sterile. The two women decide to go to a fancy-dress ball in drag, costumed as Laurel and Hardy. They do a bit of soft-shoe, they play tricks with their ties and their derbies, they get bad news before they have quite finished frittering about and one of them is left banging at the other's locked door with a tin flute. There is no moment in all of this when we can give in, when we can surrender to the fun of impersonation or the uneasiness of dancing against doom or the wistfulness of hearing a flute fail to pipe confidence back. We are always between moods, short of entering them. Our sensations are not mixed; they are sternly shut out.

That the contemporary world is in many ways afraid of feeling is obvious; feeling means commitment, and it is hard for us nowadays to imagine a commitment that may not cruelly backfire. We have been burned before; now we will stand away from the fire and take our revenge by making faces at it. This gap between warmth and wariness, between plunging and keeping our distance, has opened up in our own theater, to be sure, though it has most assertively appeared and been most fully developed in London. It poses a serious dilemma for at least one theatrical form. It is perfectly true, as both Bergson and Baudelaire insisted, that all comedy demands a degree of detachment: we should not easily laugh at a man impaled on a cactus plant if we truly imagined ourselves in his place. A degree of participation is always waived. But if comedy involves a certain lack of feeling, can it be plainly and ruthlessly defined as nothing more than a lack of feeling? Does the neutralization of emotion automatically bring laughter into being—or is our temporary detachment when we laugh a mere surface protection against an involvement so deep that we would probably burst into tears if we didn't laugh? Mr. Marcus' kind of comedy seems to propose that when we are made to feel absolutely nothing, when each response we might make is systematically undermined by an enemy response, we are obliged to regard the sterilized landscape as funny. I think I doubt *that*.

12

PRACTICAL MATTERS

FOOL'S ENERGY

BROADWAY is very brave.

Think of what it faces every time the seasonal machinery begins to turn over, productions arrange to come in in a tumble, money starts to be poured down what may turn out to be a drain, and practically everybody across the country gears himself to follow the season's course closely to see exactly how badly it shapes up.

Broadway can't win, you know. It can eat its little heart out hoping for approval; it can round up all the talent that isn't eating high off the hog in Hollywood; it can beg for money and audition for money and even get money from everybody except foundations and the government; it can scour the world for scripts and it can persuade all of its personnel to labor so hard perfecting each enterprise that nervous breakdowns are a dime a dozen. But nothing it can do will give it a fairer name. If, during any nine months in which craftsmanship and cash are spent without reserve, Broadway manages to be successful, it will be despised for being successful. If it fails, it will be castigated for having failed. Whipping is its lot, contempt is the reward it can look for; the only glee it will ever get is glee over its having done so badly. I sometimes wonder that it has the nerve to go on.

Our aesthetic mores are very precise, if peculiar. By current standards, a two-year run is proof positive that a show wasn't worth doing in the first place. If it *had* had any artistic merit, or displayed any intelligence, it would have failed instantly. Quick failure, however, is a little trickier. No snap judgments here, because there are really two kinds of quick failure, and they must be differentiated. If a quick failure *looked* as though it had meant to try for a run, and had in its secret heart itched for success, then it was obviously worthless and represents exactly what is wrong with Broadway. If, on the other hand, it positively invited failure, carefully and conscientiously eschewing any values that might—God forbid—have interested more than twenty friends of the author, then it was clearly distinguished work and its demise represents exactly what is wrong with Broadway. (Broadway, brace yourself; you're in for it either way.)

My purpose in these remarks is not to contest the prevailing ethos. I've tried that before, and I can't win, either. (I do take quiet, furtive comfort in the fact that during the week in which I am writing, Shakespeare has done $70,000 in one house and $50,000 in another. I worry for Shakespeare, though. He's playing fast and loose with his reputation with these long runs and high grosses.)

What really interests me—stuns me, in fact—is Broadway's blind, bull-like persistence. The *energy* it gets up every fall, all on its own! Around the country, theater has to be pushed a lot. Bankers have to be badgered, communities harangued, sluggards routed out of their beds and strong-armed onto committees; subscription campaigns have to be mounted and then given fresh vitamin shots regularly as first ardors begin to flag; matching funds must be lobbied for with art, sweat, and tears. And then, every year, new terror strikes: the subscription list is faltering, the supporters who pounded pavements last year are footsore or committed to the Community Chest this year, the whole beautiful dream needs a recharge. With a sigh, loins are girded, shoulders squared: momentum must be gained, if the starter button can be located, all over again.

Not on Broadway. Too dumb to know what is in store for it, as hopelessly incorrigible as a kid who is climbing back up a tree with his arm in a sling, Broadway generates its own heat, aflame, it would seem, with folly. Under the promptings of nobody, with handouts from nowhere, with memories of disaster behind it and what must look like the void ahead, it compulsively goes back to work, literally unable not to work.

Whether it is a lemming or in love, it *wants* to do what it is doing, wants to scrounge for its mad money, wade through those interminable piles of intolerable scripts until it has found one just a little less bad than the last, connive with agents and fight with actors and wheedle directors and cope with designers and go out on the road where it knows perfectly well it will break its neck and have to do its very hardest work while in traction. After that, the critics. Not just the first-night critics, who have claws enough, but second-guessers stretching to infinity. Moss Hart once thought he'd finally cleared his head of a particularly distressing notice, after approximately three years of trying to forget, when, spending a relaxing weekend in the country with friends, he was delighted to find an anthology left considerately by his bedside for late-night reading. Opening the book, and settling down comfortably, he of course came upon the notice, reprinted for its very special wit and wisdom, providing him with yet one more sleepless night. I never asked him, but he probably started another play the next day.

Now, some people will suppose that Broadway eternally goes back to the fray, building up its independent head of steam and counting on encouragement from no one, because all of its people are money-grubbers hoping for a kill; some will suppose that so much spontaneous combustion occurs because moths *are* attracted to candles and because Broadway, brash and brainless though it be, is still the most brilliantly lit theatrical corner in the country; I suppose it keeps going its hyperthyroid, self-propelling way because the people who live along it are professionals.

There is one awkward thing about being a professional. Once you've committed yourself to a profession, you're no longer fit for anything but to follow it. Your hand reaches, when you crawl out in the morning, for the tool that has betrayed you a hundred times; it's the tool you know, and if it weren't there you'd be on relief or in the booby hatch. Habits are desperate acquisitions: if you have a habit of threading your way through Shubert Alley, or doing your thinking while sitting on theater fire-escapes, or surviving by being the fittest in a hotel-room fracas immediately after a play's first indecent exposure in New Haven, you don't stop to think about how ignoble your work is, or how middle-class your aspirations are, or how likely you are to be both despised *and* poor by November. (Robert Anderson has been heard to say that you can make a killing in the theater, but not a living. The remark is true. You will notice, though, that however Mr. Anderson makes his living he is still in the theater.) Broadway uses a skill, well or ill, gratefully or ungratefully; the man who's picked it up, in any degree at all, behaves like a drunk, heading unerringly and with uncritical affection for the bar he's last been thrown out of. He doesn't need a shove to get him going, either. He knows his own drives and has a certain practical respect for them.

There's something else. While I was curving around the lakes of Killarney one summer, expecting the car to hit a careless leprechaun any minute, I had a chat with the driver, who, it turned out, had spent eight years in New York before returning to a less fun-loving land. It also turned out that he'd read some of my reviews. He proved it by quoting from them (a rare bird, as you can see). In fact, he said, he'd always read *all* reviews of new plays as they opened in New York. Eventually I asked him if he'd ever gone to see one of the plays. The answer—and I knew it—was no.

Now, what fascinated me was not that he'd succeeded in staying out of theaters—an enormous number of people succeed in that objective nowadays—but that he'd clung for the whole time to the practice of keeping in distant touch. Clung to the skirts, you might say, without ever clasping hands. Why? Why should any man in his right mind who is *never* going to go to the theater keep reading about the theater, persistently, systematically? I suspect that my man has a thousand, or a million, duplicates in this country right now. Broadway is followed, daily, weekly, monthly, religiously, if only to be lambasted. In newspapers and magazines Broadway still takes precedence—in position and in space—over films, though heaven knows more people go to films. Why and why again?

I suspect they're waiting for something, and don't want to miss it when it happens. I suspect that, buried fairly deep in the mass subconscious, there lingers a conviction that somewhere, somehow, the stage is going to do or say something extraordinary, and that, when it does, the deed or speech is going to be more extraordinary than its equivalent in a rival medium. Something is expected of the stage, and of the Broadway stage. (Something is expected of other stages, too, though not so much; notice how we really do not demand as much of other stages and are grateful for almost any flash.) And I suspect that as the pros go back to work each year, battered but under their own power, they go with a little tingling sensation that the long-expected, the unexpected, might—just *might*—happen this year. That's where fool's energy comes from.

BURNING DOWN BROADWAY

We are always sentimental about what does not exist.

The commercial theater of Broadway, mess that it is, exists, and that is why I am prepared to defend to its death and mine its continuing claim to a decent measure of attention. There are those among us who would deny it this claim. Almost any day in the week —pick a day—you can read in one journal or another not simply the statement that the American commercial theater is in a state of galloping senility but that the gallop should be intensified, by a constant flick of the whip, until the beast drops in its tracks. The general implication is that when what is left of the commercial theater is at last happily exterminated, we shall be free—free!—to make a new and beautiful and original and wholly respectable theater to stand in its place. There is a further assumption that this new and beautiful, original and respectable, theater will move in the very moment Broadway moves out.

I have my doubts. Broadway is indeed in a decline, a decline so steep that night after night one has the sensation of sitting on the rim of a long-dormant volcano, and of slipping. Some nights it seems as though the very seats in the auditorium have come unbolted and that, as soon as everything on stage is sucked through the floor with a *whoosh*, all the rest of us will go plummeting into the open hole after it, never to be heard of again.

Broadway is often not a cheery place. Still, it is a stubbornly, obtusely, wistfully, energetically active place, kept alive by innocence. Should it be swept away with a giant hand so that something purer might come to birth? There are three reasons why I don't think so.

The alternative we hear most about these days is the regional repertory theater. Everyone knows that across the country municipalities are putting together acting companies and importing directors to provide communities with fare that Broadway won't or can't send them. Everyone is in favor of the maximum theatrical activity from coast to coast, and so am I. But while we are dreaming, or even while we are doing, we must remain realists. It is every bit as difficult to achieve first-rate work—and certainly as difficult to achieve genuinely contemporary work—in regional repertory as it is on Broadway.

Conceivably you have read in the newspapers during recent years of many shifts of directors from one community playhouse to another, generally after disagreements with what are called "boards of directors." In several notable instances—notable because the disaffected or just plain fired men in charge have reputations behind them—the artists who have been staging the plays have clashed fatally with the community solons who have been responsible for fund-raising. Either the companies have not become solvent quickly enough, or, when solvency is not required because endowment is plentiful, artists and their overlords have locked horns on matters of judgment. In short, the problem that is supposed to vex Broadway, and to lower its standards—the problem of dealing with "backers"— is precisely as troublesome in regional theaters as it is on what I think of as home base. The regional "backer" is apt to wear a different cut of clothes, and read different weekly magazines. But he is, in the last analysis, the same man. He may be, from a theatrical point of view, a worse man. That is to say, he may be less knowledgeable about the theater and less foolishly in love with it than the typical New York investor.

Community "boards" are made up of all sorts of people, but among them there are going to be bankers. And bankers, in some curious way, are devoted to money, as mayors are devoted to their personal popularities and leading businessmen to their cultural-corporate images (which may be a contradiction in terms). Good stage directors are hard to come by in any case, anywhere, including Broadway. Good governing boards may be even harder. I have talked with one extremely intelligent producer of plays who had *had* it with councils composed of community figures rather than catch-as-catch-can Broadway investors. "Compared to dealing with a board of directors," he remarked, "Broadway is like running an art house."

I bring this up not to discourage the burgeoning new movement now leaping state after state, but to bring the issue into sober focus. We must always remember that all dreams are booby-trapped, and we must set about realizing them with open eyes and strong nerves. I bring it up, too, to say that the dream will not be realized tomorrow and since the day after tomorrow may be slow in coming, Broadway had best be encouraged to live through its present torments, too, as mother hen, reminder, or stopgap—however you choose to regard it.

Another, somewhat bitterer but less practical (in the stone-and-mortar sense) attack upon Broadway comes from an earnest, and honest, intellectual elite which imagines that the moment the Morosco and David Merrick are both torn down, a flourishing drama of some literary dignity will at once win the hearts of the finer-grained populace. The assumption here is that as soon as we can drive *The Impossible Years* out of the theater, a movement which will get no resistance from me, we will immediately have entire seasons devoted to de Ghelderode, Arrabal, and Brecht.

This position is a bit more realistic than the first because it does not ask for a mass audience or a thriving box office. It conceives of a limited theater for an audience even more limited than the one we now have: raising sights higher, it imagines a small audience of more refined sensibilities and it generally expects that subsidy—from government or foundations—will pay the costs that no minority audience could possibly pay. This view does, of course, overlook the difficulty outlined above: that governments have committees and foundations have "boards" and the energies of the creative people concerned can be exhausted once more, quickly, by policy contretemps before very much goes into rehearsal. But that is not my point in this instance. The point here is that the destruction of Broadway is utterly irrelevant to the plan in mind. The plan is wasting its breath despising Broadway so vehemently because it is not after the Broadway audience at all; it is not after Broadway money; it is not even after Broadway know-how. Broadway could vanish over-night and the new dispensation would not be one whit nearer its cherished goal. On its own terms and by its own standards, the new dispensation must bring itself into being, create its own audience, find its own financing. If it is truly vital, and if it means what it says, it can do this—must do this—whether Broadway lives or dies.

Which brings me to my third observation. Bad as Broadway is just now, there is no reason under the sun why it should not coexist—for as long as it can—with every kind of regional repertory company or specialized theater growing alongside it. My own view, which I do not mean to press here, is that the most substantial and most complex work is ultimately going to be done in the presence of the largest and most diverse possible group of spectators, that the biggest play is going to be built in front of the biggest audience, and that both regional companies and minority theaters historically act as feeders, as pointing fingers, as seminal influences.

But even if we dismiss this view, we are left with a truism: Broadway, such as it is, takes care of itself, neither interfering with the growth of forces outside it nor denying its contemptuous cousins anything those cousins really want.

The notion that beauty will automatically flower once we have leveled the present weed-choked garden to the ground is a sentimental one. Things are not that easy. We are not guaranteed good theater the moment bad theater ceases to be. We may simply get no theater, perhaps for a very long time.

I would rather *some* theater, at an unmistakably professional if less than celestial level, and that at the moment is what Broadway provides. If we are realists, we will go on wrestling with it.

WHO'S IN THE HOUSE TONIGHT?

I don't know about you, but I find it exceedingly difficult to read through an entire column of newspaper type devoted to the latest pronouncements from Albany about the control of ticket scalping, the regulation of prices, and all of those things which occupy the minds of people who wish to improve the theater without going to it. It's not that I'm skeptical about the good intentions of public officials, or even about the possibilities of reforming the human heart. I'm an uplift type, really, a firm believer in the proposition that some good will come of the whole rotten mess sooner or later, and I suppose it's worth while to nudge the moral evolution along now and then.

But I do always have the feeling that what I'm reading about is irrelevant. With each succeeding paragraph I feel more and more remote from what is actually happening on Broadway, from what is important on and about Broadway, from what is really going on in the minds of theatergoers. Theatergoers do want to be protected, I'm sure. But what they want to be protected from is bad plays, not malfeasance in the countinghouse, and the deeper I go into a column devoted to malfeasance and/or high prices the farther away I seem to be from the world of the living.

Having this sensation, I hate to add so much as a sentence to it, which is why I am reluctant to deal with two questions posed for reviewers by Abel Green, editor of *Variety*. I will give you the questions and try to hedge on the answers. (1) What do you think of the proposal to legalize the sale of "very choice" seats at perhaps $25 a head in order to cut down scalping and put the money directly into the producer's exchequer instead of into an outsider's pocket? (2) What effect do you think the boost in prices for top seats, which is coming anyway, will have on the theater in general?

You can see how abstract these questions really are. Actually, I'm in favor of *anything* that will put going money (I mean money that is going to be passed from hand to hand regardless) into the production pool. That's where it belongs, that's where it is desperately needed, that's where it is earned. If some idiot wants to pay $25 for a seat, I would like him to pay it to all of the nice people who put shows on and not to some otherwise unemployed sneak in a hotel lobby. Given that first "if," there's no argument. Nor is there anything very interesting about the question. What other attitude would a sane man take?

As for the next boost in prices, I suppose it's going to have about the same effect on the theater as the last boost did, and the boost before that. Everybody is going to sigh about it, and some few are going to be shrill about it, and it isn't going to make any difference to the theater whatsoever. If a show is in demand, the increased price will be paid all too willingly. If a show isn't in demand, it won't increase its prices—also to no effect. The issue can be discussed, but its facts and figures will be trampled to death the minute people decide to move toward or away from an entertainment.

You see, I am calm about such things, and don't tell me it's because I don't have to pay for my seats; I have to pay for my relatives' seats and my friends' seats and my children's seats (the children are permitted to pay so much and no more, or stand at the back), and if my wife writes a play she has to pay for *every* seat she hands out and also for the one she sits in (I insert this informative tidbit in order to help dispel a popular superstition to the contrary, really on behalf of all authors), and so I do know what life at the box office is like.

But it's like that because we are quirky human beings who abandon our high moral and budgetary principles the minute we hear Carol Channing has a good show again, and the fact of the matter is that our "the hell with it" mood is very much the mood of abandon appropriate to all theatergoing. If you're not cutting loose and overdoing things one way or another, what fun do you think you're going to have?

But these are wormlike observations that wind up swallowing their own tails and let's dispense with them. Behind all of the waste breath there *is* something that worries me. It has to do with both of Mr. Green's questions, but not really with money. It has to do with people.

Here is the catch I see in charging $25 a seat to those who will cough up. Only one kind of person—or one kind of audience—will cough up. You can call it an expense-account audience, or an out-of-town-buyer's audience, or a first-six-weeks audience (meaning the smart audience that *must* see a hot show early in order to score handsomely at competitive cocktail parties). You can call it anything you like so long as you recognize one thing about it: it is an audience whose motive in going to the theater is extraneous in exact proportion to the increase in price. That is to say, no one shells out $25 simply to see the show. He pays the extra fee for an extra, highly irrelevant consideration: to see it incredibly early in the run, to brag about so seeing it, to impress his guests, perhaps to waste his substance before the government can get hold of it. Et cetera and so on. There is a giant gap between the purposes of the play and the purposes of the man going to see it. The pleasure such a man takes in the experience has little to do with the pleasure the playwright intended.

Under the $25 dispensation we are not merely going to get a rich audience, for as long as the largesse shall live; we are going to get an indifferent audience—an audience indifferent to the precise nature of the occasion, an audience preoccupied with the side benefits it has bargained for with every dollar above 10. The theater becomes a pawn in the situation, not a principal.

And when this possibility is put together with the constant rise in prices generally, we do have to think of the dangers of falling heir to a rich audience—more and more, and then exclusively. Producers, of course, aren't exactly going to avoid rich audiences, or drive them away with sticks; and sometimes rich audiences have been known to support very good things. The danger isn't defined by saying that the audience will be rich; the danger is that its members will be all of one kind.

The single-level house seems to me an eventuality to be abhorred, at all times, in all weathers. The level itself doesn't matter much. An exclusively proletarian audience is going to produce a partially crippled theatrical experience; so is an exclusively intellectual audience; so is an exclusively church-bazaar audience; so is any audience too readily defined. For instance, I never liked being in the *lobby* of The Living Theater because I felt an outsider, an intruder, there. The people milling about me either constituted a cult or strained every hair frond to look like one. I'm not trying to hint that there was an air of studied grime about them, though there was. I have not been asked to model Hathaway shirts myself. What distinguished them was their aura of sharing a secret, of belonging to a caste, of existing in mannered isolation from any other thread in the social fabric. Look-alikes spoke to look-alikes here, and to look-alikes alone; one could not see how there was ever going to be much cross-fertilization.

In the end, of course, they *were* sharing a secret. The Living Theater died of its secretiveness, of its failure to invite, or to hook, any other segment of the body politic. Having done some good work (and much bad), it closed because its single-level audience made up too narrow a level to support so public an activity as the theater.

Once again, it is not costs that count most. It is the sustained will, and the ability, to deal with two or more audience levels at once. That is what the theater's auditorium was shaped for: to lure disparate persons into it, to accommodate various kinds and to weld them—in a hypnotic act of breathing together—into one. Isolated peoples do not require an auditorium; they can be isolated at home, or wherever they like. Theater is, in its open arc, a communal form. Strangers come to it, and may depart again as strangers; while they were there they were blood brothers, courtesy of an act of art. Whenever a fresh welding takes place, in however small a way, costs tend to take care of themselves (not discounting subsidy, which is most often granted after successful fusion has been demonstrated).

Is there any way to describe an ideal audience? Probably not, but I'd do it this way. When you don't know who's in the house tonight, the audience is right. If you stand at the gate and can't identify the faces, if the mixture is baffling beyond any quick trick of naming categories, if, just before curtain time, the house manager finds himself hopelessly unable to say to the actors that it's *this* kind of house or *that* kind of house, then conditions are perfect for the work the theater is meant to do. Now the actors must go out and find the audience, probing, poking, testing, teasing, until at last new acquaintance is made and all portions of the house discover each other. Better plays, better performers, better audiences are bred of the exploration.

But to know for certain the composition of tonight's house is to dull challenge and to kill adventure. If the audience knows the kind of gesture that is to be made, and if the actors know that the audience knows, what can the actors do but make the expected gesture, and soon stale it? The big-money theater we are rapidly galloping toward, and which we are even thinking of formally acknowledging, threatens to become a one-face theater. And how bored one becomes looking at the same old face!

HOW TO BE AN AUDIENCE

The theater is not a foreign city. It often feels that way, even for people who live within a subway ride of it or work not thirty feet from a lighted marquee. It seems a world of apartness, where all the tickets are passed from hand to hand by the members of a secret society, where headwaiters speak only to those who know the language and push tourists into corners already preempted by cobwebs, where the good or bad "word" on a show is a most mysterious matter of inflection and where the outsider who attempts to chance a statement of his own will no doubt find himself fumbling, inadequate, presumptuous and gauche.

Thus the theater is either avoided out of sheer nervousness or it is attended only under the aegis of a well-paid archangel. One must first come to know someone who "knows" the theater. Everything from the choice of a show to the purchase of tickets to the summoning of a cab to the selection of the nearest restaurant to the amount of applause that is appropriate at curtain fall is thereafter dictated by a heaven-sent baby-sitter, or an interlocked succession of them.

The non-New Yorker who comes to New York passes several dozens of theater marquees between Forty-first Street and Fifty-ninth, either to the west or to the east of Seventh Avenue but mostly to the west, without supposing that the open doors beneath them are openly open to him. A certain radiation emanates from the interior of the lobby and the focal point of the box office, but it is a discharge that shoulders him away more than it entices him toward it; he does not feel insidey enough to go inside. He looks at the posters, he reads some of the shrill quotations that leap across the door tops, and he wonders. Perhaps he yearns. But he feels that he might embarrass himself if he opened the one door that isn't marked "Use other door," stepped up to that brass rail (which side of the brass rail are you supposed to come in by and which side are you supposed to go out by, and if you don't get it right won't you be excommunicated?), and simply asked for two tickets. So he sidles past the playhouse, trying to look as though he owned real estate in the area and was simply checking to see that all foundations were secure, and goes back to his hotel or motel or friend's house in Brooklyn. If he goes back to a hotel, he now checks with the porter or the newsstand or wherever this particular hotel's archangel may be stationed, and hands his soul over to him, lock, stock and wallet. If he is visiting a friend in Brooklyn, his friend probably knows a broker who takes care of *his* visits to the interior of the sacred city, and that will be that again. Would the archangel suggest a show? Would the archangel get the seats? Would the archangel recommend a restaurant? Would the archangel tuck him in at night?

The visitor is now doing all of the things calculated to make him despise not only the theater and New York but himself as well. He is going to the management instead of going to the theater. (Sometimes the management is kindly and wise, and I am not trying to injure the reputation or the profit of brokers or concierges. I am only trying to indicate that, by surrendering to his own unnecessary helplessness, he is well on the way to having somebody else's good time.)

Here are some of the things that are going to make him discontented:

(1) The absence of potluck. The theatergoer hasn't picked his own lemon or selected his own lollipop. Because playgoing is meant to be a pleasure, personal responsibility is essential. One can always shirk responsibility in one's work; after all, there is a chain of command where forced labor is concerned and one may readily defer to orders from above; one can always say later, when all those mistakes have been made, that he did only what he was told to do. With theatergoing, one must be free to say that he did what he wanted to do. That compensates him for a bad show and makes a mighty genius of him for having picked a good one. It is terribly distressing to have a dull evening for which you are in no way to blame.

There are only two intelligent ways to pick a play: by hunch or at random. It's no good trying to be scientific about it, looking to see how long a show has run (some shows run, I think, only because no warehouse will have them), or looking to see what the reviewers said about them. The first thing anyone notices as he studies the reviewers' quotes is that everything on the list has utterly enchanted someone, and you'd have to stay around for twenty years to be certain

whether Someone was your favorite reviewer or merely the producer's. Nor is research profitable. The visitor who took the time to
go to the New York Public Library's back newspaper files to see what
all of the reviewers had to say about the particular prospect he has in
mind for the evening would discover, to his horror, that great minds
had not met. What had proved tasteless to the *Times* had proved
tasty to the *News* and delightfully so-so to the *Post*. Vertigo is to be
avoided at all costs when in the city, and the newspaper files had best
be kept tucked away. (I should not, as a reviewer, be advising you of
this lesion in the intellectual life of New York, but on last New
Year's Day I promised myself to tell the truth during one twenty-four-
hour period in the coming twelve months and you just happen to
have hit me, shortly after sunrise, on that day.) The reviewers, because they are proud and happy to disagree, are unhelpful.

Hunch is the best method. The man who runs his finger down the
list of shows until his heart hesitates or his finger balks is the man
likeliest to succeed in the lottery that is theatergoing. After all, he
probably married his wife out of instinct, and if he can get through
all those evenings with her he ought to be able to get through one,
spurred on by idiot impulse and the chanciness of love, in the
theater. As he says "my wife" or "my evening" he ought to be able to
say "my show." Possession is nine-tenths of the fun.

If no hunch stirs, then window-shopping will do. The man who
wanders aimlessly past theater fronts where gleaming grimaces and
prancing torsos are so persuasively blown up in the panels provided
for the purpose and who wanders past enough theaters—three or four
won't do, one must be serious about window-shopping—will finally
be willing enough to go into one of them, where he can sit down. In
an art gallery, one often sits down not because a nearby painting is
arresting, but because physical collapse is imminent and one would
prefer not to be carried out by the attendants; seated, one often
discovers an arresting painting. Neither theater nor galleries need be
guided tours, unless one is thinking of giving paid lectures on his
return home. Affection is very often engendered by surprise. Men
have become passionate about Uccello because it was five minutes to
five, and there was one Uccello hanging near the door to the street.
And disaffection is decreased when one has not been promised the

moon. The pleasant state of maybe needs to be investigated more thoroughly.

By the way, it is generally assumed that theatergoing on these hunch and/or random terms is not possible in New York, where, legend has it, arrangements must be made in the way that one puts down a three-week-old son for Andover. The legend is a lie, possibly propagated by hot-dog concessionaires who want people walking the streets all night. During the first half of the season in which this is written, there were never more than two out of thirty entertainments selling out every week. Unless it is already 8:40 on a Saturday night, the chances are generally fifteen to one that a theatergoer can go where he wants to go.

But we have almost lost track of our list of discontents due to superplanning, or heavenly management. Discontent can also be due to:

(2) Making an occasion of it. By a process of superb illogic, modern man in New York has decided that anything so expensive as theatergoing must be compensated for by spending as much again before the theater, after the theater, getting to the theater and, if possible, between the acts. The cost of playgoing must be fifty dollars a night, even though the theater tickets cost only fifteen, or the playgoer will have nothing to write about to his congressman. It is like getting into a taxicab, leaning over the front seat, and urging the meter to "Go, go, go!" hoping to break the world's record, or the meter. This is a compulsion, and if it can't be licked I advise seeing a doctor.

Dinner is the main thing. Dinner with drinks. I am not really against dinner with drinks, but I am in favor of it on the continental plan. If you want a couple of drinks and a really good dinner, give the evening to it. It's worth it. And on that particular evening you'll only have to pay for the dinner and drinks, not for the show you can't see through the blur.

Too often we want to pack our pleasure into a pressure cooker. We think of dinner *and* a show. This calls for preparation on a massive scale, rather as though we were synchronizing our watches on D-Day. It means making certain in advance that we have theater seats for a certain night; it means making certain in advance that we have a reservation at a reasonably nearby restaurant (perhaps not the one we'd have preferred if we could have gone anywhere) not only on that same night but at a particular time and not forty minutes later; it means bribing someone to make certain that a taxicab will be on hand to get us to the restaurant not forty minutes later; it means clock-watching over drinks ("Hadn't we better order?" "No, I want one more." "Oh, dear, we'll be late") and panic over dinner; it means soul-searching and public wrangling over the matter of whether or not a taxi to the theater is advisable if the restaurant happens to be just three blocks farther away than it ought to be; it means apprehension through traffic due not to speed but to the absence of any motion whatsoever in the midtown theater district at 8:30 (8:40, ye gods, 8:50!) and perhaps jumping out of the cab to run the rest of the way; it means arriving in the playhouse possibly late, possibly to be cursed by the people we must crawl over, possibly unfocused as we blink at the bright lights on stage, and certainly unrecovered from the digestive effort our systems are so nobly making. In all of this no one thing is ever fully attended to, and afterward we can decide which was worst, the ineptitude of the hotel doorman, the rushed dinner, the unrushed traffic, or the play to which we sat down exhausted. My own strongest recommendation is to go to dinner on a Tuesday, go to the theater on a Wednesday, and take a cab ride during the whole of a Friday evening if that is the sort of thing you enjoy. On Friday the cabbie will bless you, he may even sing to you, when he learns that you are not going to take him into the theater district.

In short, zero in. Anything that is worth devoting two and one-half hours to is worth a clear head, an unshattered state of nerves, and some physical trim. No play should have to bear the burden of a cross-country track meet and an apple-pie eating contest just prior to it, with the residual fatigue or even the residual excitement of these things occupying the forefront of the customer's brain. Ask an actor which audience in any week is hardest to wake up, hardest to play to, and he will tell you Saturday night's, when business is at its very best and when one might hopefully expect the audience, smack in the middle of its weekend holiday, to be at its most relaxed, gregarious, exuberant. Saturday night responses are generally leaden to begin with because Saturday night is the night when most people cram most of their experiences into a single, presumably festive, three-ring splurge. By the time they get to the theater, they don't want to be in the theater; they want to go home. It takes a lot of wooing by actors to recharge the batteries out front.

Nor should the theater have to bear the cost burden in the name of "theatergoing." Not long ago a television program illustrated the high cost of playgoing by ringing up all the items of a night out on a cash register: the taxi fares, the tips, the checks in fashionable restaurants, and so on. Total: fifty dollars. All of this was lumped under the general heading of "theater" expense. But it wasn't. The money that went to the theater was fifteen dollars. The rest was the result of our desire to stampede ourselves into doing too much too late.

London wouldn't hear of such a thing. Many of the best London restaurants simply refuse to open their doors early enough to feed anyone who is thinking of going to the theater. If someone is thinking of going to the theater he should think about that and catch his nourishment when he can: after the theater, perhaps, sustaining himself meantime on tea biscuits at intermission. Result: London theatergoing is easy, pleasant, more popular as a pastime than it is in New York, and—what is more important—in London you will generally find people looking at the play. I'm not certain I have ever seen anyone asleep in a London theater; in New York you sometimes have to lift your neighbor out of your lap.

As for the entertainments themselves, the quality is going to vary, which is fair enough: the quality of meals varies, the quality of wives varies, the quality of the work anyone does at the office by day varies. The theater is not supposed to sound the one perfect note in a noisome world.

If it is attended without undue harassment, even its imperfections can become interesting. To speak for myself, I have been deeply interested in some of the least successful shows I ever saw. The best performance I ever saw on a stage was given in a three-day failure. A contest with the playwright, tracking him down to see what he is doing and challenging him intellectually about what he has done, can be as stimulating—may even be twice as fascinating—as sitting in quiet assent before a workmanlike vehicle that stakes its greatest claim to fame on the fact that it doesn't need oiling.

The materials at hand are as variable as the quality. A third discontent that may harry the theatergoer stems from:

(3) Knowing exactly what he wants. There is a legend to the effect that Broadway fare is composed of nothing but musicals and light comedies. There is a further legend to the effect that people who come into town with the theater in mind wish to see nothing but musicals and light comedies. If both legends were true, the millennium would have been reached, the two parties to a contract would have been mated happily forever after, the Broadway theater would be wildly solvent, and all Broadway customers would be deeply, deeply satisfied. So much for legends.

Facts: there are generally one or two successful light comedies on Broadway each season, along with, say, two more that are medium-funny; there are generally one or two major musicals in unmistakable demand, along with three or possibly four others that are good enough to span a season without setting fire to it. Let's say that we have accounted now for nine or ten of the entertainments available at most times. (Actually, my figure is high.)

At most times there are thirty entertainments available. What can the remaining twenty be? They can be anything from courtroom melodramas to biographies of Luther or Sir Thomas More, anything from a bewigged artifice by Jean Anouilh to a savage portrait of contemporary marriage by Edward Albee, anything from a revival of Shaw to an attempt to do Brecht, anything from a visit from Kirk Douglas or the Comédie Française to the return of Charles Boyer or Eugene O'Neill. In short, anything.

Now one of the real pleasures of theatergoing lies in not being too strict about preferences. The theatergoer who says "All I want is a good musical" is the theatergoer who is going to be most miserable most of the year. He's going to see more bad musicals than he should see because he is going to devote too much of his available time to going to musicals. And he is going to spend the rest of his time fretting because there aren't more of them to go wrong on. But it is he who is making himself miserable, not the theater. The theater is turning up all sorts of other pleasures while he is merely being stubborn. I was a bitter man when the Marx Brothers broke up; but if I had decided to sit it out until the Marx Brothers came back I should have missed Nancy Walker and *La Plume de ma Tante* and *Beyond the Fringe*. More than that. If I'd decided it was only zany comedy I liked, I should have missed the off-Broadway production of Euripides' *The Trojan Women*.

I mention the Circle in the Square production of *The Trojan Women* for a particular reason. It is that a revival of the Greek playwright Euripides is about the farthest out of all playgoing possibilities in our time (consider how few of what we consider the greatest of all plays we have ever seen produced by professionals) and about the furthest from the mind of the playgoer who supposes that he is looking for pleasure. The customer who does nerve himself to Euripides normally goes out of a sense of cultural obligation, not out of a desire to be wholly and memorably absorbed for an evening. And the customer who stays away stays away because he is certain that, however virtuous he may be made to feel, he will be bored virtuous. His certainty, however, is without foundation because he has in fact never exposed himself to the experience. Until he goes, he cannot know. So long as he is certain, he can never be surprised. The moral: One can never be sure of what he likes until he's been there.

I know a woman who, when traveling, always orders lamb chops because she is certain she likes lamb chops. How can she be certain, I always ask, when she's never compared them to anything else? They may taste terrible, even to her. I don't say they do, only that she doesn't know whether they do or not.

So much for the things we may do in the name of pleasure that actually succeed in depriving us of pleasure. I have only one thought to add: pleasure is its own reward. It is not supposed to make anyone brighter, richer, more beautiful, better educated, better equipped to cope, or neater in his personal habits. It is supposed to account for itself as pleasure: did it engage me in such a way that I wasn't sorry I went? If it doesn't do this, no incidental trimmings or promise of profit will justify it. If it does, the trimmings will have been unnecessary and the promise of profit irrelevant.

I hate disinterested affirmation. I often hear people speaking of the **theater** with approval. Sometimes they are speaking of a particular

play with approval. But nothing stirs in their eyes as they so thoughtfully stir their coffee and acknowledge that such-and-such an entertainment was very good indeed. Their mouths do not become
animated as they speak, except for such animation as is necessary to
articulate the words and, between words, to sip the coffee. They
behave as though they had spent all of their lives impartially on the
bench. The law is the law and emotion is no part of it. They speak of
an objective reality that can be determined by evidence, and they are
willing to abide by the evidence presented. The show was presented.
Yes. Very good. More sugar?

I don't believe them. I don't believe that they admired the show
they saw. I think they were utterly indifferent to it, and, since indifference is not a quality that can ever be associated with pleasure, I
think they secretly hated it but have kept the secret even from themselves. I don't think they knew that they were supposed to have
enjoyed it.

The best way to shock oneself into a state of possible enjoyment is
to know when one has not enjoyed something, and not only to know
it but to confess it, to insist upon it, to shout it. Boredom should be
announced; dissatisfaction should be advertised; at the risk of spoiling
the party, voices should be raised. If one does not speak one's own
truth, who will speak it? And if it isn't spoken, where shall its bones
be laid?

Neutrality where pleasure is concerned is a sign of real death. Let
us be animated one way or another. If our first experience is de-
pressing, let us be animated about that—candid and, if necessary,
cantankerous. It will give our muscles tone. Then, having acquired a
habit of speaking up and having all the equipment for speaking up in
sound working order, we shall be ready to make a noise that announces our pleasure and announces it in such a way that it reflects
it. A man who is saying he has liked something should look as though
heaven had blessed him and sound as though heaven might hear him.
An actor on stage doesn't want the audience to nod approval; he
wants approval howled. (And he won't mind terribly if something
else is howled; after all, he didn't write the play, and now at least he
knows you're there.)

A theater is an open place in which people should be open with
one another.

TOYS

The Laurel and Hardy dolls are on the shelf and the summer is over.

Possibly you have never run across Laurel and Hardy dolls. I hadn't until I turned one more corner in Venice and saw them smirking at me through a shopwindow. There is nothing very special about them, even if their derbies do rise from their heads when they are squeaked, although Hardy looks remarkably like Hardy. The only thing that struck me as special about them, and sent me into the store for one more wrapped package that would eventually have to be opened by a stunned customs inspector, was the fact that they'd turned up in Venice. Perhaps they are on sale in New York even as I chatter; but I have never seen them on sale in New York—they are clearly stamped "made in Italy," in English—just as I have never seen a ceramic figure of Charlie Chaplin except in Florence, which is also in Italy.

What I am getting around to is that once someone has given the Italians a certain amount of visual pleasure the Italians are not apt to forget it. (Parisians don't entirely forget it, either; there is an ancient Laurel and Hardy feature film running on the Champs-Élysées as I write.) Americans tend to scrap what has been used up; or perhaps they simply surrender it with a sigh and look forward greedily to what comes next. Europeans make a little picture of it and shelve it in full view, perhaps dusting it now and then. Death by repetition on television is not enough; a small totem must be fashioned and put among the household gods, or at least among the gods of the playpen.

The next thing that struck me was the appropriateness of turning the memento into a toy. For Europe in general has not yet wholly lost the sense of toy theater, of theater that is capable of turning adults back into children. Wherever you go, you're apt to run into something idiotic, infantile, and splendid.

Outdoor opera at the Baths of Caracalla in Rome is no doubt too obvious an example. Anyone who goes there knows that he is going to see the Saturday-matinee-only-twelve-thrilling-chapters serial version of *Aida*. But I was touched on my last visit by the camel, deeply touched. At the Baths of Caracalla *Aida* goes along for several acts content with plunging white steeds heading directly for the footlights (my wife worried about the singers who were riding the chariots behind; I worried about the musicians who were playing beneath: one false hoof and no concertmeister).

Then, as we prepared for the sequence in which all guilty secrets come out, the lights slowly rose on the night desert. Before we had quite decided, under the false moonlight and the real, which lumpy shapes before us were dunes and which staircases to temples, one lumpy shape lurched, staggered to its feet, and with a haughty, stately tread departed. It was a real camel and its work for the evening was now done. It had sat still for about ten seconds and staggered across the echoing floorboards for another fifteen; camels probably come high, and this camel had had an easy evening for his money. But he was worth it. The audience had been given its bauble.

The response was delighted and delightful. Everyone present, no doubt including the camel, knew precisely how silly the whole brief business was. And everyone, the camel excepted, grinned like a fool, like a conspiratorial fool. They had, and they hadn't, come for this.

They had come to give serious attention to an opera, and, as it happened on this particular evening, the performance deserved decent attention. But they were also charmed to have been reminded of certain things: that they were on holiday, that they were somewhere interesting (somewhere so interesting that real camels might join the group), and—above all, I think—that all theater, no matter how sober, is at root artifice. Life and death may occupy the stage tonight; but—dare we forget?—we are *playing*.

The moment, and the quiet hilarity it produced up and down the bleachers, did not in the least disturb or diminish the sobriety of what followed. It simply relaxed it, freed it. Earnestness, after all, is the great enemy of open response; a completely earnest audience gets in its own way, and in the actors', whereas a relaxed audience is ready for anything, including the tragic. In any case, a bit of visual nonsense—irrelevant, unnecessary, and probably expensive—had placed the audience in space. It was not in a temple, not in a museum, not in a study hall; it was in that very foolish place, the playhouse, to which all of us graduate from the nursery.

The playhouse is an important place, but it can be important only on its own terms. And every once in a while a degree of innocence, even of idiocy, is essential if we are to grasp, and be happy with, those terms. As it happens, I am opposed to too much scenery. As it happens, Italian opera is today in serious financial straits, partly because of all that scenery. But there comes a time when there can be so much scenery that it explodes in your face like a whoop of laughter and squares everything. The time came for me in the Roman amphitheater at Verona, where 22,000 people in the auditorium sat gawking with enchanted disbelief at what seemed 22,000 extras on a stage built seven stories high.

None of this was plausible, mind you, or even well managed. When a director has that many extras to contend with, and when they are all so far away that only interstellar communication could possibly convey his messages, a certain sloppiness of detail comes to exist. During a performance of *Carmen* at the Verona arena there were so many displaced persons wandering vaguely through the upper reaches of scenic Spain that you felt they must be latecomers and you wished ushers would seat them. But the very preposterousness of having tiers upon tiers of buildings that neither Carmen nor Don José would ever use, the very absurdity of hiring people off the streets to put on costumes and do nothing all night but walk five hundred feet to the left and then five hundred feet to the right, suddenly reduces the theater to what it everlastingly is—man's biggest toy.

I thought of this all over again—couldn't get away from it, it seems—at Vicenza, where Palladio's sixteenth-century playhouse-in-perspective still stands. To put the matter bluntly, Palladio's playhouse-in-perspective is insane. The audience sits in a graceful arc facing a platform pierced with three doorways. Beyond the doorways streets recede in those perfect diminishing proportions so beloved by the late Renaissance. The essence of this particular playhouse, its *raison d'être*, lies in the optical illusions made possible by craftily foreshortened bits of carpentry. (In some performances dwarfs have been used to inhabit the remotest areas, so that the forced perspective would not be exposed for the jolly fraud it is.) In any case, most visitors who now come to the playhouse come to goggle and grin at the vanishing-point streets.

The only catch is that there is no seat in the house from which you can see all three streets and in order to see so much as *one* street you must be strategically placed exactly in front of it. In short, there are three good seats in any one row—or, if you want to be a bit more generous and allow for a bit of neck stretching, say nine—which means that approximately seventy percent of the people who come to see a performance in this auditorium will probably never catch a glimpse of the one feature that has made the playhouse celebrated enough for them to want to come see a performance in it.

Now, I suppose a functionalist architect could become angry about something like that. And, to speak for myself, I don't care whether I *ever* see a vista through a doorway on a stage anywhere. But I can't resist the crazy playfulness that brought an apparently irrelevant stage-wall into being. Someone was toying about, someone hit upon something ingenious that was scarcely more than a joke, someone put up a building to house a small and unnecessary daydream. I find I am grateful for that because it makes me laugh, and also because it points directly at that one aspect of theater we are so quick to forget—its cheerful, shining, profound unreality.

It is absolutely essential for the theater to be unreal in order for it to do its most profound work; otherwise we should be slaughtering real innocents, or real gladiators, or real animals, as the Romans once did before they became interested in theater. It is also essential for us to remember that it is unreal; otherwise we should not know what we were about. And it sometimes requires a gesture of great preposterousness, of radical absurdity, of utterly wanton fun, to ram the point home again.

Toys have their place. In our seriousness—a rather thin and anxious seriousness—we don't make enough of them.

THE CLEAR-HEADED CAD

I find myself very, very puzzled by a new aberration of human nature. Not long ago there was a great ruckus in our community over the fact that a young writer who had been permitted to "observe" a production during its entire rehearsal process had thereafter sold his observations to a national magazine. The ruckus ostensibly had to do with the fact that these observations reached print at all: when an outsider is graciously permitted to eavesdrop on anything so unformed and tremulous as the rehearsal process, it is more or less assumed that he will go to his death with his lips sealed. Actually, the storm blew up because the observations were unfriendly, or at the very least decidedly detached. If they'd been glowing, we mightn't have heard another word about the matter—except for a hearty "*Amigo!*" to all those other observers who might be waiting in line at the stage door.

Now, I don't want to get into this fight. Any man who would sell somebody else's soul for a few paltry pennies is obviously a scoundrel, and, as Dogberry might say, it is better to take no notice of scoundrels. You never know when one will start observing *you*. So I shall bypass the moral issues involved.

It's not the moral issues that bother me. It's the human issue that does. At what point did the human race lose its power of losing perspective?

Here is what I mean. A man who attaches himself to a given production, who goes day after day into the darkened auditorium to share deliciously in the most secret of rites, who becomes the familiar of those glamorous midwives who know how to get a play born, who watches the baby take its very first steps and then sees it imperceptibly grow into some sort of creature—this man normally acquires the attitude that has given faithful dogs such good reputations.

With every little advance he wags what tail he has. He would no more think of taking a nip out of the infant he has godfathered than he would out of his own dear brother. No matter that the growing child has scanty hair and bowlegs, no matter that new imperfections begin to appear with adolescence: this child is beautiful. It is beautiful to the constant observer because, by virtue of his constancy, it is half *his*.

Certainly all theatrical people behave in this way, at least through rehearsals. Every day in every way the project grows dearer and dearer because every day in every way the project shines brighter and more blindingly into the critical eye. Isn't that a wonderful bit of business

Marjorie Whoever does? So deft. Besides, I've just had lunch with Marjorie and she isn't like what they said at all, she's a darling. The possibility that Marjorie's delightful bit of business is fundamentally unrelated to the structural articulation of the play is an abstraction; it vanishes from the mind quite easily as Marjorie, in the flesh, makes herself ever more real. And hasn't the restaging of that scene doubled its effectiveness? It has. The fact that the scene was only about five-percent effective to begin with, and has now reached a majestic ten, is as nothing beside the actual improvement that can be actually seen, almost touched. The scene is better, the seats in the auditorium are more comfortable, the sandwiches in waxed paper are delicious. No more coffee, thanks. I want to watch this scene again. There are directors who watch only the *improved* scenes, it gives them such deep satisfaction.

In any case the director is now turning to the playwright to confide, on impulse, that "No matter what happens, Jim, I love this play." Nor does Jim notice the unbidden suggestion from the director's far subconscious that something might very well happen, something awful; like all the rest of us, he has ears only for love.

The producer, having for ten days watched his play take dancing lessons, spreads the word around town that he's got a dazzler coming in. He means it, and spends more money on costumes. The stage manager, so ready to explain to his wife how badly the director is botching things, eventually permits himself a hesitant but meaningful "I . . . begin to hope."

When the whole thing is over—let's say, just for argument's sake, that it's bombed—the one thing you are certain to hear a director or producer say is "If I had it to do all over again, I'd do it exactly the same way." And he means that, too. For as he runs his mind back over the entire period when he was doing it—the rehearsal period— he can remember nothing but *gloire*. Obviously no wrong turnings were taken in those days; whatever went wrong went wrong after the opening, in the audience, in the newspapers, in the star's loss of nerve, somewhere. Experienced hands know, of course, that the rehearsal flowering is not to be trusted; and they do all they can to force themselves not to trust it. "I don't trust it," they say; "it's going too well."

There are very good reasons why all theatrical people should behave in this way. Quite apart from the natural myopia that comes of being in the loved one's company day and night for three weeks, there is literally no other way for theatrical people to behave. What kind of performance would you get from a star who spent half her thinking time thinking that her part was a rotten one? A rotten one, of course. Even doubt is dangerous. Unless an actress is *sure* that her next line is brilliant, she is not going to deliver it brilliantly enough to fool you. Not just confidence is wanted; divine certainty is required if the performer is not to collapse in a little pile at center stage.

The director can believe no less firmly. He can, of course, whinny steadily before rehearsals begin, badgering the author and waking up nights to make feverish notes to himself on the obvious pitfalls he has been overlooking. But he cannot put the show into work as though he had Hamlet's time to achieve certainty. Now he is the one who must convince everyone else that the text is just the thing ordered to make stars out of all of them. He is the father of assurance, defender of the faith. Every director must come to a moment, not later than the night before the first morning of rehearsals, when he says to himself, "This is a good play and I know why and I know how it can be made to work. Amen." The director who cannot bring himself to such a moment, and mean it, is honor-bound to quit.

Very well. In addition to a natural myopia there must be a self-induced myopia if anything so given to fits of insecurity as a play is to be shouldered, nervelessly, across that glaring open stage. Second thoughts can be reserved for New Haven, or Elba. Now, it is really quite customary for anyone who is close to a production—even in an observer's capacity—to catch something of this necessary disease. The bug is in the air, and anyone who cares enough about the theater to *wish* to observe rehearsals should be especially vulnerable to it.

But clearly our man, this fellow who started all the fuss, didn't catch it. He came, he saw, he was not infected. There he sat, sandwichless no doubt, resisting the virus that leaps from bloodstream to bloodstream in the temporarily enchanted auditorium.

The baby began to coo, and he did not coo back. He kept his wits about him while all about him fell in love. With detachment sublime, and heart of quartz, he stood clear-eyed outside the experience, not having any. It is a remarkable case of successful alienation, and I think the man should be preserved for study. He may be a mutation, the beginning of a species incapable of myopia, invulnerable to hypnosis, not susceptible to the delusions which assure the theater that another play can be got on tomorrow night. Breed him and you will have more sanity. I wonder if you will have much theater.

INDEX